THE ENTHYMEME

The Enthymeme

Syllogism, Reasoning, and Narrative in Ancient Greek Rhetoric

JAMES FREDAL

The Pennsylvania State University Press
University Park, Pennsylvania

Material from chapter 5 previously appeared in "Enthymizing in the Orators," *Advances in the History of Rhetoric* 19.1 (2016): 31–49. Reprinted by permission of the American Society for the History of Rhetoric, https://ashr.org/.

Material from chapter 8 previously appeared in "The Enthymizing of Lysias," *Advances in the History of Rhetoric* 20.1 (2017): 1–27. Reprinted by permission of the American Society for the History of Rhetoric, https://ashr.org/.

Library of Congress Cataloging-in-Publication Data

Names: Fredal, James, 1961– author.
Title: The enthymeme : syllogism, reasoning, and narrative in ancient Greek rhetoric / James Fredal.
Description: University Park, Pennsylvania : The Pennsylvania State University Press, [2020] | Includes bibliographical references and index.
Summary: "Examines the concept of the enthymeme in ancient Greek rhetoric, arguing that it is a technique of storytelling aimed at eliciting from the audience an inference about a narrative"—Provided by publisher.
Identifiers: LCCN 2019059723 | ISBN 9780271086132 (hardback)
Subjects: LCSH: Enthymeme (Logic) | Syllogism. | Rhetoric, Ancient. | Narration (Rhetoric)
Classification: LCC BC185 .F74 2020 | DDC 808.00938—dc23
LC record available at https://lccn.loc.gov/2019059723

Copyright © 2020 James Fredal
All rights reserved
Printed in the United States of America
Published by The Pennsylvania State University Press,
University Park, PA 16802-1003

The Pennsylvania State University Press is a member of the Association of University Presses.

It is the policy of The Pennsylvania State University Press to use acid-free paper. Publications on uncoated stock satisfy the minimum requirements of American National Standard for Information Sciences—Permanence of Paper for Printed Library Material, ANSI Z39.48-1992.

CONTENTS

Introduction *(1)*

PART ONE   3.0

1   Enthymeme 3.0: The Truncated Syllogism *(23)*
2   3.0 and Its Problems *(45)*

PART TWO   2.0

3   Aristotle, *Sullogismos*, and 2.0 *(59)*
4   2.0 and Its Problems *(75)*

PART THREE   1.0

5   Enthymizing in the Orators *(87)*
6   Oratorical Enthymizing in Context *(109)*
7   Enthymizing and Adversarial Narratives *(128)*

PART FOUR   LYSIAS AND THE ENTHYMEME

8   Enthymizing in Lysias 1, *On the Death of Eratosthenes* *(147)*
9   A Many-Layered Tale *(163)*

Conclusion *(179)*

Notes *(189)*
References *(201)*
Index *(213)*

The past is a foreign country.

—L. P. HARTLEY (1953)

Rhetoric is the *antistrophe* to dialectic.

—ARISTOTLE (~330 B.C.E.)

I deny that the enthymeme properly understood is a truncated syllogism.

—FACCIOLATI (1728)

What then was an Enthymeme?

—DE QUINCEY (1897)

The first type of enthymeme is a truncated syllogism.

—WIKIPEDIA (2019)

The immediate cause of the greatly increased consciousness of rhetorical techniques in fifth-century Athens was the application of the democratic process on a large scale to judicial procedure.

—KENNEDY (1963)

The law always begins in story ... and it ends in story.

—JAMES BOYD WHITE (1985)

Narrative reasoning is ubiquitous and lies at the heart of legal reasoning.

—DESANCTIS (2012)

Introduction

1. THE *RHETORIC* AS GUIDEBOOK

If we were to travel à la Hartley to the sprawling city of Rhetoric in ancient Greece, we would need a guide.[1] We could do worse, it seems, than to take with us the popular and perennial guidebook provided by Aristotle: *On Rhetoric*.[2] It has the advantage of having been written by one of the greatest philosophers of his age, perhaps of any age, and one who also happened to be a rough contemporary of some of the greatest orators of the ancient world: Demades, Lycurgus, and Demosthenes. Of course, Aristotle is not a native of this city and may never have lived there—that is, he was not himself a practicing rhetor. But he was an experienced teacher, an astute observer, a skilled writer, and a practiced scientific explorer and researcher—the philosophical Pausanias of the Greek intellectual landscape. And perhaps his not being a practitioner, his having remained unsullied by the seedier districts of Rhetoric, made him that much less partisan and more objective about its landmarks and dangers, its traps and tricks, its strengths and its manifest weaknesses.

Let us play out this conceit and consider the *Rhetoric* as though it were our guidebook to an unknown country. There was in his time, says Aristotle, no proper map of Rhetoric, merely some rough sketches of a few alleys through the legal district—Reply by Comparison, Recapitulation, Supplementary Narration, and the like—and most of those were inaccurate or useless.[3] Immediately, though, Aristotle offers the generative clarity of a novel insight: the city of Rhetoric, says our guide, is in fact a colony. Rhetoric was built after the plan and in the model of its greater and

2 THE ENTHYMEME

more important mother city, Dialectic. Rhetoric is the *anti-* to Dialectic's *strophē* (1.1; 30 and n. 4).[4] Citizens of Dialectic refer to Rhetoric as the city of "reasoning-of-a-sort." Though sprawling and populous, Rhetoric is not so fine or august, its streets not so straight, its edifices not so secure as those of the metropole.[5] Rhetoric was built to be populated by a rougher class of citizen—less patient, more volatile, less disciplined, and to be sure, intellectually inferior to the great families of Dialectic. Nevertheless, Aristotle asserts, in essence, that "any Greek familiar with dialectic would immediately acquire a fundamental though common notion of the nature of rhetoric" (Crem 1956, 235). The similarity is not simply structural but functional. Rhetoric does what Dialectic does: it relies on topical forms and reputable premises to invent arguments, or "proofs," on both sides of a question or topic that has no science of its own. It is a lay art for bilateral proving.

Rhetoric is said to be notable for a pair of landmarks that are similar to originals well known to citizens of Dialectic: the two towers of induction, or *epagoge* (here called *paradeigma*), and deduction, or *sullogismos* (called *enthumēma*; 1.2.8–10; 38–39). Also recognizable will be its estimable premises (endoxa; 1.2.11–13; 40–42), though these are limited to probabilities or signs (1.2.14–18; 42–43), and the robust variety of its topical forms (1.3–1.15, 2.22–23; 46–110, 168–84), some of which are said to be quite faithful copies of the prototypes in the metropole. The twin peaks will of course be a bit of a disappointment to denizens of Dialectic, and few of Rhetoric's premises and topoi display the structural rigor of those in Dialectic, much less the adamantine axioms and figures of Demonstration.[6] But with these premises and topics, Rhetoric is able to produce examples and enthymemes in abundance, and with these enthymemes and examples, its citizens craft a kind of disposable knowledge that is useful for their legal, political, and ceremonial contests.

Of course, Rhetoric's knowledge will not equal the rigorous mode of learning being built in Dialectic, much less the peerless truths forged in the capital city of Analytic. It will be a simpler, rough-and-ready kind of knowing, suitable for public use (and, many would say, abuse) by the assorted busybodies and sycophants easily found on every thoroughfare and square in Rhetoric. But this logic-of-a-sort is a central ingredient in all of the city's primary exports: legal, deliberative, and epideictic arguments for the democratic agon. Since its founding, Rhetoric has grown organically and after its own fashion, with the result being that Rhetoric's layout necessarily departs from the dialectical model Aristotle imposes.

For example, many of Rhetoric's topoi differ from those used in Dialectic, and the city's output is found to contain several extralogical ingredients, including intoxicating quantities of emotional appeal (pathos) and character appeal (ethos). And so, having initiated this comparison, much of Aristotle's guidebook has to account for these differences and demonstrate that they can be accommodated by his colonial scheme. This has led some to view his observations as contradictory.[7] For example, early on he says that Rhetoric's enthymemes and examples are suitable for emotion and character appeals as well as for factual appeals, and he speaks of both emotion and character as though they were just another kind of proof (1.2.3–7; 38–39). But later he says that if you want to generate an emotion or character appeal, you shouldn't use enthymemes, or you'll ruin it (3.17.8; 243). Nevertheless, and despite these differences, we are assured by Aristotle that a familiarity with Dialectic will prepare us admirably for a tour of Rhetoric.

Unfortunately, if we ever happen to make the trip to Rhetoric armed with Aristotle's guidebook—that is to say, if we read the legal and political speeches of Antiphon, Lysias, Isaeus, Demosthenes, and the rest through the lens of Aristotle's *Rhetoric*—we are likely to become disoriented and uncertain about how to proceed. We discover that the terrain looks very little like that described by our guidebook. This city seems to have been built on an entirely different plan, with strange landmarks, an unexpected layout, and very little logic to be found—or if there is logic, it is logic of a form quite unlike the inductions and deductions of Dialectic or the syllogisms of Analytic. Only with difficulty and a fertile imagination can we convince ourselves that we are looking at a colony of Dialectic. Where are those towering edifices Induction and Deduction? Where are the orderly ranks of premises Major and Minor advancing every proof? Where are the sure-footed conclusions marching forward? In fact, had we not been yoked to the sure guidance of Aristotle, and were some questioner to ask us about our visit to ancient Rhetoric, we wouldn't think to compare it to Dialectic at all.

Rhetoric does remind us of someplace, a place we find somehow very familiar, though we can't immediately put our finger on it. Like trying to think of a song when another is playing, as long as we are guided by Aristotle's dialectical tour book, we won't recall that we have actually seen terrain like this before, many times. Only when we put down the *Rhetoric* and look again does it strike us: the polis of Rhetoric—which is to say, the practice of ancient Greek rhetorical artistry—does remind us of a place. Not of Dialectic but of a city much less regular, larger, more populous, more famous, and much older. If ancient rhetoric is a foreign country, we will recognize it not as a colony of Dialectic but as a suburb of Narrative.

2. RHETORIC AS NARRATIVE

Perhaps it is time to speak plainly: our understanding of rhetoric has been rendered in the language of dialectic and our view of logos described in terms of logic so frequently and for so long that we forget that this is the language and these the terms of a *model*, not the *reality*. Rhetorical logos is not logic as it is commonly understood, though it has been and can be so described. This model is useful, but as I hope to show in this work, it conceals as much as it reveals. Fortunately, there is another powerful and well-developed model for exploring and understanding rhetorical reasoning, argument, and proof. We can—and I argue that we should—begin to read early rhetoric as legal storytelling. Its legal arguments are not set in premise-conclusion (PC) logical forms, and its logic is neither formal nor universal. Ancient rhetorical reasoning arises from narratives set in adversarial juxtaposition as required by and specific to the democratic polis and its unique social, political, and legal culture.

Ancient rhetorical artistry is built on narrative artistry, and ancient rhetorical reasoning is a special form of narrative reasoning. Aristotle's treatise, for all its inestimable and enduring value, remains a partial and incomplete guide to ancient rhetorical practice—especially legal practice—in part because the prominence that he gave to dialectic and deductive form overshadowed the centrality of story creation to rhetorical craft. This bias was exacerbated by subsequent generations of readers who assimilated Aristotelian logos to formal logic, elevated it to a dogma, and then retrofitted it onto Rhetoric's native landscape, in the process ignoring both the patterns of narrative artistry native to all ancient oratory and the traces of narrative reasoning still latent in Aristotle's *Rhetoric*. Rhetoric was not built on a dialectical plan; it was just seen through dialectical lenses. And to the degree that modern rhetorical theories rely on Aristotle and on the exaggerations typical of neo-Aristotelian logos, they too will misconstrue both ancient rhetoric and its foundational paradigm. Ancient rhetoric, we might say, is the antistrophe of poetics. In the words of James Boyd White, it "begins with story" and "it ends with story" (1985, 168).

It is story, and not dialectic, that provides the primary framework necessary for understanding ancient rhetorical artistry, including rhetorical invention and argument. The orator's use of rhetorical techniques, from canons of speech, parts of speech, the many terms and concepts pertaining to appeals, and tropes and figures to characteristics of the speaker, the audience, the opponent, the case and issue, the situation, the purpose, the genre, and the larger social and cultural context, including the nature of the persuasive goal itself—all of these will be significantly clarified and brought into an easily assimilated and productive whole when we begin with a narrative framework and an orientation toward story. We can paraphrase Bennet and Feldman to say that the ancient legal trial, and ancient rhetorical artistry more generally, "is organized around storytelling" (2014, 3).[8]

It will be helpful to begin by defining some terms. By *ancient rhetorical artistry*, I do not mean "theory." The term *theory* will immediately be read as meaning (above all) Aristotle, and then Plato, the sophists, and perhaps Isocrates, Cicero, and other writers of treatises, and with them the whole panoply of neo-Aristotelian and classical rhetorical terms and systems. I will speak of Aristotle in chapters 3 and 4, but I do not mean for this work to be a commentary on ancient rhetorical theory, much less a commentary on Aristotle.

Nor do I mean simply "oratory" or "rhetorical practice," as represented in the speeches of a Protagoras, Gorgias, Plato, Thucydides, Lysias, Antiphon, Demosthenes, or Cicero. I will refer to oratory in order to describe an alternative approach to rhetorical reasoning, but I am not claiming simply that orators used narratives. I argue rather that orators developed a stable set of rhetorical/narrative techniques prior to and independent of later theory, that this technical ability was rhetorical (not simply pre- or protorhetoric or eloquence), and that this body of knowledge was fundamentally rooted in the skill of telling a good story. I mean to explore the detectable regularities of expertise that lie beyond theory and the treatise.

These techniques constituted a type of knowledge that could be called theory, though it was never encoded in any treatise and cannot be cleanly abstracted from its cultural and legal setting. The process of encoding and theorizing this knowledge, as by Aristotle, resulted in its being distorted.

6   THE ENTHYMEME

I will refer to it instead as artistry: situated knowledge derived from and oriented toward practical experience. These techniques were known in one form by experienced speakers and speechwriters and in another by experienced auditors of public oratory, especially in ancient democracies like Athens. This is what Bourdieu might call the regularities of a habitus, the logic of practice, a "feel for the game," or "practical mastery" (1990, 66–67).

Narrative and *story* are famously fraught terms; their meanings are field-dependent, and their boundaries, features, and differences are difficult to capture. To make it more difficult, I'll be using a set of fairly idiosyncratic definitions. By *narrative*, I mean any text that prompts in the audience a story. By *story*, I mean the experiencing of a plot by an audience immersed in a normative storyworld. By *plot*, I mean the linked actions and consequences of humanlike actors whose telling prompts a holistic and teleologically oriented response in the audience, from an initiating or catalyzing state in the beginning; to one or more intermediate, delaying, or transforming states in the middle; to a concluding or resolving state that satisfies the others at the end. The former brings about the latter, and the latter resolves and explains the former. Together they form a bounded unity that can be seen "in a single glance" (Mink 1970, 554).

Students of Aristotle will recognize in this the movement described in the *Poetics* (7), though in this case, we look not for the events that initiate, continue, or end the action but rather for the events that initiate and orient the audience's response. Plot will name the connected set of events, characters, choices, and actions that prompts this responsive cycle, cadence, or *periodos*.[9] This cycle takes up the whole of human experience; it is at once cognitive and inferential, affective and emotional, appetitive and aesthetic, ethical and normative. These layers are interconnected: cognitive curiosity and reasoning generate emotional and aesthetic expectations and responses, which themselves trigger normative judgments.

If a story is the full experience of movement prompted by a plot set in a storyworld, then a narrative is any text that prompts such a story movement, however short or fragmentary. Hemingway's alleged six words count as narrative because they prompt, even if they do not describe, a story:

For Sale: Baby shoes. Never worn.[10]

This text reads like a classified advertisement. It mentions no characters, no action, no sequence or causation, but it is a narrative because it is capable of prompting in audiences a plot cycle and thus a story, even if most of this plot and story must be inferred by the reader. It evokes characters, linked events, emotion, sympathy, and in the taking out of the ad and sale of the shoes, a kind of tragic resolution, a letting go.

I use this definition because I will be focused on the rhetorical features of legal narratives. The kinds of stories I am interested in, the kinds of stories that ancient rhetoric concerns itself with, are anthropocentric: they involve humans or nonhuman actors that are given human characteristics and are oriented toward a human lifeworld. I will be concerned with the ethically ordered storyworld, the *nomos*, within which humans act. This is the realm of adversarial narratives, of what Lucaites and Condit (1985) call "rhetorical narratives," and of legal stories.

Ancient Greek rhetoric is the art of legal storytelling. Not only did orators regularly deliver narratives, but every nonnarrative portion of an ancient speech either refers to an existing narrative or is built upon it. In the same way, decisions made by juries or assemblies depend upon their understanding and acceptance of a logos as the narrative account. One of the first and most important tasks facing an orator or speechwriter was discovering and assembling a set of facts that was capable of supporting a plot and thus capable of generating a story of the case, and one of the most important aspects of a successful story was the discovery and arrangement of narrative details that could catalyze a complete intellectual, emotional, sensory, and normative *periodos*, the story movement. The speaker sought to immerse the listener in this movement, to make it not just a speech, not just a narrative, but a story experience.

The most reliable and powerful way for an ancient orator to find and utilize all the "available means of persuasion" was to find the legally sanctioned story. Every one of the many familiar and frequently individualized concepts and terms that were familiar to ancient rhetorical theory gains clarity and power when it is situated within an overarching framework of legal narrative, and each of these elements achieves its full effect only in coordination with other elements as part of a larger narrative whole.

Ethos will name portrayals of character within a narrative. The ethos of the speaker will be shaped by his portrayal of the first-person narrator as a character, and the ethos of this character will be shaped by his narrated motives, choices, actions, and words; his relationship to other characters; and his contribution to the plot. Pathos is also aroused primarily through story—through the normative motives and choices of characters embedded within a storyworld; through their actions and the consequences of those actions; through what they want, what they do, and what is done to them; and through the plot and its manipulation of time and sequencing of anticipation, delay, suspense, surprise, and resolution. Rhetorical situations will largely be narrative situations, the world in which the narrative is set will merge with the world of the jury and their deliberations, and the world they imaginatively inhabit as auditors will reveal itself to be continuous with the world where they live as participants and judges. They will carry out the final act of a story-become-drama in which they have a pivotal role.

Similarly, a narrative framework will encourage us to view other rhetorical concepts in the context of story: rhetorical *kairos* as the opportunity for action and advantage presented by the unfolding of a plot, by the decisive moments recognized and acted upon by characters in the narrative, and by participants in the courtroom drama. *Enargeia, ekphrasis*, and *phantasia* will all make sense as the narrative creation of a storyworld that listeners can imaginatively inhabit and experience as virtual witnesses. The parts of the speech will be understood to prepare the audience for the narrative and its proper conclusion and to help the audience interpret this narrative correctly, see it clearly, and accept it as the only possible account. The argument portion of a speech, the confirmation and refutation, is required by the need to comment on the story, to highlight its coherence, and to demonstrate the impossibility of the opposing narrative.

3. NARRATIVE REASONING

In the same way, logos will refer primarily not to formal logic, to deduction and induction, but to narrative reasoning about the facts of a case. I will be interested in how orators used narratives to argue, specifically to argue against opposing narratives. This will require attending to inference-making and to the space or "gap" between what is said and what is inferred and imagined, including the gap between the narratives as told and the story as felt and experienced. Based on what the speaker says, the jurors attempt to think, feel, and experience what "really happened" beyond the narrative and within the parameters of the law. To do so, they make inferences from important plot details in the narrative—scenes, characters, acts, motives, instruments—to their own internal feel for "the story." These inferences are the links that prompt additional known and felt but unnarrated story features that fill out and give meaning to the story. These links connect narrated and unnarrated details together into a complete and fully experienced whole, and they connect this felt story with other similar and familiar storyforms. Narrative linking is the body of rhetoric.

Terms like *logos*, *logic*, and *syllogism* can refer to a range of different activities and call up a number of different models. They traditionally refer to the serial laying down of propositions that lead to a conclusion or to the rules or abstract models governing the formation of this series. We could call this a formal model of reasoning. But logos can also refer more broadly to the process of explanation, of making links or inferences between one thing and the next, and to the audience's ability to understand and accept something as true or likely based on something else that has been said or understood. A logos is an account, a story, and a narrative—especially a narrative that seeks to explain.[11]

Audiences make inferences not only from premises to conclusions but from one portion of a narrative to another and from stated narrative elements to unstated story elements: from scene to character and from character to motive, from motive to choice and action, and from choice, action, and consequence to aesthetic and moral judgment. Audiences reason from facts that are admitted or proven to those that cannot be proven or that are disputed and from these to imagined scenes, emotions, attitudes, character assessments, and aesthetic and moral judgments. *Narrative reasoning* means the following of narrative details to locate or invent links among story elements and from story elements to the outside world.

Rhetorical reasoning is necessarily narrative reasoning because the issues taken up by ancient rhetoric, unlike the issues taken up by dialectical argument or logic, are necessarily situated within the human lifeworld that stories evoke. Rhetorical reasoning is temporally and spatially situated reasoning about human events and their consequences. It must take into account "the facts," and these facts link human actions, motives, and goals to choices and consequences, and they link the reasoning of its actors to a course of action in time and space. They link the actions of characters to the interpretations and choices of others, and they link the narrative told to the story felt and to the myths of a culture and these to the judgment of the audience. Rhetorical logos is situated human reasoning about situated humans and their reasoning. Every rhetorical argument will involve some form of narrative element. And since narratives prompt a holistic response in audiences, every aspect of this human response—cognitive, emotional, characterological, kinesthetic, and aesthetic—will be involved in rhetorical reasoning.

Rhetorical reasoning is also always normative reasoning. These characters, the speakers who conjure them, and the auditors who pass judgment on them are all embedded within a *nomos*—a world not of "one damn thing after another" but of patterns formed by an established hierarchy of significance, a moral order. Rhetorical narratives unfold in the context of this culturally sanctioned order and the archetypal or foundational "myths" or scripts that populate this *nomos* and give it life. Things happen for a reason, and similar things can be expected to happen again. We can guess what probably happened based on what usually happens, on who we are and who they are, and we can respond to what happened based on what ought to happen. We make ethical, legal, and practical judgments of right and wrong, innocence and guilt, expedience and inexpedience, or praise and blame by drawing on our knowledge of our normative world—some of which is encoded in law, written and unwritten—and on our attitude toward the law. Most of this knowledge is encoded as story: both the daily expectations of character, traits, and social scrips and the archetypal storyforms that come from foundational myths.

It is this order that makes possible normative decisions about what ought to happen in a particular case, and these decisions in turn rest upon the narrative construction of a storyworld. In fact, narrative is the only way to immerse an audience within a *nomos*. No legal or deliberative case can be decided outside an accepted moral order within which a set of facts and a legal instrument can be situated and applied, and no moral order can be invoked without in some way calling up for the audience a storyworld within which are situated nested strata of mythic, historical, and legal narratives.

Thus narratives prompt a wide range of inferences, from a stated set of facts to the felt and imagined storyworld in which the narrative occurs, from an understanding of "real life" and how it unfolds to the emotional and characterological responses to the stated and inferred facts, from the narrative as heard to ethical and aesthetic judgments about the story and its proper end. The speaker must convey and the audience must grasp what happened in the context of what happens (typically or normatively), what is happening (now), and what will or ought to happen (in the future). The verdict of the jury is based on the story that they infer from the narrative told and the arguments about it and the fit of that story with a law and a way of life.

But the range of possible inferences in a given narrative will always be much larger than the number of relevant inferences that were intended by the narrator to produce the proper reading. If the plot traces the thread of linked actions that complete the story, connecting the end to the beginning, then the speaker will want to generate a parallel thread of audience response, restricting the inferences, reactions, and judgments that the audience makes to those that forward the plot. The speaker will want a way to highlight or mark important factual statements so that the listeners notice them and form the relevant links between and among them, tying the speaker to the narrator, his account to the law, and his actions to the proper verdict. This narrative inference marker is what I will call oratorical enthymizing, the narrative enthymeme, or simply 1.0.

This is the enthymeme of early rhetorical practice and artistry. This early enthymeme began not as a truncated syllogism, an argument missing a piece, or as a rhetorically salient ideological silence but as a moment of narrative reasoning—a technique for prompting and guiding narrative inference-making in legal storytelling. With the enthymeme, the speaker draws the attention of the audience to a narrative detail in order to highlight its significance, to clarify its meaning and narrow its effect, and to enhance the plausibility of the plot and the effectiveness of the story. The enthymeme is a rhetorical tool of adversarial narrative.

Detective fictions are an excellent place to find this kind of enthymizing. They are adversarial in the sense that they develop an ambiguous set of details that can support two or more possible narratives, only one of which can be true. The detective (like Sherlock Holmes) can then enthymize, or explain and interpret, key details (for Watson and the reader), showing what they mean and how they link together—at the same time making all other narrative interpretations impossible.

For example, at the beginning of Sir Arthur Conan Doyle's 1893 short story "Silver Blaze," a prize racehorse has been stolen from the King's Pyland training stables just a week before the Wessex Cup, an important race in which he was to run as the favorite. Tavistock, the nearest town, was two miles away, as was Capleton, a larger training establishment. Three stable boys worked at King's Pyland stables. On the evening of the crime, two of the stable hands had a supper of curried mutton in the trainer's kitchen. The third, Hunter, was on guard, so the maid brought his supper to the stable. As she was returning to the house, a stranger and track agent, a Mr. Fitzroy Simpson, arrived at the stable wearing a cravat and carrying a cane. He attempted to bribe Hunter for information on the horse but was chased away by Hunter and the stable hound. Hunter and the dog returned to the stable, where Hunter finished his supper, locked the door, and went to sleep. The other boys slept in the loft.

During the night, Silver Blaze went missing along with his trainer, John Straker. Hunter was found the next morning "in a state of absolute stupor" (2005, 394). He had obviously been drugged and remembered nothing. Simpson was apprehended the next day by Inspector Gregory, who was assigned to the case. Simpson had in his possession his walking stick with a large, heavy head, but no cravat.

Straker was found a quarter mile from the stable in a depression on the moor, dead. His forehead had been crushed by a heavy weapon and his thigh lacerated by a sharp instrument. He held in one hand a bloody surgical knife and in the other a cravat that Hunter positively identified as having been worn by Simpson. The newspapers and Inspector Gregory suspect that Simpson stole the horse and killed Straker, perhaps accidentally in a scuffle. Holmes visits the scene of the crime and speaks to the principles. With this information and a few other details (including a clothing receipt found in the pocket of Straker's coat) in hand, Holmes decides to return to London. Watson reacts: "I was thunderstruck by my friend's words. We had only been in Devonshire a few hours, and that he should give up on an investigation which he had begun so brilliantly was quite incomprehensible to me" (410).

Before his departure, Holmes guarantees to Colonel Ross (Silver Blaze's owner) that the horse would run in the Wessex Cup and recommends to Inspector Gregory that the inspector see about a "singular epidemic" of lameness in the area sheep.

"You consider this to be important?" asks the inspector.

"Exceedingly so," Holmes replies.

When the inspector asks whether there is "any other point to which you would wish to draw my attention," Holmes points "to the curious incident of the dog in the night-time."

"The dog did nothing in the night-time," says the inspector.

"That was the curious incident," replies Holmes (411).

Holmes returns to London and four days later travels to Winchester for the race. Silver Blaze, his characteristic white markings hidden by brown dye, wins. On the train back to London, Holmes explains himself just as an attorney would do in a closing argument or a rhetor in the argument portion of his speech. Holmes calls attention to important details and explains their meaning to quickly construct a coherent, plausible, and complete story. Two details were crucial for Holmes in this case. First, the curious incident: the stable boys reported hearing nothing during the night, but if the thief had been a stranger, the dog would have barked. Second, the drugging of Hunter. Holmes knows that curried mutton is one of a few dishes that would mask the taste of opium. The other boys suffered no ill effects, so the opium was introduced only onto Hunter's plate by someone who knew or planned that a curried dish would be served. The thief must have been in the household, and suspicion falls upon Straker himself.

The knife found in Straker's hand, the receipt in his pocket, and the lame sheep explain the motive and the events of the evening in question: he was planning to inflict "a slight nick upon the tendons of the horse's ham, and to do it subcutaneously, so as to leave no trace" (417). Straker would bet against, Silver Blaze would lose the race, and the lameness would be put down to a strain. He took the horse out to the moor for the surgery but practiced on the sheep first. The clothing receipt provided the motive: it was for an expensive dress that did not belong to his wife. Straker fell behind buying expensive dresses for his mistress and needed the winnings. "Wonderful!" exclaims the colonel. "You have made it perfectly clear, Mr. Holmes" (418).[12]

The process of seeing a series of apparently inconsequential details take on meaning and watching each piece fall into place to form a complete and credible story is indeed wonderful. It is intellectually, emotionally, and morally rewarding to see how the pieces fit, the mystery solved, the criminal found out. And it is persuasive. Feeling the suspense of the story build and then resolve as its details are explained, questions are answered, and plot comes into focus is aesthetically satisfying as well. All of this is accomplished by narrating a series of details and then enthymizing some of them to reveal how they link up into an experiential whole, a story. The enthymemes link the details to their meanings, but they also link them to each other and to familiar storyforms. The expensive mistress who drives a simple man to crime and the easy-money or gambling scheme gone wrong are common enough moralizing plot structures to make this case readily grasped and easily believed, at least for the nineteenth-century British imagination.

4. THE QUESTION OF THE ENTHYMEME

> What then was an Enthymeme? Oxford! Thou wilt think us mad to ask.
> —DE QUINCEY (1897)

Of course, this "narrative enthymeme" is not the enthymeme of Aristotle (what I will call 2.0).[13] I will argue in chapters 3 and 4 that Aristotle's enthymeme as a topical deduction is a good deal more flexible and unstructured than the truncated syllogism of traditional and current scholarship (which I will call the "standard view," or 3.0). In fact, although Aristotle's discussion of the enthymeme deflects from a narrative understanding of rhetorical artistry, it does not preclude such an understanding. Aristotle's rhetorical topoi cannot all be reduced to syllogistic form, but they are largely compatible with a narrative view of rhetorical reasoning. Still, it must be admitted that Aristotle's premise-driven, deductive model of *sullogismos* has historically led us away rather than toward a narrative framework for rhetorical inference. Neither is the oratorical enthymeme much like 3.0, the modern audience-added, missing-piece argument (chapters 1 and 2) or its later modifications of Bitzer (3.1) or Barthes (3.2).[14] These and other manifestations of the neo-Aristotelian enthymeme have dominated scholarship for centuries, but they are in their own ways more restrictive, less cogent, and less useful even than Aristotle. They cannot adequately represent how orators argued.

Unfortunately, Aristotelian views dominate the discussion of this technique. In fact, he has been credited with inventing the enthymeme, and his *Rhetoric* is universally accepted as the authoritative source on the subject. But the enthymeme was developed and used by orators long before Aristotle's treatise. I am saying not only that early Greek orators used enthymemes to guide narrative reasoning and that the enthymemes they used differed from Aristotelian and neo-Aristotelian models but that they did so as a conscious and deliberate rhetorical technique, as artistry. Understanding the early history of rhetorical artistry through the lens of narrative provides a fresh perspective on the "body of persuasion," as it does on every other aspect of rhetorical artistry.

There are thus three different models of the enthymeme to consider: the traditional truncated syllogism or argument missing a piece (3.0), the Aristotelian topical deduction (2.0), and what I am for now calling the narrative enthymeme (1.0). The history of the enthymeme is long, its traditional formulation popular, its Aristotelian pedigree well established, and the problems with this formulation and its pedigree well rehearsed. But the enthymeme's history, the reasons for its popularity, and the problems with its formulation have not yet been explored in the context of an alternative model based on ancient oratorical practice. Therefore, it will be worth reviewing each of these theoretical models, 3.0 and 2.0, before introducing 1.0, the narrative enthymeme. I will address them in a historically reverse order here, beginning with the standard view (3.0) and then turning to Aristotle (2.0) and finally to ancient oratory (1.0).

This will not be a complete reinvention: 1.0 will introduce important alterations to a traditional understanding of the enthymeme, but the narrative enthymeme has some important elements in common with prior theoretical concretions. Most importantly, they all place inference-making at the center of rhetorical artistry, and they all attempt to describe the particular features of rhetorical inference-making to answer the question, What is specific about the reasoning process in the domain of rhetoric? Since I will be explicitly challenging the traditional PC framework, I will use the term *inference* in its broadest possible sense, but I claim Aristotelian authority for doing so. What Aristotle says about the enthymeme at *Rhetoric* 1.2.9 will serve as a satisfactory definition: "To show that if some things are so, something else beyond them results from these because they are true, either universally or for the most part."[15]

The central focus of any study of the enthymeme, and of rhetorical artistry generally, has to include this central process by which something results in the audience from some other things being shown by the speaker to be so. We typically translate and interpret this definition in the language of premises and conclusions, but Aristotle avoids this terminology. *Sullogismos* here is not restricted to any logical form; it can apply as well to narrative as to deduction. An action can be seen to result from a motive and an opportunity, a character trait or moral quality from a repeated action, the proper ending of a story from its beginning and middle, the meaning of an earlier action from a later result. Aristotle rightly places the inferential move at the center of persuasive artistry, and he wisely keeps his definition of inference-making as broad and all-encompassing as possible, even if this breadth will subsequently be compromised by a commitment to deductive topical forms. We could with Perelman and Olbrechts-Tyteca say that the narrative enthymeme forms a liaison between some narrative fact or detail and another—between narrative fact and storyworld, real world, or audience response.

3.0 defines *inference* even more narrowly in syllogistic terms that are entirely inappropriate to ancient rhetorical practice. 3.0 is described as a conclusion from a premise; 1.0, on the other hand, leaves the nature of the inference rather broadly unspecified other than saying that it arises from a plot set in a human storyworld. If it arises from strings of premises, these strings are simply the stated and imagined details of a narrative. They have no preordained formal requirements in order to qualify as an inference. Plus, in narratives, the rational or cognitive element of reasoning cannot be separated from other aspects of the inferential movement. A narrative inference will include every kind of effect that an audience thinks, feels, and experiences in the storyworld and that they receive from the narrative that is told. It is not restricted to "logical" conclusions understood as mentally affirmed propositions. If the "things" that are "the case" are told in a narrative, then the "things that result" will include emotional reactions, assessments of character, sensations, moral and aesthetic judgments, and attitudes as well as mental beliefs or affirmations of truth.

Thus inference-making as an element of rhetorical artistry does not require that the "things that result" be articulated as propositions or even that they take a verbal form at all (e.g., rather than arising as an attitude, emotion, desire, or aversion; a mental model or imagined scene or object; or a moral or aesthetic feeling or movement). Inference-making will have to involve all manner of narrative effects, including many (though perhaps not all) forms of implication, suggestion, association, and bodily affect, all of which lie outside the rigidly formal PC model ensconced in 3.0 and suggested by Aristotle more loosely as 2.0.

There are other similarities among 3.0, 2.0, and 1.0. All are said to include items that are left unstated. The enthymeme is able to prompt a response in the audience beyond what was said. 3.0 describes this in terms of the "truncated" or "suppressed" major premise of a syllogism that is known as a popular opinion or cultural assumption (*doxa* or *endoxa*). 2.0 says simply that for rhetorical arguments, not all of the premises that are strictly necessary for reaching a conclusion must be stated or demonstrated and that we should use as few as necessary. 1.0 similarly works across "gaps" that separate the narrative as told from the story as experienced. Narrative gaps are a ubiquitous feature of narratives, and they are central to story comprehension and enjoyment.

In legal stories, narrative gaps separate facts that can be proven or attested to and those that can only be inferred and felt. More generally, they separate the end of the narrative as told by the narrator from the conclusion of the story and its *periodos* that the jury must grasp and put into effect. Narrative enthymemes guide audiences to see the proper narrative details in the proper light and to draw from them just those inferences and responses that will further the plot and win the verdict. Only by seeing rhetoric as situated within narrative can we see rhetorical artistry in the proper light and the enthymeme for what it is.

5. PLAN OF THE PRESENT WORK

My goal in this work, then, will be to describe the narrative enthymeme as it was developed by practiced Greek logographers for adversarial legal arguments and to demonstrate regularities of use that suggest the development of a deliberate technique. Before I unpack this argument, I'll want to clear the space for it, space currently occupied by the two currently operative models of the enthymeme: 3.0 and 2.0. To that end, I will begin in chapters 1 and 2 with a discussion of the familiar and traditional neo-Aristotelian truncated-syllogism enthymeme. The standard view of the enthymeme—though well known and well supported in the fields of logic, argumentation theory, rhetoric, and composition and communication—is entirely inappropriate to ancient Greek oratory and makes a poor model of rhetorical argument generally.

A full exploration of the development of 3.0, its attractions, and its flaws has not yet been compiled, but some of the problems with 3.0 are well rehearsed. Despite this, 3.0 remains the standard view: it is taught in textbooks, advertised on rhetoric websites, applied in rhetorical criticism, and explored in scholarly research. In light of this continued support, a fuller exploration of its development, its flaws, and its improbable survival seems warranted. Thus in part 1, I will examine 3.0. In chapter 1, I'll describe the standard view and review the history of this rhetorical concept to understand how it evolved from its Aristotelian origins and how it more recently accrued its contemporary features, and I'll explore some reasons for its current appeal. Then in chapter 2, I will review some of its practical difficulties. I want to demonstrate that this enthymeme survives not because it is useful or faithful to Aristotle but because it is old and familiar, traditional and teachable.

In part 2, I turn more specifically to Aristotle to explain in some detail what Aristotle says about the enthymeme. In chapter 3, I will attempt to show that *enthumēma* is not a kind of syllogism; it is simply explanatory reasoning. It has no essential features that differentiate it from dialectical *sullogismos*. Also, because *sullogismos* itself means not "syllogism" but "explanatory reasoning," 2.0 is not a syllogism at all. Thus it is not limited to two premises, and its so-called missing premise is misleading at best and irrelevant at worst as a defining feature of the Aristotelian enthymeme. 2.0 is not syllogistic but topical. In fact, the rhetorical topics from which enthymemes are drawn are much more adaptable to a narrative framework than they are to a syllogistic one. While Aristotle's language leads us to view instances of rhetorical reasoning as "like" the so-called dialectical syllogism, in fact his rhetorical topics (unlike his dialectical topics) retain the imprint of their narrative origins.

In chapter 4, I discuss the limitations of Aristotle's enthymeme, *rhetorikos sullogismos*. Unfortunately, Aristotle's discussion of the enthymeme tacitly suppresses a narrative approach to rhetorical argument in part because he limits logos to *sullogismos* and *sullogisimos* to topical forms. His unit of analysis is not the narrative and its plot but the PC structure and its form. For this reason, even though 2.0 is theoretically more defensible and practically more flexible than 3.0, as a model of rhetorical reasoning, it remains unsatisfactory and misleading. Aristotle was committed to understanding rhetoric from the perspective of the dialectical framework of the *Topics*, but dialectic is not the best lens through which to view ancient legal rhetoric. It is unfortunate that Aristotle made this choice because he had at his disposal a perfectly good and more serviceable avenue for approaching rhetoric in his *Poetics*. Rhetoric is not the antistrophe of dialectic; it is an application of narrative.

I suspect that previous criticisms of the standard view have failed to erode its popularity in part because there has been, up to now, no good replacement for it. 2.0 is underdeveloped, ambiguous, in parts contradictory, difficult to apply to most rhetorical texts, and unsatisfying either as a productive technique or as an analytical tool, whereas 3.0 is clear, precise, teachable, and seems to state more explicitly what Aristotle must have meant. That it is wrong seems not to be much of a drawback. Even if you can't use it to create arguments, you can easily impose it upon unwary primary texts and students—and always with positive results. It has the support of centuries of scholarly authority, and it adapts itself well to current trends.

To claim that 3.0 bastardizes Aristotle and has marginal relevance to how people actually argue or persuade—and therefore little legitimate rhetorical value—and to claim that 2.0 itself mischaracterizes ancient rhetorical practice and ought to be set aside without not only demonstrating its failings but also offering a better model would be highly impolitic and would leave us with a rather disappointing gap in our rhetorical lexicon. If 3.0 is not Aristotelian, and if both 2.0 and 3.0 misrepresent the nature of ancient rhetorical reasoning, what, then, is the enthymeme? In part 3, I put forward my answer to this question by returning to the opening argument: it is a linking technique developed by orators specifically for the adversarial narratives of a legal trial.

In chapter 5, I look at the language of the orators that gave rise to the term *enthymeme*, deriving it not from the "passional" *thumos* or the missing premise that the audience already has "in mind" (*en-thumos*)[16] but from the verb *enthumeisthai*, or "enthymize," a term frequently used by the orators. I examine the variety of meanings and the patterns of use that led to the rise of this term as a deliberate rhetorical (and narrative) move. In chapter 6, I look at some examples of enthymizing in the context of a speech, a narrative, and a case to illustrate the varieties of its use. Then in chapter 7, I turn to the terms of narrative theory and to features of the contest or game to see whether these approaches can contribute to our understanding of rhetorical reasoning. Finally, in chapters 8 and 9, I nominate Lysias as an early inventor of the enthymeme. I argue that in Lysias 1, *On the Death of Eratosthenes*, Lysias explicitly proposes the enthymeme as a kind of reasoning and a rhetorical skill that is central not only to legal oratory but to life in a secure household and a robust democratic polis. This disarmingly simple and entertaining speech includes enthymizing, names enthymizing and highlights it as a rhetorical skill, teaches students what it is and how it works, and then encourages students to produce their own. It is Lysias, I suggest, who put 1.0 on the map. The conclusion will summarize these findings and offer a few suggestions for further work.

PART ONE
3.0

CHAPTER 1

Enthymeme 3.0
The Truncated Syllogism

THE STANDARD VIEW

For several millennia, the enthymeme has been taught, on the putative authority of Aristotle, as "a kind of syllogism" (*sullogismos tis*; *Rhetoric* 1.1.11; 33), which is to say a rhetorical syllogism (*rhētorikon sullogismon*; 1.2.8; 40). Aristotle is understood to say that there are other kinds of syllogisms, such as dialectical, demonstrative, and contentious (or eristic) syllogisms, in addition to rhetorical ones.[1] A syllogism, as explained in the *Prior Analytics*, is a three-term argument structure in which a conclusion that is different from the initial two premises necessarily follows from these premises because they are true (A.4; Smith 1989, 4). Every syllogism has two premises: a premise with a major or more general term (a major premise) and a premise with a less general or minor term (a minor premise). Each premise has two terms, a predicate and a subject, and the two premises together share one term, the middle term, which drops out of the conclusion. Every syllogism thus contains three terms in total, as in this first figure syllogism in the universal affirmative:

All A is B   (Major premise, A)
All B is C   (Minor premise, C)
All A is C   (Conclusion in which the middle term, B, has dropped out)

Unlike this standard, or what is often referred to as a "primary" syllogism (*Rhetoric* 1.2.13; 41), the rhetorical syllogism, or enthymeme, is said to rely on reputable (*endoxa*; 1.1.11; 34) or probable (*eikos*; 1.2.14–15; 42) premises rather than certain ones so that its conclusion is not necessary but true only, as Aristotle says, "for the most part" (1.2.14; 42). So a proposition might read, "A is for the most part B" or "A is usually" or "probably B." This is because human knowledge about the past and the future is not certain and because patterns and signs of human behavior are not entirely reliable (1.2.14; 42). Further, one premise of the rhetorical syllogism is "suppressed" and unstated. Usually the major premise is suppressed because it is already known to the audience; they already have it in mind (*en-thumos*), and they mentally add it in (1.2.13; 41–42). A common example concerns the mortality of Socrates:

Socrates is human
Socrates is mortal[2]

An enthymeme, then, is a three-part probable argument that is missing a piece because the audience already knows it and can supply that information for themselves. Although technically any one of the three propositions can be elided, commentators on the enthymeme overwhelmingly prefer to discuss enthymemes in which the major premise is left out (in the example above, "All humans are mortal"), because the major premise is most easily assimilated to the "common opinion" or "cultural assumption" (*doxa* or *endoxa*) that the audience already knows and accepts. Everyone already knows that humans are mortal, so it need not be stated.

By leaving the major premise unstated, the author shortens her argument; avoids boring, confusing, or insulting her listeners; and resists critical inquiry into the validity of her suppressed premise. Since it will at best be true only "for the most part," and since it is a dominant cultural assumption, it operates best when unacknowledged.[3] By remaining unspoken, the missing premise elicits the unwitting participation of the audience in constructing the very argument by which they are persuaded, achieving a shared bond—a kind of identification between speaker and listener. Thus it is the "missing piece" that renders the argument persuasive, that makes it rhetorical. I will refer to this model as the standard view, or simply 3.0.[4]

Instances of 3.0 in written or spoken text can be found by looking for (1) a proposition as conclusion with (2) a reason as premise connected by (3) a stated or implied causal conjunction (*because, for, since, so, therefore,* etc.).[5] "Socrates is mortal because Socrates is a man," or "since Socrates is a man, Socrates is mortal" (Corbett and Connors 1999, 46; see Knudsen 2014, 42).[6] Its expressive form can vary considerably: "What man is immortal? And is Socrates not a man?" We'll see below that the modern enthymeme has been broadened to include any argument missing a piece or an argument that, when a piece is added, becomes clearer or logically valid: Moms love the added vitamins! Kids love the taste! Get Frosted-Os for breakfast!

However it is expressed, the enthymeme is widely agreed to be logically reducible to the three-part structure described above. Levi calls the truncated version a premise-conclusion (PC) sequence: conclusion because premise, or premise therefore conclusion (1995, 70). In each case, a premise making the sequence logically complete is implied and assumed.

3.0 thrives in contemporary rhetorical scholarship. The presentation of the concept and its use as an analytical tool in an essay by Young is typical and can stand in the place of many similar examples that could be cited:

> According to Aristotle (2001), an enthymeme is "a sort of syllogism" (p. 180). Bitzer (1959) further explains enthymeme as "a syllogism based on probabilities, signs, and examples" in which the premises are "supplied by the audience" and "whose function is rhetorical persuasion" (p. 408). As an abbreviated logical argument in which one premise is not explicitly stated, an enthymeme requires audience and rhetor to have shared unspoken assumptions (Burnyeat, 1994; Cronkhite, 1966; Emmel, 1994). An essential component of a successful enthymeme, then, is that the audience inserts the argument's premise as intended by the rhetor. (2015, 333–34)[7]

I cite the passage at length to illustrate the familiarity of the standard view and the constellation of its parts: an enthymeme is (1) a sort of syllogism (2) based on signs or probabilities (3) that is persuasive because (4) it includes a premise that is shared by the rhetor and audience such that (5) it need not be stated by the speaker but (6) is supplied by the audience. Young can tick off all these elements in rapid succession because they are not controversial; all are widely known and accepted features of the concept. For rhetoricians, 3.0 is, we might say, *endoxa*.

THE APPEAL OF 3.0

3.0 has become the standard view of the enthymeme for a number of good reasons. First, it must be admitted that Aristotle's *Rhetoric* does seem to say that an enthymeme is a "kind of syllogism" (1.1.11; 33) and a "rhetorical syllogism" (1.2.8; 40) drawn from probabilities and signs (1.2.14–18; 42–43), that it is the function of rhetoric to present arguments "among such listeners as are not able to see many things all together or to reason from a distant starting point" (1.2.12; 41), and that therefore enthymemes ought to be "drawn from few premises and often less than those of the primary syllogism, for if one of these is known, it does not have to be stated, since the hearer supplies it" (1.2.13; 41–42; see also 2.22.3; 168–69). He gives the example of Dorieus's crown. By saying that Dorieus won a prize at the Olympics, we can show that he was crowned, since the Olympic prize is a crown. But "there is no need," says Aristotle, to say this, since "everybody knows that" (1.2.13; 42).

Later he says that the conclusion of the enthymeme "should not be drawn from far back, nor is it necessary to include everything. The former is unclear because of the length [of the argument], the latter tiresome because of stating what is obvious" (2.22.3; 169). Again, he notes that enthymemes are most effective (2.23.30; 184), and the style is most pleasing and the understanding is quicker when something is given "in brief form" (3.11.8; 224).

Now, since a syllogism is known to have two premises and a conclusion, and since a syllogism with no premises is impossible, a shorter syllogism must have one premise. And since what is probable is also likely to be widely accepted, or *endoxa*, and since what is widely known need not be stated because the audience will often share this knowledge with the speaker—that is to say, it will be known by everybody—then it would seem that you shorten the syllogism by leaving unstated the premise that is widely known and hence probable and reputable. It thus seems clear that Aristotle is suggesting, albeit via a set of admittedly peculiar circumlocutions, that enthymemes are syllogisms in which one premise is left unsaid because it is well known to the audience, such as the crown given at the Olympics.[8]

This view has found indirect support from the *Prior Analytics*, where Aristotle seems to describe the enthymeme as a syllogism from probabilities and signs with either one or both premises stated. In his translation of the *Prior Analytics*, Tredennick has, "If only one premiss is stated, we get only a sign, but if the other premiss is assumed as well, we get a syllogism" (2.27.24–25; 1962, 525). Tredennick adds a note here to observe that this is "strictly an enthymeme" (525). By this he means that if one premise is stated and the other is assumed, we get not just a syllogism but that special species of syllogism called an enthymeme. Thus the *Prior Analytics* seems to provide an independent validation of this view: Aristotle differentiates the enthymeme from the syllogism by means of the number of premises that are stated and/or assumed (see, e.g., Kremmydas 2007, 26–27).

Given the difficulties with the original text—a reading of Aristotle's *Rhetoric* reveals it to be terse to the point of obscurity and in need of a healthy dose of critical elaboration[9]—it becomes easy to understand the motivation behind and the need for 3.0, which presents itself as a fuller, clearer, and more intellectually satisfying articulation of what Aristotle must have really meant. And given the sheer intellectual force that Aristotle can still exert in rhetorical scholarship and his virtual monopoly on our understanding of the enthymeme, getting ahold of what Aristotle really meant remains of primary importance.

Besides, given the field's continuing collective commitment to ethos, pathos, and logos and the apparent importance of deduction for logical argument, rhetorical scholarship has been loath to give up its proprietary brand of deductive logic. The standard view offers a specifically rhetorical logic—sufficiently simple to fit well into one section of a textbook (under "Argument: Logical Appeals") but complex enough to make the reading substantive, boasting a close relationship to a long tradition of logical reasoning and its lexicon (major premise, minor premise, deduction) but with a distinctly rhetorical adaptation to audience. 3.0 shows itself to be quasi-logical but sufficiently different from standard syllogistic form to make it a clearly distinct and therefore demonstrably valuable piece of rhetorical real estate.

What's more, 3.0 has been in the family for generations—centuries, even—and has been shored up, elaborated upon, and reiterated by a long line of rhetorical scholars. Teachers generally teach what they have been taught, and we try not to entirely ignore long-standing doctrine, especially textbook doctrine, producing a default conservatism in the academy.[10] It seems to be a natural inclination of intellectual economy to find (or invent, if necessary) scholarly value in whatever has been arduously labored over, lest that labor prove to have been in vain.[11] Plus, maintaining from Aristotle a logical structure and set of terms (*dialectic, deduction, induction, syllogism, premise*, etc.), even if these are later abandoned and other strictures of syllogistic form are altogether ignored, affords 3.0 both a respectable pedigree and a patina of logical rigor.

Then again, loosening or ignoring the unwieldly syllogistic frame, as twentieth-century scholars have done, allows an otherwise awkward and restrictive model to fit more comfortably into contemporary tenets of rhetorical theory, including the intersubjectivity of the self, the postmodern fragmentation of discourse, and the ideological power of cultural silences and absences. It also allows rhetoricians to maintain and advance the continuing and apparently universal relevance of concepts that were ostensibly developed to describe the rhetorical output of a relatively tiny, two-millennia-old political system (classical Athens) whose workings would in other ways be strange or outrageous to us. To suggest that the enthymeme might be a kind of argumentative strategy specifically suited to the agonistic, patriarchal, slaveholding, shame-based, performance and gift culture that gave rise to it and specific to the particularities of the amateur legal-political system (if it could be called a system) that served it—that is, to suggest that the enthymeme might be a piece of local theory—has been unthinkable.

Also, it must be admitted that an updated and universalized enthymeme 3.0, unmoored from its historical context and freed of its premodern syllogistic shackles, has generated a great deal of critical and theoretical scholarship. Perhaps no ancient rhetorical term has been found as useful to as many scholars over as long a time or been subjected to as many permutations as this foundling enthymeme. Its applications have been almost as numerous and variable as its meanings.[12] "The enthymeme," says Lloyd, "can mean whatever we decide it means" (2014, 734). It will be as useful as it is protean. Indeed, its popularity may be less a function of its value as a rhetorical concept than of its malleability as a rhetorical cipher—an incomplete symbol awaiting theoretical substance that can be supplied or "filled in" as needed. It is the "something more" that can always be added to what has been said, the thing that both completes and exposes incompleteness, reveals ambiguity, and brings clarity. Finding and filling in enthymemes always shows the reader to be a sensitive and astute critic.

We will see in chapter 2 that almost everything about this view of the enthymeme is wrong. It is not faithful to Aristotle, it is not accurate as an analytical tool, and it is not useful as a productive technique. Least of all does it reflect how ancient orators argued. Before discussing the problems with 3.0, it will perhaps be helpful to begin with the story of how it evolved from Aristotle in the first place. While the full history of 3.0 has not been written (and probably need not be written), enough of it can be pieced together from the work of Bons (2002), Walker (1994), Ong (1958), Burnyeat (1994), Conley (1984), Green (1995), Poster (2003), and others to reveal the important landmarks in its historical trajectory.

A BRIEF HISTORY OF 3.0

The enthymeme did not begin with Aristotle. It was known to Isocrates and Anaximenes (author of the *Ad Alexandrum*, which may predate Aristotle)[13] and almost certainly others. The *Rhetoric to Alexander* says that enthymemes are "contraries not only in word and action but also in all other ways" (10.1; 527).[14] Even prior to this (as I'll demonstrate in part 3), it was developed as a rhetorical technique by the orators. But since so little can be gleaned of the enthymeme from the early theorists, and since other early rhetorical treatises dropped out of circulation, and since the orators do not use this term to refer to the rhetorical technique, Aristotle came to be known not only as the principal theorist of the enthymeme but as its real inventor. And it is from Aristotle alone that 3.0 derives.

I will review Aristotle's discussion of the enthymeme in chapter 2. Here it will be important to preview a few important conclusions. Primary among these is that for Aristotle, *sullogismos* did not mean "syllogism" but something rather looser, such as "inference," "reasoning," or "explanatory reasoning through the serial assertion of linked premises that would lead a listener to affirm a conclusion." *Sullogismos* and its relative *sullogizesthai* were perfectly good Greek terms that already meant something like "infer," "conclude," or "total up." Herodotus says about an Egyptian labyrinth that "if one were to total up [*sullogisaito*] for display the walls and other works of the Greeks, the sum would not amount to the labor and cost of this labyrinth" (2.148.2; see *Cratylus* 412a; Fowler 2007, 98–99; and *Metaphysics* 4.7.7; Tredennick 1980, 202–3).

Present here are both the notion of gathering items (facts or statements) together in one view, of arranging them for easy comprehension by means of juxtaposition or aggregation, and of seeing or inferring from them or linking them to something new as a result.[15] The ability to do this with statements, says Plato, belongs to the dialectician (*Phaedrus* 266b5–c1; Fowler 1982, 534–35). And it is this that Aristotle teaches his students to do in the *Topics*. Yet nothing here suggests the categorical syllogism or its limitations as laid out in the *Prior Analytics*: two terms—one subject and one predicate—per premise, with two premises per deduction, and so on. So when Aristotle is made to say that "the enthymeme is a sort of syllogism" (*enthumēma sullogismos tis*; *Rhetoric* 1.1.11; 33), and when he is said to call a "rhetorical syllogism an enthymeme" (*rhetorikov sullogismov*; 1.2.8; 40), he means simply that an enthymeme is reasoning as used in rhetorical contests.

After Aristotle, the enthymeme became both less important and more ambiguous than it was in Aristotle's *Rhetoric* or than it would be in its twentieth-century neo-Aristotelian reanimation. Its general meaning lingered (a thought), and the meaning given it by the *Rhetoric to Alexander* persisted (a pointed contradiction), but later treatises shifted their attention away from the enthymeme and toward the topics, stasis theory, and the five-part "epicheireme," which became the basic unit of argument.[16]

The enthymeme was then understood to be an abbreviated (and hence imperfect) version or element of this longer unit (*Ad C. Herennium* 2.18.28; Caplan 1989, 106–9; see also Jebb 1876, 289–90). Cicero rarely discusses the enthymeme, and when he does, it is not typically in the Aristotelian sense. In *Topica*, Cicero defines the enthymeme simply as a thought and in rhetoric as belonging to the topos "from contraries" as the most pointed kind of thought (§§55–56; Hubbell 1993, 422–25; see also *Rhetoric to Alexander*). Elsewhere, he tends to avoid the term, though he devotes careful attention to the ongoing controversy over how many sections an argument ought to have (five, four, three, or two), suggesting that already in his time, proofs were distinguished less in terms of their rhetorical context or function than in terms of the number of their parts (see *De inventione* 1.34–41; Hubbell 1993, 98–105).

The *Art of Political Speech* (Anonymous Seguerianus), quoting Neocles, vaguely echoes Aristotle, but its definition is quite broad: "Enthymeme ... is language concerning something under discussion when some other things have been posited, or concerning what is antecedent, and stating the conclusion summarily and compactly" (Dilts and Kennedy 1997, 45). In Apsines's *Art of Rhetoric*, enthymemes are treated as topical forms. Enthymemes, we are told, are derived "from either the lesser or the parallel or the contrary or the greater or by setting an honorable judgment in opposition or syllogistically or from a dilemma" and so on (Dilts and Kennedy 1997, 175–77).

In *The Orator's Education*, Quintilian lists a wide range of definitions for the enthymeme, including "a proposition with a reason," "a conclusion of an argument drawn either from denial of consequences or from incompatibles," and "an imperfect syllogism, because its parts are not distinct or of the same number as those of the syllogism" (5.10.2–3; Russell 2001, 366–67; see *Rhetoric* 2.21.2; 165). The manual *On Style* (attributed to a Demetrius) echoes Aristotle in calling the enthymeme a "kind of syllogism"—that is to say, an "imperfect syllogism" (i.e., "an imperfect sort of reasoning" *sullogismos atelēs*; §1.32; Innes 1995, 371).

Aristotle's *Rhetoric* had declined in influence by late antiquity, and rhetorical understanding of the term remained ambiguous, but the enthymeme nevertheless thrived in translations, commentaries, and textbooks on Aristotle's *Prior Analytics*, where syllogistic theory is laid out and the enthymeme is mentioned, once, at 2.27. Aristotle explains that an inference from just one premise is not a deduction but a sign; that if you add to a sign a second premise, it becomes a deduction; and that the enthymeme is a deduction from signs. This explanation was misread to say that the enthymeme was a one-premise (i.e., imperfect) deduction (Smith 1989, 102–3)

Green (1995) suggests that it was the declining importance and early loss of the *Rhetoric* that contributed to the shift in meaning of a term that was already fading in relevance. This was a shift in interpretative context as well: away from Aristotle's *Rhetoric* and the dialectic of the *Topics* and toward the syllogistic figures of the *Prior Analytics*. It was also a narrowing: the enthymeme as a contradictory thought, topical framework, or abbreviated epicheireme was lost. The enthymeme would increasingly be encountered in the context of formal logic and the developing theory of the categorical syllogism and its figures, and it thus became more definitively a "one-premise syllogism."

The phrase *imperfect syllogism* (συλλογισμὸς ἀτελής) as meaning "truncated"—that is, the enthymeme had only one premise—appeared in a commentary on the *Rhetoric* to describe the enthymeme and, not surprisingly, says Green, found its way into some manuscripts of the *Prior Analytics* (1995, 23–24). It was in this way that the tradition of the enthymeme as an imperfect—that is, a "single proposition" (μονολήμματος)—syllogism ossified and was preserved by an anonymous copyist's addition of the word *incomplete* (*atelēs*) into a copy of the text of the *Prior Analytics* possibly sometime around the twelfth or thirteenth century. The statement at 2.27, translated as "An enthymeme is a syllogism from likelihoods or signs," became "An enthymeme is an *imperfect* (ἀτελής) syllogism from likelihoods or signs."[17]

Two extant early manuscripts include the offending term: codex Coilinianus 330 dates to the eleventh century, though the passage at 2.27 was added in the twelfth or thirteenth century. Similarly, "most of Ambrosianus L93 sup. (490) dates from the 9th century, but the folios that include the present locus have been supplied by an imitator writing in the 15th century" (Green 1995, 23). The added *atelēs* continued to be included in editions, translations, and commentaries on the *Prior Analytics* well into the nineteenth century.

The textual emendation made its way into the text of the *Rhetoric* in the twelfth century, but the corrupt reading of Aristotle that made it possible gained a textual foothold much earlier, sometime between Alexander of Aphrodisias in the third century C.E., who still knew his *Rhetoric*, and Ammonius of Alexandria in the fifth, who apparently did not (Green 1995; and see Burnyeat 1994, 46–49). Of course, Ammonius was not the author of the error either, merely its transmitter and popularizer. Ammonius understood, says Green, that "rhetoricians use a syllogism that has but one premise (μονολήμματος) and that such a syllogism is imperfect (ἀτελής). Ammonius repeats the same argument in his commentary on Porphyry' s *Isogoge*, this time introducing the phrase συλλογισμὸς ἀτελής, thus making it easier for subsequent readers to understand *imperfection* as *truncation*" (1995, 22).

This view of the enthymeme was taken up by Boethius in his *De topicis differentiis*. Boethius describes the enthymeme as a syllogism whose "precipitate conclusion is derived without all the propositions having been laid down beforehand" and is therefore called an imperfect syllogism, since "it does not use all the propositions appropriate to a syllogism" (2.25; 45; Burnyeat 1994, 50). By the time of Philoponus (sixth century C.E.), the traditional doctrine was already "so entrenched as to make it extremely difficult to read [the *Prior Analytics*] correctly" (Burnyeat 1994, 48). And since Boethius "was to be an authoritative teacher of Logic for the Latin west," the Middle Ages followed Boethius's lead (50). This reading of Aristotle spread: "An anonymous scholiast on Hermongenes' *On Invention* specifies that enthymemes are syllogisms that are ἀτελής" (Green 1995, 23). Conley charts the continued use of the term down to the sixteenth century (Conley 1994, 217–42).

Absent the *Rhetoric*, the trend of logically framed thought and commentary on the enthymeme could proceed unimpeded throughout the Middle

Ages and into the Renaissance. Thus for Green, the mistaken reading is less a matter of a singularly incautious scribe than of a "continuing cultural interest in seeing the enthymeme... as an imperfect, or incomplete or truncated syllogism" (1995, 24), an inferior kind of popular logic.

During the Renaissance, two things changed. As scholars with Greek and Latin began to accumulate multiple versions of early texts, it became possible to compare manuscripts, to catalog alternative readings, and to refine methods for discerning better and worse textual variants. As a result of this "lower criticism," a few scholars began to suspect that errors had crept into some manuscripts of Aristotle's logical works. For example, in his 1584 edition of the *Prior Analytics*, Giulio Pace argued that the ἀτελής at 2.27 was not original, and he later offered nine reasons for rejecting it as a scribal insertion (Pace 1597). For example, the stray term did not appear in four early manuscripts, nor did early Greek and Latin translators and commentators betray any knowledge of this word or the doctrine it supported (Green 1995, 24–26). Besides, says Pace, though Aristotle discusses the single-premise syllogism, he never describes it as an enthymeme.

But this fusillade of erudition could not penetrate the thick hide of tradition. Even scholars who knew Pace, who knew the arguments concerning the error, and who understood the preferred reading of *Prior Analytics* 2.27 reverted to 3.0 when describing the enthymeme: "The authoritative Sylburg edition of Aristotle (Frankfurt 1585) and the great Casaubon edition (Lyon, 1590) both claim to have consulted Pace scrupulously; yet both include the supposedly offending word ἀτελής, and neither edition even bothers to acknowledge the emendation by Pace in 1584" (Green 1995, 26). Pace's corrections did periodically resurface, albeit as a minority view: Facciolati, De Quincey, Hamilton, Donaldson, and Seaton all challenged the standard view as faulty. But the majority of scholars continued to support 3.0.[18]

At the same time that lower criticism was being applied to Aristotle's works, the *Rhetoric* was being reintroduced into European schools. The enthymeme of the *Rhetoric* reentered scholarly discussions, but by then the logical tradition was too deeply entrenched to allow an unbiased reading such that "the intervening centuries of logical discussion were read back into the *Rhetoric*" (Green 1995, 37; see also Green 1994).

Ong notes that Ramus and others in the sixteenth century read Aristotle through the same reductive lens that Boethius had used earlier: "In Aristotle and everywhere else, Ramus takes enthymeme to mean a syllogism which is 'imperfect' in the crude *simpliste* sense that one of its premises is suppressed" (1958, 187). 3.0 was also the enthymeme of the Port Royal Logic (1662): "An enthymeme, is a syllogism perfect in the mind, but imperfect in the expression, since some one of the propositions is suppressed as too clear and too well known, and as being easily supplied by the mind of those to whom we speak" (Baynes 1850, 224; see also 177). A century and a half later, Whately in his *Elements of Logic* could assert much the same thing without having to refer to Aristotle: "An argument thus stated regularly and at full length, is called a Syllogism; which therefore is evidently not a peculiar *kind of argument*, but only a peculiar *form* of expression, in which every argument may be stated. When one of the premises is suppressed (which for brevity's sake it usually is) the argument is called an enthymeme" (1848, 44; italics in original).

Jevons adopts an ersatz etymological interpretation of the term: "A syllogism, when incompletely stated is usually called an enthymeme, and this name is often supposed to be derived from two Greek words (ἐν, in and θυμός, mind), so as to signify that some knowledge is held by the mind and is supplied in the form of a tacit, that is a silent or understood premise" (1888, 153; see also Green 1995, 36 and n. 72). He also goes on to describe the three "orders" of enthymeme according to whether the major premise, minor premise, or conclusion is suppressed (153–54).

Poster (2003) refers to Whately, Jevons, and other eighteenth- and nineteenth-century champions of 3.0 as "traditionalists" because they reject or ignore textual criticism of corrupt texts (biblical or secular, like the *Prior Analytics*) in order to maintain widespread and respected textual traditions. Just as traditionalists retained Jerome's Vulgate despite its textual errors, so in the secular realm traditionalists like Whately and Jevons retained 3.0 despite scholarly rejection of the ἀτελής in the *Prior Analytics* and despite demonstrable differences between 3.0 and Aristotle's *Rhetoric*. Whereas textual critics from Pace to Hamilton saw 3.0 as patently un-Aristotelian, "traditionalists" like Whately and Jevons defended 3.0 not, says Poster, for its fidelity to Aristotle (since Whately never mentions Aristotle) but for its longevity and its "immediate utility" (2003, 75).[19] Traditionalists, Poster continues, viewed the enthymeme as "an evolving usable set of ideas, gradually working itself out in history" (75).

Whatever we might think of the quixotic wisdom of defending 3.0 for its utility, we can see the inertia of tradition prevail against the engine of philology in Cope's commentary on the *Rhetoric* (1867, 103). In this work, Cope follows the criticism of William Hamilton, who argued, beginning with remarks from Rodolphus Agricola (1521) and including the scholarship of Pace, that the *atelēs* was a late interpolation into the *Prior Analytics*, that the "vulgar doctrine" of 3.0 had been illegitimately "fathered upon the Stagirite," and that the "truncated syllogism" could not be Aristotle's view of the enthymeme (1852, 151–56). Based on Hamilton's arguments, Cope finds that the "distinctive difference" between the enthymeme and the syllogism is not truncation; it is not a matter of form at all. Rather, "its premises and conclusions are never more than probable" (1867, 102). In fact, says Cope, a syllogism based on signs and probabilities "expressed at full length, with all its terms and premises and conclusions complete, would be just as much an enthymeme as the incomplete one" (102–3).

Unfortunately, Cope later recalled that dialectic also uses premises that are neither certainly nor universally true. And so, believing that rhetorical and dialectical must be distinct species of reasoning and that they therefore required some essential difference, he had to recant his previous position. Since rhetorical syllogisms must differ in some definitive way from dialectical syllogisms as two species of the same genus,[20] and since this difference could not be the probability of the premises, Cope peremptorily threw out the baby with the bathwater, rejecting Hamilton and the whole line of scholarship that Hamilton represented and reverting back to 3.0. Cope declared his change of heart in a now infamous and influential footnote. He rejected 3.0, he says, "in deference to Hamilton" but is now "convinced that he is wrong" (1867, 103). The probability of the rhetorical syllogism cannot distinguish it from the probability of the dialectical syllogism. Therefore the difference must be one of form: "The syllogism," says Cope, "is complete in all its parts, the enthymeme incomplete; one of the premises or the conclusion is *invariably* wanting" (103; emphasis in original). Cope's *Introduction to Aristotle's Rhetoric* (1867) and his posthumously published translation of *The Rhetoric* with commentary (revised and edited by J. E. Sandys, 1877) became standard resources for twentieth-century rhetorical scholarship. And so Boethius and Ramus's enthymeme became Cope's enthymeme, and it was Cope's noteworthy reversal that set the stage for the improbable modern resurgence of the standard view.

In the twentieth century, 3.0, maintained by traditionalists and propped up by Cope's footnote, retained its dominance. This is the view, says Madden, "which is always present in the textbooks" (1952, 373). This is the view of Corbett and Connors (1999, 52–53), and more recently of Crowley and Hawhee (2004), and of Keith and Lundberg (2008, 37). It reappears in twentieth-century logic texts as well, such as Copi, Cohen, and McMahon's *Introduction to Logic* (2014, 274–76). It is this very "Boethian and Ramist notion of enthymeme," says Ong, "which prevails today" (1958, 187).

The later twentieth century has also introduced a few modifications to the standard view. Brandt et al. (1969), for example, saw the enthymeme as the structural principle behind an entire composition (see also Gage 1983). In what follows, I'd like to focus in a bit more detail on two recent scholars who further modified Aristotle's enthymeme: Lloyd Bitzer and Roland Barthes. If Aristotle said that enthymemes were "often" shorter than "primary deductions" and that "if a premise is known, it does not have to be stated" (*Rhetoric* 1.2.13; 41–42), Bitzer will prove that to be persuasive, an enthymeme *has* to be shorter and that this brevity *must* be a consequence of leaving a premise an audience member knows unstated. Bitzer and Barthes together will further prove that an enthymeme gains its persuasive power *only* by leaving unstated those *endoxa* that the audience silently or unconsciously assents to. They will in the process pull the enthymeme further out of the orbit of Aristotle, remaking it into a distinctly modern and postmodern argument form.

BITZER: THE INTERACTIONIST ENTHYMEME

In his now famous essay "Aristotle's Enthymeme Revisited," Bitzer does not merely repeat the standard view; he detaches it from its Aristotelian frame and cements it onto a more recent foundation of modern social theory. Bitzer takes as the defining feature of the enthymeme the idea that the speaker must "ask for" and the listeners must supply some of the premises supporting the speaker's argument, and thus it is this "supplying" that makes the enthymeme persuasive (1959, 404). Of course, Aristotle says nothing of the kind in the *Rhetoric*, but he does say this about dialectical reasoning in the *Prior Analytics* (A.1; Smith 1989, 1): the questioner asks and the respondent answers a question or "lays down" a proposition for the questioner. Bitzer takes what is true literally of dialectical reasoning to be in some sense true also of rhetoric: the speaker must "ask" and the audience must "supply" premises for the argument. Again, Aristotle says nothing like this in the *Rhetoric*, and it is an unusual if not downright misleading way to characterize the ways in which speakers rely on or adapt to an audience's knowledge and beliefs.

On the face of it, this characterization looks like the standard "truncated syllogism" view of the enthymeme sponsored by logicians for centuries. But two things change here. First, the missing premise goes from being useful or helpful (to avoid boring listeners) to being strategically necessary: it is the missing premise that makes the enthymeme persuasive. Also, the definition shifts attention from the premise that was truncated to the one that was supplied. By saying the listener must supply a premise, Bitzer means not merely that the speaker "omits" a logical proposition but that the listener must "give" a premise to the listener. The listener's contribution and the resulting interaction are emphasized over the syllogistic form (which becomes irrelevant) or the selective truncation. This is not a logical but a social enthymeme.

From the perspective of symbolic interactionism, social reality, knowledge, and selfhood occur only through symbolic interaction with others, and so the basic methodological unit of analysis is never the individual but the dyad in interaction. A person becomes a "self" capable of knowing and interacting with others and the world only by developing the ability to mentally view things from the perspective of the other. In fact, a "self" is nothing but the accretion of internalized social interactions and patterns of interaction with specific and generalized others (Goffman 1959, 252–55). Since the speaker must anticipate the premise that the listener will be able to supply, she must take up the position of the listener. Reciprocally, the listener must adopt the perspective of the speaker in order to supply the premise required to produce a new understanding. Enthymeme becomes an argument that requires give and take, an interaction. If social life, including persuasion, is built upon interaction, then the rhetorical argument will be persuasive to the degree and in the way that it prompts interaction.

The implications of this perspective to rhetorical argumentation and its utility to Bitzer are clear: only when the listener adds back in the premise that the speaker has elided can the dyad make the enthymeme. In this way, the knowledge and the persuasion that is produced becomes a thoroughly social act. For Bitzer, the generation of rhetorical argument is a function not of syllogistic form or rhetorical "invention," as the enthymeme is no longer understood through the elision of a premise. It is now a function of the symbolic interaction between a socialized speaker able to place herself in the position of the audience, on the one hand, and on the other, of an audience able to understand and supply what the speaker has left out.

This results in a view of the enthymeme as an incomplete argument in what Bitzer calls "a special sense." For in fact, says Bitzer, in an apparent departure from the standard view, whether or not the speaker suppresses or omits a premise from his argument is "of no logical importance" (1959, 407).[21] What matters from the perspective of rhetoric is that the speaker cannot complete the syllogism by herself: "An orator or a dialectician can *plan* a rhetorical or dialectical argument while sitting at the desk in his study, but he cannot really *complete* it by himself, because some of the materials from which he builds arguments are absent. The missing materials of rhetorical arguments are the premises which the audience brings with it and supplies at the proper moment" (405).[22] A finished speech occurs only when the audience takes up what the speaker said and completes it, and an argument becomes an enthymeme only when the auditor puts it back in.

This way of understanding the enthymeme, while superficially similar to the standard view, is actually quite new. It draws more from Mead (1943) and Blumer (1969) than it does from Aristotle. The enthymeme will no longer be defined by its syllogistic frame, the nature of its premises, its logical or topical forms, the premise that is omitted, or any deliberate rhetorical technique on the part of the speaker. It is not "invented." It will refer to a naturally cooperative act between speaker and audience based on the social nature of human development and intersubjective selfhood. Enthymematic reasoning won't be a logical achievement of rhetorical artistry; it will be a discursive consequence of human interaction. For Bitzer, "Aristotle calls enthymemes the 'substance of rhetorical persuasion'" because "the audience itself helps construct the proofs by which it is persuaded" (1959, 408).

It is Bitzer, and not Aristotle, who "proves" that the supplied premise is functionally necessary. Bitzer's continued use of the term *premise* and other terms of syllogistic form should not lull us into a belief that he is still speaking of Aristotelian logic, which has already faded into irrelevance. He is referring not to syllogisms but to any kind of argument or reasoning, a part of which is supplied by the audience. Thus *enthymeme* will henceforth name not the truncated syllogism but the persuasive power of any audience-added "piece" of argument. Bitzer's enthymeme will in this way become a sort of negative image of the Aristotelian model, a product not of the rhetor's art but of the listener's interaction.

Again, none of this is Aristotelian, nor is it implied by what Aristotle says. This is not to say that Bitzer's views on the participation of the audience in constructing arguments are not useful or important. In fact, Bitzer here anticipates a range of later discussions about personae, the implied reader, and reader response criticism. Audiences, we now recognize, do play an important and active role in constructing and interpreting the texts that they hear or read. In fact, in part 3, I will also discuss how readers and audiences contribute to the texts they take in. Bitzer recognized social interaction as a necessary analytical feature of all rhetoric and interpretation, and Bitzer was right to argue that aspects of every rhetorical technique take place not simply in production but in interaction and reception. This is especially true, as we will see, in storytelling. For while "adding a piece" to an ongoing argument is difficult and counterproductive, filling in narrative gaps is an inevitable and fundamental aspect of a narrative's appeal and its persuasive power. Bitzer's enthymeme was the first clue toward a better understanding of the interactive basis of rhetorical reasoning. But this is not simply a matter of the enthymeme; it is characteristic of all textual interpretation and all argument, including narrative. If the enthymeme is to be a distinctly rhetorical kind or use of argument, it cannot be defined by audience participation, since some form of audience participation is a necessary quality of all symbolic interaction.

Nevertheless, Bitzer's views would come to have a lasting effect on twentieth- to twenty-first-century rhetorical theory and on the treatment of the enthymeme.[23] Fisher uses Bitzer's definition of the enthymeme to make an argument about teaching argument: "By teaching the enthymeme ... students become conscious of the fact that reasoning usually rests on unstated assumptions, which if an audience grants, the reasoning is persuasive" (1964, 201). Within two decades, a reference to Bitzer was unnecessary because his views had become the new standard. Thus Gage could echo Bitzer without citing him: "The enthymeme cannot be constructed in the absence of a dialectical relationship with an audience, since it is only through what the audience contributes that the enthymeme exists as such" (1984, 157).

Later authors will continue to explicitly affirm Bitzer's modifications, including dropping the language of the syllogism and emphasizing the audience-supplied assumption. Raymond, for example, observes simply that "enthymemes may be defined as assumptions used in public discourse" (1984, 144). Welsh similarly asserts that "it is the unstated portion of the argument that gives rhetorical enthymeme its persuasive power," and he will repeat Jevon's etymological hook: "Enthymemes need not explicitly state those premises that are anchored in common sense. They are already there, in the spirit (*en-thumos*)" (2014, 9).

BARTHES: THE IDEOLOGICAL ENTHYMEME

Bitzer's interactionist version of the standard view (we could call it 3.1) remains influential, but it has more recently been overlaid with a neo-Marxist frame. For Barthes, an enthymeme is an argument that relies on ideological knowledge that is taken for granted and remains unspoken. The ideological enthymeme derives from *S/Z*, Barthes's literary analysis of Balzac's *Sarrasine*. In Balzac's story, the narrator has brought a beautiful young woman, Madame de Rochfide, to a party at the home of the nouveau riche de Lanty family. A question is whispered by the guests: Whence their newfound wealth? The family all speak French, Spanish, English, and German fluently. Were they freebooters? Gypsies? Here we have a narrative puzzle[24] and a rumored solution: gypsies are known to possess ill-gotten, hidden wealth, and in their travels, they would acquire the languages of Europe, so perhaps . . .

A second hermeneutic riddle is posed by the narrator himself: Will he succeed in seducing Mme de Rochfide? At the party, an ancient man looking like death itself is seated beside her. The Madame whispers to him a third question: "Who is he?" This prompts the narrator to bargain his problem for hers: he will tell her the story of the old man if she will accept his advances. The following evening, the narrator tells Mme de Rochfide an intradiegetic story about the titular character, Sarrasine, an artist who travels from his native France to Rome to study sculpture. There he visits the theater and falls in love with and pursues the beautiful, pale, Italian singer Zambinella. A final hermeneutic puzzle for readers and for Mme de Rochfide parallels the narrator's own: "Will Sarrasine acquire Zambinella?" Zambinella looks, sings, dresses, and behaves like the perfect woman. She is talented, charming, brilliant, timid. She startles at the sound of popping champagne corks, and of course she rebuffs Sarrasine's advances, so he determines to abduct her.

Sarrasine gets himself invited to a salon where Zambinella is in attendance. He searches for her and asks someone where she is. But he uncovers an unfortunate hermeneutic setback: "'She? What she?' asked the old nobleman to whom Sarrasine had been speaking" (Barthes 2002, 184). The Frenchman Sarrasine does not know that women are prohibited from the Italian stage and that in Italy, all female roles are performed by castrati. Upon hearing the truth, Sarrasine carries out his plan to abduct Zambinella not out of passion but out of rage. He threatens the castrato's life, but he is discovered and killed by Zambinella's patron and protector.[25] The old man at the party, says the narrator, is Zambinella himself. After discovering this truth, the woman at the party is scandalized and declares her disgust for life and for passion. She refuses to keep her bargain with the narrator.

Both the narrator and Sarrasine fail in their quest, says Barthes, because they fall victim to the "snare" of ideology. They rely on faulty reasoning drawn from unspoken, ideologically informed premises in the form of *endoxa*. Faulty reasoning: the Lantys must be gypsies or freebooters because they speak many European languages and enjoy newfound, mysterious wealth (2002, 32). But they speak the languages of musical Europe because their benefactor and great-uncle Zambinella was a famous singer. Faulty reasoning: Zambinella is pale, beautiful, timid, and startles easily; therefore, she must be a woman. The truth: she was, like all performers in Italy, male (84, 148, 168, 171, 172). Faulty reasoning: Mme de Rochfide is passionate and will thus respond to a story about passion. The truth: she is disgusted by the violence of the story and rejects her suitor.

For Barthes, the premises for this kind of reasoning come from "the Book of culture, of life" (2002, 21), a macédoine of bourgeois common sense and internalized school-manual learning: the polyglot are gypsies, only women are timid, and women are easily aroused by stories of passion. Beliefs like these, bits of a "naturalized" ideology whose authority is taken for granted, complete the reasoning of the characters and the narrator. As already spoken from the "book of Life" or the school manual, they can remain unuttered while still functioning as part of any argument's interpretative dynamic. Here we have an argument, part of which is unuttered because it is well known by the audience and taken for granted as *endoxa*: What could this be but our old enthymeme, now revealed to be the textual mask of hegemony?[26] This faulty reasoning, drawn from a "nauseating mixture of common opinions, a smothering layer of received ideas" (206), which is also known as "endoxal truth," is simply enthymematic reasoning (184).

For Barthes, enthymematic reasoning encodes not knowledge but power. The enthymeme will be a tool not of rhetorical logos, dialectical argument, or social interaction but of naturalized, cultural self-reification. The enthymeme prompts the reader to act upon and so reproduce all the traditional "truths" that she already "knows"—truths that the culture has itself generated and relies upon for its operation. The ideological enthymeme is the snare in the hermeneutic code; it is the false clue, the textual manifestation of false consciousness (2002, 32, 84). It is truncated because it appeals to the authority of bourgeois ideology—the predictable, parochial "truth" that everyone already knows—but it is false. Because the ideological enthymeme is fundamentally hegemonic and works to maintain the status quo, audiences do not fill in the silences so much as they are *operated on* by them: Sarrasine, Zambinella, the narrator, and Mme de Rochfide.

Like Bitzer's enthymeme, Barthes's quickly gained traction. It informed McGee's (1990) influential work on textual and cultural fragmentation and on the silences of *doxa*. And it supports Ratcliffe's observation that, as the voice of ideology, the enthymeme "possesses a conservative power" (2007, 280): "Unstated assumptions not only drive thought, communication, and action, but they also drive the status quo; they hinder change because change is dependent upon changing not just thoughts and actions but assumptions. Unstated reasons drive the status quo because the speaker/writer assumes the reasons to be self-evident; if someone does not find the reasons to be self-evident, then that someone is an outsider to the powers-that-be-that-decide-assumptions" (281).

This postmodern version of the enthymeme (3.2) is much more dangerous than the traditional version because it is much more powerful. It is not a scaffold for logical deduction or a stitch of social interaction but a cog in the machine of political domination. And unlike the earlier models, this enthymeme is driven not by the structure of a syllogism, the premise that the speaker "asks for," or the one that the audience "adds" but by the broad expanse of taken-for-granted cultural and moral authority that undergirds any epistemic or moral assertion. The missing premise will now be but the blank trace of a massive, subterranean discursive realm—the invisible and dangerous depths of an expressive iceberg (Prenosil 2012, 209) or the "dark matter" of discourse (Ratcliffe 2007, 276). The unspoken premise silently evokes the invisible-because-naturalized workings of a preexisting ideological code (Jackson 2006; Scenters-Zapico 1994, 71).

This version of 3.0 thus marks another kind of reversal: an already buried needle in a haystack of bourgeois learning, the missing piece of the argument need not be truncated by the speaker, nor will it be mentally "supplied" by the listener. It is always already and must be kept silent (McGee 1990, 281). The unspoken premise as a cultural imperative is a submarine: it can perform its function only if it remains submerged.

If the rhetor does not suppress a premise and the audience does not "supply" the missing piece, then what point of rhetorical intervention will characterize 3.0? It will be the task of the critic to crack open the oppressive machine and reveal what lies within, to expose for scrutiny the cultural codes upon which the enthymeme depends and through which hegemony operates. If the premodern enthymeme belonged to the rhetor and his technique and the modern enthymeme belonged to the audience and their participation, the postmodern enthymeme would belong to the critic and her insight. It will be for the critic to carry out the work of "unmasking cultural imperatives, giving voice to the silences of *doxa*" (McGee 1990, 281). For this reason, Ratcliffe can observe that "in the practices of everyday life, people rarely know the concept or use the term, even as every single person regularly composes enthymemes in writing, speech, and body language" (2007, 278). Only the critic can point out to both speaker and listener the deep enthymematic undertow that imperceptibly channels the flow of their thoughts along the paths of hegemony.

The insights of Barthes (and his rhetorical translators like McGee) have been enormously influential and useful in pointing out the political operation of cultural texts and the crucial function of seeing the interpretative threads that connect any text to the discourses and ideologies that inform them and from which they are made. This poststructuralist semiotic showed why it was necessary and generative to read what is not said as carefully as what is. But again, this is a quality of all texts and all discourse: every argument remains immersed in hegemonic and counterhegemonic discourses unequally competing over the unspoken interpretative frameworks through which any text will be read. Thus the "missing piece" cannot be a distinctive feature of the enthymeme unless all discourse is enthymematic.

If the term is to mark a distinct quality of rhetorical argument, then we will have to look elsewhere for its features. Both Bitzer and Barthes aid our current understanding of how texts work upon audiences within a cultural setting. Both also helped entrench the notion that an enthymeme is an argument missing a piece. And both tied the enthymeme to features of discourse and interpretation that are far too large for it to support.

The standard view claims an Aristotelian lineage, a long history of scholarly support, and robust theoretical and analytical fecundity. It offers a convincing account of a kind of reasoning recognizably within the realm of logic but suited specifically to rhetorical topics (human affairs) and purposes (persuasion or identification). But 3.0 has problems. In chapter 2, I'll comment on some of the problems with 3.0, its Greek roots, and its use in arguments and will then discuss Aristotle's *rhetorikos sullogismos* in part 2.

CHAPTER 2

3.0 and Its Problems

There are several problems with 3.0, its departure from Aristotle being only one—and that not the worst. I'll discuss Aristotle's enthymeme (2.0) and implicitly demonstrate its departure from 3.0 in part 2. Its other problems I'll examine here. If 3.0 departed from Aristotle by way of reflecting more accurately how argument actually works in rhetorical discourse, then the departure would be valid and welcome. Instead, 3.0 turns out to be less relevant to rhetorical practice, including ancient rhetorical practice, than is Aristotle's enthymeme. We can take the problems with 3.0 one at a time.

1. IT'S NOT GREEK

In addition to its Aristotelian lineage, 3.0 gets support more generally by unfortunate translations and faux etymologies. One is the idea that *enthymeme* is derived from the commonly held opinion that the audience already has "in mind" (*en-thumos*). This popular etymology appears nowhere in Aristotle and is not supported by ancient Greek usage; it was instead reverse engineered and retrofitted to explain the already firmly entrenched and widely accepted chimera, 3.0. The *en-thumos* derivation is widespread but unsupportable and as valid as is the belief that the missing premise makes the enthymeme persuasive (Jevons 1888, 153; Welsh 2014, 10; Crem 1956, 241; Burnyeat 1994, 3). The term *enthumēma* almost certainly derives from the verb *enthumaomai*, which is used to refer not to the idea already in the mind of the audience but to the idea *placed in the mind* of the audience by the speaker, as when we say "keep in mind, members of the jury..."

Another is the notion that since *thumos*[1] means "heart" or "gut," the enthymeme is essentially emotional or "passional" and embodied (Miller and Bee 1972, 202; Rossolatos 2014, 4; Crowley and Hawhee 2004, 141; Walker 1994, 49–53; Grimaldi 1972, 82).[2] Walker says that enthymemes generate "passional identification" (1994, 53), and McHendry notes how they "strike at the heart" (2017, 314). But in his review of this topic, Mirhady finds the relationship between *thumos* and the enthymeme to be a "dead etymology" (2007, 54–55). We could call it a dead metaphor. The *thumos* root in *enthumēma* demonstrates the enthymeme to have a seat in the emotions about as convincingly as holding a *suitcase* means that one is carrying suits or that in a *cupboard*, one must be storing cups. "It is usage," Adkins reminds us, "not etymology that gives words their meaning" (1970, 16). Nor is it clear why a syllogism that relies on probable rather than certain premises, or one that omits one premise, should render the remainder especially "passional." Categorical syllogisms, truncated or not, must be among the least passional forms of discourse available. It is clear that for Aristotle at least, the enthymeme reasons about facts and deeds (*pragma*) whether or not it also manipulates emotions or portrays character (Grimaldi 1972, 62–63; see also Gaines 2000, 8–10).[3] Examples of enthymemes from the *Rhetoric* show no tendency to rely particularly upon emotional rather than logical or character appeals.

Those interested in pursuing an etymological or connotative link between the enthymeme and emotional "arguments" might instead have pursued *enthumios*, the adjectival form of the term, which does in many instances seem to refer especially to emotionally charged thoughts or concerns. When, in Homer's *Odyssey*, Odysseus learns from Athena that Telemachus has taken to sea to find out about his father and that the suitors are hunting him, he worries. But Athena urges him not to take the danger to Telemachus too much to heart (*enthumios*) because she is watching over him and will see to his safe return (13.421; Murray 1995, 32–33). Some three centuries later, in his *History of the Peloponnesian War*, Thucydides tells us that the Athenians in Sicily took to heart (*enthumios*) the lunar eclipse they saw; they feared it as an ill omen and begged the generals not to set sail until the required thirty days had passed (7.50.4; 100–101).[4] In these and other cases, *enthumios* clearly implies a strong emotional response—an anxiety, regret, or "burden" (as it is often translated)—whereas the uses of *enthumēma* do not.[5] The meaning of *enthumios* aside, suffice it to say that if the enthymeme is essentially emotional or passional, it will not be because of its *thumos* root or its syllogistic structure but because of its narrative framing.

2. AUDIENCES DON'T SYLLOGIZE WELL

The bigger problem isn't simply that 3.0 departs from Aristotle or from Greek usage but that it has little practical use. Burnyeat notes that the standard "doctrine of the enthymeme is comprehensive, orderly, and totally useless" (1994, 4). Other critics similarly remark that 3.0 cannot aid in the construction of arguments. Green suggests that "trying to turn Aristotle's syllogism to practical account and, at the same time, to preserve its status as an inferential categorical proceeding leads quickly to absurdity" (1995, 40).

Not even its staunchest supporters suggest that they compose arguments by finding syllogisms and then suppressing premises or stating conclusions and then adding a "because clause." Nor has anyone ever seriously pressed or examined the claim that hearing a rhetorical argument elicits from listeners premises, opinions, or "pieces" that they mentally "think" or "supply" to fill its "gaps"; that doing so makes an otherwise less persuasive argument more persuasive; or that such arguments necessarily succeed by relying on universally "known" but unspoken cultural opinions. To my knowledge, there is no research to support such claims; they rest purely on tradition. Though comfortable and familiar, these claims are useless in practice. My guess is that no research has ever supported these kinds of claims because they aren't true and nothing of the sort ever happens.

The first problem has to do with the categorical syllogism as a tool of persuasion or explanation. The issue is that audiences don't process syllogisms very well. If audiences really did have to "fill in" or "think" the missing piece of an enthymeme to complete the syllogism, then the resulting inference would more often than not be wrong, or else the truncated argument would simply confuse rather than persuade, since listeners are notoriously bad at comprehending all but the simplest kinds of first-figure syllogisms. Rhetoric scholars have examined only one syllogistic figure—the universal affirmative in *Barbara*—and a wide range of research has demonstrated that audiences have little difficulty in interpreting this and a few other primary forms. But outside these self-evident forms in the first figure, audience comprehension and correct interpretation of syllogistic reasoning plummet drastically.

Evans summarizes much of this research, observing that "when actually confronted by exercises in syllogistic reasoning, people make a large number of errors" (1993, 215). Johnson-Laird adds two additional general results: individuals vary widely in their ability to draw valid conclusions from syllogisms, and different figures and modes of syllogism differ widely in their difficulty (2006, 144–46). Research subjects are rather unsuccessful at grasping valid conclusions warranted by many syllogistic forms, but they are particularly bad at spotting invalid syllogisms and frequently draw conclusions that are not warranted by the form (Dickstein 1978, 537). Johnson-Laird offers this example: "None of the artists is a beekeeper. All the beekeepers are chemists" (2006, 145). What valid conclusions can be drawn? Much of the research about the psychology of syllogistic reasoning uses problems that are written down for subjects to examine and answer questions about. Listening to a running speech would make the task even more difficult.

It's also difficult to see how comprehending complex syllogistic forms could be improved by leaving out one of the premises, and it is equally difficult to divine how the variable ability of audiences to process second- and third-figure syllogisms might or might not be impacted by speakers whose own syllogizing ability is likely to be equally fallible. Nor is there any research that examines how well audiences interpret enthymemes made from truncated nonprimary syllogisms or what difference it would make which proposition was suppressed. If Aristotle meant that only the universal affirmative first-figure syllogism was to be truncated for enthymemes, he unhelpfully fails to say so.

3. IF THEY DID, IT WOULDN'T BE PERSUASIVE

But even if audiences could be relied on to accurately solve syllogisms in all figures and all forms, it's hard to see how truncating one premise from a categorical syllogism, or suppressing from an argument one "piece" that an audience has to "fill in" for themselves, could possibly make the argument *more* persuasive. I can demonstrate this conclusion with an extended dilemma: 3.0 can be written out as one of two varieties of the kind of imaginary dialogue that Bitzer says characterizes the enthymeme. Either the listeners know the conclusion already or they don't.[6]

Here, for example, I declare my conclusion: syllogisms with missing premises and arguments with missing pieces are less persuasive, not more so. If the speaker has declared (or the audience already knows) the conclusion at which the argument is aiming, then whatever missing premises are needed can be supplied in the spaces or momentary gaps between one sentence and the next of a spoken or written text.[7]

SPEAKER: Socrates is mortal because Socrates is a man.
LISTENER (*THINKING TO SELF*): And all men are mortal.

Perhaps some portion of readers or listeners on a few occasions have thought something of the sort to themselves. Perhaps it is not uncommon. It is surely not so common as to be a defining feature of rhetorical reasoning. But suppose this was a universally accurate portrayal of how people listen to these kinds of arguments. In that case, then since a known or familiar proposition is suppressed for strategic and not simply formal reasons, it will also apply to a known conclusion.[8]

According to 3.0, the speaker ought to suppress a known conclusion as easily as a known major premise: repeating it within the syllogism will make the argument more tedious and less persuasive, and thinking the conclusion piece will achieve as strong a bond of identification between the audience and speaker as thinking the major premise piece. In this case, rhetorical arguments with a known conclusion can be reduced to the serial assertion of minor premises. This clearly departs from version 3.0 and would make a hash of the whole syllogistic suppressed-premise model.[9] But perhaps this does happen, and the audience, already knowing the conclusion, does indeed think these pieces, supplying all known premises and conclusions to arguments to make them complete. If enthymemes work this way, then since I have stated my conclusion above, readers should be able (without looking back) to fill in here the major premises they mentally supplied to this portion of my argument, which includes several instances of 3.0.

In other cases, the listener won't yet know what the conclusion will be. Then the missing premise cannot be mentally supplied by the listener until the enthymeme has been completed. Of all the cultural assumptions that we might be able to supply to the claim that Socrates is a man, only one will turn out to be relevant to the deduction that he is mortal. Supplying any other premise will avail us nothing.

In this case, supplying the missing premise can occur only after the conclusion is known to the audience, and it will require the listener to backpedal to a prior statement in order to insert a thought that will provide the middle term, or "missing piece," required to arrive at the now apparent conclusion. Perhaps this too does happen. It nevertheless cannot stand as the central element of a persuasive argument. Anyone who has experienced having to think back to fill in necessary but unstated earlier pieces of a speaker's argument can attest that this kind of listening—requiring the audience to divert their attention away from the ongoing argument to fill in prior steps—detracts from the persuasiveness of the argument; it doesn't produce it. Pausing to fill in the missing premise destroys the very rhetorical interaction upon which the speech depends for its effect.

The imagined "filling in" of premises corresponds to no recognizable psychological process on the part of the listener because no one could complete the enthymeme and remain a listener. We can maintain the fiction that listeners "fill in" enthymemes to make them valid arguments only on the pain of admitting that they absent themselves, however briefly, from the unfolding rhetorical encounter. Creating such a break cannot possibly be considered a rhetorical skill; it is the opposite, a rhetorical failure.

Perhaps the supporters of 3.0 will object to my admittedly literal characterization of the rhetorical encounter. Perhaps they will maintain that the audience doesn't "supply" or "think" the missing piece in so many words. Rather, they supply it tacitly and automatically, without conscious awareness (either during or after its utterance). This departs from how the enthymeme is typically described ("filling in" or "thinking a piece"), but even if we accept this modification and maintain that "supplying" a missing premise is accompanied by no conscious awareness on the part of the listener, then it will also resist any method for validation or invalidation on the part of the researcher. We may as well assume that persuasion depends on audiences supplying to arguments images of pastel-colored zoo animals. That none of us is ever aware of imagining pink elephants as we listen to rhetorical arguments simply demonstrates the process to be tacit and unconscious, perhaps drawing upon a universal albeit subterranean and suppressed aspect of Western zoo-chromocentric culture.

If we agree to overlook the language of "supplied" *endoxa* or any "filling in" of "pieces" and say simply that enthymemes rely on some preexisting and taken-for-granted contextual knowledge to be effective, we are on firmer ground: textual comprehension certainly does require a base of knowledge beyond what is said. Some of this existing knowledge will be "ideological," from Barthes's "book of Life," while some of it will be drawn from previous parts of a text; from knowledge of a language, a code, a regional dialect, or a way of life; from previous related (perhaps even nonideological) texts; from lived experiences; or from encounters with others. Contextual knowledge that is useful to decoding a text can take myriad forms. This version really amounts to the rather unremarkable claim that meaning depends on context.

Armed with this view of the enthymeme, we are forced to acknowledge that every argument, every text—indeed, every utterance, image, act, or object—is enthymematic because every meaningful thing, picture, act, or word can be shown to rely for its comprehension or effect on some associated body of contextual knowledge or belief (linguistic, generic, situational, social, or cultural) that is not encoded within the artifact, event, or text.[10] This was the very problem with Bitzer's and Barthes's innovations: they described features of symbolic interaction and audience or readerly interpretation generally but nothing specific to the enthymeme as a rhetorical technique.

Unstated cultural knowledge cannot be the hallmark of enthymematic reasoning for the simple reason that no piece of communication, however small (a sigh or a wink) or exhaustive (Proust), contains the keys to its own decoding. The ideal of the fully independent, self-elucidating text is the semantic equivalent of lifting oneself by one's own bootstraps. If the enthymeme is defined by being incomplete, then every piece of communication will be found to be an enthymeme, and the enthymeme will cease to demarcate any distinct rhetorical technique or feature of language use at all.

But even if we could make all these textual, practical, and interpretative difficulties vanish, it would remain the case that 3.0 is a clumsy and simplistic model for persuasion. Proponents of 3.0 should be able to illustrate the power of this model from good arguments, even their own arguments. This suggestion was made by Cooper (1932), rejected out of hand by Bitzer (1959), and called for again implicitly with McGee's (1982) "materialist" approach to rhetoric. But rather than looking for and offering moving examples to showcase the power of this model,[11] textbooks in rhetoric and argument typically either borrow or invent their own two- or three-part premise-conclusion (PC) sequences that are stripped of any rhetorical exigency, situation, genre, or context. Socrates's mortality is common (see chapter 1). Hamilton in his *Lectures on Metaphysics and Logic* made Caius almost as well known: "Every liar is a coward, and Caius is a liar" (1860, 392; see also Burnyeat 1994, 4). In *Classical Rhetoric for Modern Students*, Corbett and Connors argue, "He must be a Communist because he advocates civil rights for minority groups" (1999, 54). Keith and Lundberg observe in the recent *Essential Guide to Rhetoric* that "Bob is a student, therefore Bob is registered for courses" (2008, 37). These are clearly instances of 3.0, but are they powerful, persuasive arguments? Can they be Aristotle's "body of persuasion"? It's hard to imagine a case in which examples like these could exert the unique rhetorical power for which the enthymeme is famed.

4. IT ISN'T RHETORIC

Powerful examples of 3.0 may be hard to find because rhetorical arguments always occur within the context of a speech or text; the speech or text always comes from a situated speaking source and is always delivered within a set of genre conventions, an issue or situation, a lexicon and a language or discourse; and all these occur within the context of a normative cultural setting, or *nomos*, but 3.0 does not. The standard view and its textbook exemplars are context-free; they function and are meant to function independently of the surrounding text and situation. That these examples of 3.0 lack context is, as they say, a feature, not a bug. 3.0, like the syllogism from which it is derived, is defined by the nature, arrangement, and number of its parts. The figures were designed to abstract the logical form of an argument from its content and context, and thus from its rhetorical setting, in order to test and illustrate its validity. As an abbreviation of this form, 3.0 too enjoys the benefit of being entirely context independent. Its meaning and effect depend not at all upon any of the traditional elements of rhetorical interaction. It will work wherever it is placed.

Thus whether a piece of text is a version of 3.0 depends only upon whether one statement (a premise) connected to another (a conclusion) by a "because clause" can be made logically complete through the insertion of another premise. Even though champions of 3.0 assert that the audience must know and accept the missing premise so they can "fill it in" and that 3.0 is in this way responsive to audience and therefore rhetorical, the fact remains that 3.0 cares not at all about the nature of the audience or situation beyond their collective acceptance and uniform mental insertion of one particular preformed "piece" of opinion. 3.0 is rhetorical in the same way that Procrustes is hospitable: anything that doesn't fit into the frame must be cut off.[12] It offers, at best, a thin and fairly mechanical model of audience participation and a shallow view of rhetorical interaction.

Because it neither has nor needs any rhetorical context, 3.0 is capable only of flat referentiality; it ignores how context shapes the meaning and force of utterances, including argumentative utterances, in subtle but significant ways—through various emotional or attitudinal registers; through manipulation of form and convention; through varying degrees of reliability, sincerity, irony, sarcasm, humor, diffidence, understatement, or exaggeration; and through framing devices, tropes, and other markers of style, tone, or mood. All these factors introduce subtle (and not so subtle) nuances into the meaning of any rhetorical utterance that alter, sometimes significantly, its rhetorical effect. In any living rhetorical encounter, the meaning and effect of a symbolic act never coincide exactly with what is said. Not only are layered refractions of meaning possible; they are inevitable, as Burke makes clear.[13] If there were such a thing as an uninflected word or statement, once placed within a rhetorical encounter, it could not avoid being colored by its surroundings.

But isolation from any rhetorical context or coloring is exactly what makes 3.0 so popular and attractive: because it has no setting, it can be easily transported intact into textbooks and handbooks and fixed on the page as an example of the form. Given the structure, I can formulate enthymemes identical in form anywhere and everywhere. But the result is a construct that is as artificial and unreal as an ornamental plaster Corinthian column: it can support nothing.

Not surprisingly, this feature infects the work of logic and argument scholars as well. Levi observes a persistent "failure on the part of logicians to appreciate the importance of the rhetorical context of an argument" (1995, 67).[14] To illustrate the problems with textbook enthymemes (the PC sequence), he offers this example:

Benny confessed to the crime;
So, Benny is guilty. (68)

The apparently missing (and generalized) premise would be, "A person who confesses to a crime is guilty," or, more realistically, since rhetorical syllogisms are only probable, "A person who confesses to a crime is *likely* to be guilty." But, says Levi, "it is hard to imagine an arguer who could be thinking something that is to apply so generally" (1995, 69). We cannot imagine such an arguer because we cannot know how to take this passage. The example has no speaker and no context, and we never interpret actual texts independent of some context.[15] What kind of crime was it? What kind of person is confessing and to whom? What kind of confession was it, or under what conditions did he confess? How much time has passed between the crime and the confession, or how long was the suspect in custody and under questioning? In what conditions was he held? Did he have a lawyer present? Who is making this argument, in what venue, and for what purpose? What is the relationship of this speaker to Benny, or to the victim, or to the interrogator, or to the audience? Where do the speaker's interests lie?

The example illustrates 3.0. It looks like a realistic slice of argument, but without the context, this cannot be a rhetorical argument because it is not planted in any rhetorical interaction. In any real rhetorical encounter, the context would fundamentally shape the contours within which such an assertion would be interpreted and understood. The terms *Benny*, *confess*, *crime*, and *guilt* would all take on specific content colored by our views on age, race, gender, criminality and policing, punishment and justice, and responsibility and circumstance—colored by the identity of the speaker and our view of him or her, and of the interrogator, and of Benny himself. 3.0 can capture none of this.[16]

Any attempt on the part of a logician or rhetorician to supply a hypothetical context, even a true or documentary context for the example, does not help, in part because the logician or rhetorician is still merely "substituting his own voice for that of the speakers in the situation" (Levi 1995, 73). It remains, in Bakhtin's language, monologic regardless of the invented context. We do not yet have an encounter of divergent voices or distinct parties with divergent interests contending for an adequate understanding of what happened and where culpability lies. Again, this is not a defect in the illustration or a by-product of its being taught through textbooks; it is rather a central feature and a virtue of 3.0 that it does not need for its effectiveness any actual rhetorical context. If rhetoric is the study of language in use, then a theory of argument based on logical forms cannot be rhetorical.

It is for this reason that the illustrative enthymeme of the textbook is always available but also always already a dead thing. The PC sequence never serves the purpose of persuasion—only of illustration. Benny and his confession will stand in as well as Caius and his lying or Socrates and his mortality because the purpose of the example and its conclusion has nothing to do with Benny or Caius or Socrates. It only ever endlessly speaks about its own structure and function. But the PC model of the enthymeme cannot describe a rhetorical argument because it is not a piece of argument but the hypothetical illustration of a logical model.

PART TWO

2.0

CHAPTER 3

Aristotle, *Sullogismos*, and 2.0

According to its many critics, and despite its apparent Aristotelian bona fides, the standard view constitutes a significant departure from Aristotle's view of the enthymeme. The pedigree of criticism is not as well established as that supporting 3.0, but as I have noted above, it is long and includes Agricola (1521), Giulio Pace (1584, 1597), Facciolati (1728), Aldrich (1750; Mansel trans. 1856), Hamilton (1852), De Quincey (1897), Seaton (1914), Conley (1984), Walker (1994), Burnyeat (1994, 1996), Green (1995), and Gaines (2000). All of them reject 3.0 or define the Aristotelian enthymeme in other ways.[1]

Many of the problems with the standard view are well rehearsed and widely known: that Aristotle nowhere defines the enthymeme in terms of the suppression of a premise,[2] that suppressing a premise changes nothing about the form of reasoning that structures deductive argument,[3] that Aristotle never suggests that either suppressing a premise or mentally putting it back in is necessary or that it renders the enthymeme persuasive, that "imperfect" or "truncated" syllogism was not Aristotle's language or definition for the enthymeme, and that when Aristotle does call a syllogism imperfect (*atelēs*), he means not that it lacks a premise and is therefore an enthymeme but that the validity of the syllogism cannot be determined in its current form.[4] The imperfect or "incomplete" (i.e., second- or third-figure) syllogism must first be "reduced" to a perfect or "complete" first-figure syllogism (*Prior Analytics* A.1, A.5; Smith 1989, 1–2, 9; and see Flannery 1987).

The conclusion that we might draw from this body of work has already been observed by Gaines: "Much of the scholarship that purports to be Aristotelian either obscures Aristotle's thought, by reducing it to an unrecognizable abstraction, or subverts it, by misappropriating Aristotle's authority for conceptions that are alien to his view" (2000, 19).

Yet despite the repeated objections of Aristotle scholars, "the determination to understand the enthymeme as a mechanistic and deductive formula" persists (Green 1995, 20). For example, after criticizing the syllogistic view of the enthymeme as overly simplistic, Walker reviewed ancient sources, including the works of Isocrates and Anaximenes; considered the problems with 3.0; and crafted a definition that invoked *kairos* and the relevance of style, *exetasis* and opposition, the psychological impact of the enthymeme on the hearer, and the concept of the argumentative "cap" of a fuller epicheiremic argument form—all without any reference to missing premises or audience supplied *endoxa* (1994, 53). Yet not two decades later, the enthymeme could still be defined as "a rhetorical argument in which one or more premises or the conclusion has been left unstated" (Welsh 2014, 7). Prenosil discusses scholarship on the enthymeme, including Walker, and then explains the enthymeme this way: "The rhetor communicates his or her piece; the audience thinks theirs. If the rhetor is successful, the audience thinks a piece that brings them nearer to identification with the rhetor's position" (2012, 284).

Any problems with 3.0 will apply as well to the innovations brought by the interactionist enthymeme (3.1) and the ideological enthymeme (3.2), since both work from the 3.0 framework and graft onto it a branch of more recent theory. Bitzer and Barthes, like Whately (1848) and Cope (1867) before them, accept 3.0 despite a long tradition of criticism. Since 3.0 is itself a manifest distortion of Aristotle, these cannot but be distortions as well, albeit theoretically more interesting and profitable distortions. Here is Gaines again: "In both the communication and English fields we find theoretical research that attempts to justify modern and postmodern predilections by appeal to Aristotelian 'certification,'" making Aristotle an "unlikely participant in a wide range of positions" (2000, 19).

The full extent of the problem has never been widely taken up or fully explored, and given that the standard view has never lost its dominance and continues to be described as Aristotle's enthymeme (Kremmydas 2007; Goddu 2016), a fuller discussion of 2.0 and how it departs from 3.0 is merited. Because my goal is to establish a framework for thinking about a pre-Aristotelian (and nontheoretical) enthymeme, I will only briefly explore 2.0 here and in chapter 4. Much of the problem, I think, stems from two errors in reading Aristotle. The first concerns Aristotle's definition of *enthumēma*. The second concerns his definition of *sullogismos*. Once these are successfully misunderstood, 3.0 become almost inevitable.

We can begin with *enthumēma*, but to do so we have to take a detour back to dialectic, the method Aristotle uses as the model for understanding rhetoric. *Topics* is Aristotle's treatise on dialectic. In the *Topics*, at the very outset of the treatise, Aristotle unsurprisingly says that he must first say what *sullogismos* is. This will be its definition. It is, says Aristotle, "an argument in which, certain things being supposed, something different from the supposition results of necessity through them" (1.1; Smith 2003, 1). The explanation and topics that follow are all elaborations upon this definition.

So when Aristotle says in the *Rhetoric* that rhetoric is the antistrophe of dialectic, and when—shortly after his "second beginning" at 1.2.1—he stipulates that "to show that if some things are so, something else beyond them results from these because they are true, either universally or for the most part, in dialectic is called syllogism and in rhetoric enthymeme" (1.2.9; 40), students of dialectic will understand that here he is giving the definition of both *sullogismos* and *enthumēma*. Though the wording in *Topics* is slightly different, here Aristotle tells us that for his purposes in the *Rhetoric*, he is going to treat the definition for these two terms as functionally identical. What separate them will be the particular features of the contexts within which they operate. Thinking of enthymeme as a "kind of syllogism from probable premises with one premise missing which the audience supplies" is not Aristotle's definition for the enthymeme. By the time he speaks of "fewer premise" (1.2.13; 41–42), he has already stated his definition.

The defining features of 3.0 were never Aristotelian, beginning with the traditional understanding that the enthymeme is a "kind of syllogism" that differs in some way from other species (like "the dialectical syllogism") of the same genus. According to this line of thinking, if the "rhetorical syllogism" is a species of the genus "syllogism," then it must differ in some consistent way from the "dialectical" or "demonstrative" syllogisms.[5] We've seen Cope return to 3.0 because (as he thought) truncation was the only feature that could reliably distinguish dialectical reasoning from rhetorical reasoning (1877, 2; 1867, 102–3).

The tendency to see enthymeme as a "species of syllogism" is understandable and appears to have Aristotelian support. Aristotle developed the idea of "essential predication"—of genus, species, and differentia.[6] And

Aristotle places rhetoric alongside dialectic even if their respective treatises look very different (Brunschwig 1996, 38). If rhetoric is the antistrophe of dialectic and both rhetoric and dialectic utilize a "kind of *sullogismos*," which in dialectic is said to be syllogism and in rhetoric is called enthymeme, then it's natural to suppose that there ought to be some essential features they share as members of a genus and some differentia that separate them as species. Unfortunately, Aristotle doesn't give us any. He gives us many differences, all of which are situational and strategic, none essential. Neither the missing premise, nor the probable premises, nor individual versus universal or particular subjects, nor any particular logical form, nor any other single feature of 2.0 will reliably distinguish rhetorical from dialectical reasoning. Both rely on reputable opinions that are widely accepted to be true but are capable of being opposed and (in the event) are so. I will suggest in part 3 that the enthymeme is an attention-management technique of adversarial narratives and is actually quite different from the dialectical *sullogismos*, but Aristotle treats them as functionally identical.

The difference between these applications of *sullogismos* is simply, as Burnyeat says, "the context in which they occur" (1994, 21).[7] There were several socially sanctioned and epistemologically useful venues for masculine performance in competitive argument. Aristotle breaks them into two large categories. If you have two or more people arguing in response to current affairs before a mass audience by giving speeches that the audience will vote on in favor of one and against the others, such as occurs in legal cases, assemblies, and other occasional game and ceremonial contests, then you have a rhetorical context. If you have two people arguing over a posited proposition—something predicated of something else—with or without an audience by having one person question the other such that the respondent must agree to the propositions offered and the inferences drawn from them until either the respondent is led to affirm a proposition contrary to the stated proposition (in which case, the proposition is refuted) or the questioner fails to bring this about (in which case, the proposition is not refuted and, while not yet proven, gains in confidence), then you have a dialectical context. The former was a ubiquitous feature of ancient Greek democratic life. The latter was a popular pastime among sophists and their elite sponsors and was refined by sophists and philosophers into a tool of inquiry.

Both "argue from premises which the audience would accept" (Smith 2003, xv), both obtain propositions and draw inferences from them on both sides of an issue, and neither are restricted to any particular topic or field of study. I'll argue below that (if rhetorical reasoning is indeed a manifestation of *sullogismos*) these two contexts do differ in one central way: dialectic contests concern themselves with coming to know a subject by predicating something of it (a definition and properties), whereas rhetorical contests concern themselves with coming to know a series of events by telling a story, demonstrating its coherence, and disnarrating alternative accounts.

But for Aristotle, *rhetorikos sullogismos* is not a species of the larger genus *sullogismos* but more like a tool used in a particular setting. I can use a tool—let's say a knife with a short curved blade—in the context of cooking, or crafting, or surgery. These functionally identical tools will be called a paring knife in one context, a hobby or X-Acto knife in another, and a scalpel or lancet in the third. They are not three species of the genus knife but rather three different names and contexts for use of what is essentially the same instrument. In fact, Aristotle did develop a specialized kind of *sullogismos* tool for the exacting process of demonstrative or scientific reasoning, like a specialized surgical blade, but the categorical syllogism (*sullogismos* "in the figures") was never intended to be used in either the rhetorical or dialectical agon.

The same is true of rhetorical and dialectical *sullogismos*: they differ only in where and how they are used.[8] Enthymeme is not "a kind of syllogism" but an instance of it. As Aristotle says in the *Posterior Analytics*, *sullogismos* is what the enthymeme is (1.1; 71a11; Barnes 2002, 1).[9] When in the *Topics* Aristotle says that he must say not only what *sullogismos* is but also "what its different varieties are, so that the dialectical *sullogismos* may be grasped," he describes demonstrative *sullogismos*, dialectical *sullogismos*, contentious *sullogismoi*, and "false reasoning" (1.1; Smith 2003, 1–2). "We may," he concludes, "let the aforementioned be the species of deductions" (101a17; Smith 2003, 2). He does not mention rhetorical *sullogismos* in this list because he does not see rhetorical reasoning as a distinct species of reasoning.[10]

Any further light to be thrown on the Aristotelian enthymeme will be cast by the definition, features, and forms of *sullogismos*. *Sullogismos* is a double compound built from the verb *logizomai*. *Logizomai* means "to count, calculate, reckon, or account for something," "to consider," and also "to infer or conclude," with reference to both numerical and nonnumerical "accounting," and *logismos* is the abstract noun from the verb for an account, a calculation, a reasoning, or an explanation (again with both numeric and nonnumeric meanings). *Logizomai* and *logismos* with the *su-* prefix (meaning "together," "with," "joined") is to join or collect and arrange together a set of statements to bring them at once before the mind for the purpose of explaining, accounting for, or summing up something and so comprehending the whole: a ledger or register, summation, or geometrical proof. The term can refer to the process generally, not just one inferential step in it. The key is to find and arrange the statements so that they lead the group through a series of inferences to a new understanding. This is the term Aristotle uses for dialectical debates, for demonstrative reasoning, and for rhetorical argument. I will suggest later that this term should be understood to include the construction of (and commentary on) a narrative as well. What is a legal story if not the collecting and setting out of a series of facts to craft an account for the purpose of explaining an event, generating knowledge, and enabling comprehension and judgment?

We can also look at the *Topics* to enhance our understanding of Aristotle's *sullogismos*. I've mentioned above Aristotle's definition of *sullogismos* in the *Topics*. In this work, Aristotle discusses the generation of *sullogismoi*. Since for Aristotle *sullogizomai* proceeds via propositions, he begins by analyzing propositions and their elements, the four predicables (definition, property, accident, genus), and the ten categories (essence, quantity, quality, relation, place, time, position, state, activity, passivity). Every *sullogismos* will be composed of propositions that predicate something (the predicate) of something else (the subject). There are ten kinds of subjects (the categories) and four kinds of predication. He discusses dialectical propositions (or questions), problems, and theses. He then discusses how to obtain premises and build *sullogismoi* through the topoi.[11] The topoi are headings and forms, or rules, as well as instructions for constructing *sullogismoi*.[12] They seem to be logical rules, but in fact they function less like purely formal rules than like rules of thumb or practical tips to guide students.

Some topoi will always generate true conclusions, some only usually do so, and some have important exceptions, but Aristotle does not explain why this is or how to know in advance what kind of validity any given topic will have. In fact, says Smith, "we do not find instances in the *Topics* in which he argues for the validity of a rule, nor does he give us any indications that he conceived of a general deductive system with basic rules from which more complex deductions could be derived" (2003, xxxiii). The validity of a topic, or the extent of its validity, seems to depend primarily upon whether Aristotle has found exceptions to its application. Just as they are guides to practice, they seem to have been generated from experience. The *Topics* and the "game" of dialectic are not governed by or operate within a purely logical system; rather, the game is a set of guidelines for generating productive arguments.

Aristotle discusses topoi from accidents (books II–III), then from genera (IV), from properties (V), and then from definitions (VI–VII). Some of the topoi are common to each section: topoi from opposites and contraries, topoi from coordinates and cases (involving grammatical transformations like *just* to *justly*), and topoi from more and less and equals (Smith 2003, xxxi–xxxiv). Finally, in book VIII, Aristotle offers advice about how to organize one's argument and how to present it for greatest effectiveness: "First, then, the person who is going to be devising questions must find the location from which to attack; second, he must devise the questions, and arrange them individually, to himself; and only third and last does he ask these of someone else" (155b4–7; Smith 2003, 20). This is a familiar order for students of the *Rhetoric*: first find (*heureîn*), then arrange (*taxai*), and then deliver (*eipeîn*) your argument. Invention and arrangement are both important. Dialectic, like rhetoric, is a contest. Because he does not want the questioner to reach her goal, the respondent is likely to resist inferences and conclusions that will allow this to happen. Thus the questioner will not want to forecast the direction that she plans to take—to "tip her hand," so to speak—but will rather attempt to prevent the respondent from recognizing the path to the thesis by concealing the line of argument, proceeding inductively, and in general moving as far off from the desired conclusion as possible until that conclusion is inevitable and unavoidable.

To this end, Aristotle offers ways for "keeping your opponent in the dark about what your argument actually is until it is too late" (*Topics*; Smith 2003, 105). Aristotle offers advice on how and when to invent logically unnecessary but strategically useful premises both to support weak deductions and to prevent the respondent from anticipating the questioner's strategy. This important strategic move means that while respondents infer conclusions through and because of the things laid down, not all the propositions will be strictly necessary to arrive at that thesis.

In fact, says Aristotle, to conceal your final conclusion, you should postpone it as long as possible: establish by deduction not only the required premises but some of the other premises necessary for obtaining them—and also some of the premises necessary for obtaining those (thus moving "backward" and "standing off" from the premise you need).[13] Deduce not the desired proposition but what necessarily follows from it (since if the respondent admits this, he has admitted the desired proposition as well).

Arrangement is important as well. Aristotle recommends mixing up the natural order of deductions to obscure the trajectory of your inquiry. Follow up a deduction leading to one conclusion with a deduction along a different line of inquiry, one that you will come back to later. Try establishing a universal premise using the definition not for the term you want but for a coordinate term: speak not of "justice" but of the "the just person." Later you can easily link these coordinate terms in another deduction. In general, says Aristotle, "stretch out your argument and throw in things of no use towards it" (*Topics* 8.1; Smith 2003, 23) in order to "get as many [premises] as possible" (8.1; 21). The invention of premises should be excessive and the arrangement complex. This is followed up with further practical advice on how to handle objections, what to do with a poor definition, how to ask and answer questions, how to prevent an arguer from reaching a conclusion, and the like.

Aristotle considered his *methodos* to be a significant achievement. Though the *Topics* conveys no general method for proving the logical validity of any topical form, Aristotle's achievement did enable disputants "to advance from 'This conclusion follows from these premisses' to 'A conclusion of this *form* follows from a set of premisses [*sic*] having this *form*'" (Smith 2003, xxiv). Because of the achievement of the *Topics*, Aristotle can claim that his topical method for reasoning (*Topics* 1.1; Smith 2003, 1–2) constitutes an original discovery (*Sophistical Refutations* 34; Forster 1965, 154–55). Since each form can produce valid conclusions from its premises, and since the forms together cover the full range of kinds of propositions (of predicables and categories), everything *endoxa* should be assimilable to a topic and thus to a number of valid conclusions. This, in short, is the dialectical *sullogismos*.

There are a few things worth noticing. The first is that the *Topics* says nothing at all about the categorical syllogism. The treatise does aim to provide students with a method for finding premises and forming valid deductions, and it does offer "forms" into which premise-conclusion (PC) deductions can be cast, but this method and this form are topical, not syllogistic. In fact, says Barnes, in the *Topics*, "there is no whiff of the Syllogism. The characteristic terminology of Syllogistic, which pervades the *Analytics*, is entirely absent from the *Topics*: here there are no moods and figures, no middle terms and extremes, no majors and minors, no conversions, no expositions, no reductions. The *Topics* never uses a Syllogism; it never hints at Syllogistic technique" (1981, 47). Dialectical deduction is nowhere limited to two premises, or two terms per premise, or three terms across the two premises. It requires none of the other trappings of syllogistic form. There simply is no such thing as a dialectical syllogism.

The lack of reference to the figures and to the syllogistic framework in the *Topics* means that this work was almost certainly "put into its final form before ever Syllogism was dreamed of" (Barnes 1981, 48). Dialectic could be considered an early logic, with the categorical syllogism and modal syllogistic form being "second" and "third" logics developed later (Bochenski 1961, 43–44). Nor is the irrelevance of syllogistic to either the dialectical *sullogismos* or the enthymeme a new discovery. Solmsen argues against seeing *sullogismos* as syllogism and suggests about the enthymeme of the *Prior Analytics* "that what Aristotle here discusses are earlier, i.e., pre-syllogistic 'forms' of reasoning" (1951, 568). Barnes made the argument about *sullogismos* as it relates to dialectic in 1981. Conley expressed frustration with the limitations of syllogistic form in 1984, and Burnyeat reminded us that the enthymeme was not syllogistic in 1994 (14–15). But the inertia of tradition and the strong pull of 3.0 overrode this important insight as easily as Cope abandoned the criticisms of Hamilton—just as others had done for centuries—maintaining 3.0 and its logical frame as the majority view.

It is also the case that Aristotle never revised the *Topics* (or the *Rhetoric*) to adhere to the standards of the syllogistic framework because these treatises deal with different kinds of arguments and have different goals. "The *Analytics*," says Smith, "is a theoretical treatise which aims at giving a theory of science and resolving the puzzles which arise in connection with that theory. The *Topics* has no such theoretical aims but instead offers an 'art of dialectic': a set of procedures which will bring about success in dialectical argument" (1994, 140). The method for dialectical deduction is topical and strategic; the *Analytics* is theoretical and scientific. The absence of the syllogistic framework from dialectic is both chronological and strategic, but it is also necessary. Topics and syllogistic figures are not only different but incompatible. Not only does the *Topics* contain "virtually nothing that can be construed as a reference to the figures"; it also "makes use of many argumentative patterns... which cannot be put into syllogistic form" (136).

All of this applies equally to the *Rhetoric*. There is no whiff of the categorical syllogism.[14] There is no discussion of figures or modes or other trappings of the categorical syllogism. *Sullogismos* is defined similarly in the *Rhetoric* and the *Topics*, and the topics in the *Rhetoric* overlap significantly with those in the *Topics*, such as those involving contraries, more and less, and grammatical cases.[15] Rhetorical topics include headings, inference rules or principles, and instructions much like dialectical topics.[16] But topics in the *Rhetoric* are even less regular than in the *Topics*. They are empirical and referential rather than methodical and programmatic (Brunschwig 1996). They can be accommodated to syllogistic form no more successfully than can dialectical topics. For example, we might consider the topic "from contraries," which figures in both the *Topics* and the *Rhetoric*. Syllogisms employ three terms distributed across two premises linked by a copula (A is B or B belongs to A). One of the terms, the middle term, drops out of the conclusion: if A is B, and B is C, then A is C.

The topic "from contraries," though, requires three premises, four terms, and two different relational connectors, *contrary to* and *belongs to*:

If B is the contrary of A,
and if Q is the contrary of P,
and if A belongs to P,
then B belongs to Q.

There is simply no way to reduce this set of statements to three terms instead of four or to two premises instead of three and maintain its logical structure as "from contraries." Yet this is clearly a relevant topical form for both rhetorical and dialectical argument.

So it isn't simply that Aristotle had not yet fully developed deduction in the figures when he wrote the *Topics* or *Rhetoric*, or that by *sullogismos* he really meant "syllogism" but simply assumed familiarity with the figures instead of attending to all of their details in this work, and therefore that for Aristotle, *sullogismos* simply meant "syllogism." Nor can we say that syllogistic form is there implicit, lying in the background of the topical reasoning of both works. *Sullogismos* as employed in dialectic and in rhetoric is a formal model that is different from and incompatible with what we find in the syllogistic figures of the *Prior Analytics*.

In short, *sullogismos* cannot mean "syllogism" in the *Topics* or the *Rhetoric*. Rather, it must be read more broadly as "deduction" or "explanatory reasoning" (Moss 2014). Deduction in both rhetoric and dialectic will use propositions with more than two terms and arguments with many more than two propositions. In some cases (as in dialectic), not all of the propositions that are used in the deduction will be strictly necessary to arrive at the conclusion; it will be longer than necessary. In other cases (as in rhetoric), not all of the propositions that are strictly necessary will be stated; it will be shorter than necessary. The length and path of a *sullogismos* will be determined not by logical necessity but by context and practical utility.

Even the term *deduction* is too restrictive, since some enthymemes reason not from universals but from particulars, such as topic 10: "from induction" (*Rhetoric* 2.23.11; 177).[17] Later Aristotle will include examples (*paradeigma*) in the sources for enthymemes (2.25.8; 190). For this reason, I prefer *explanatory reasoning* or simply *inference*.[18]

Unfortunately, this view—that the enthymeme is not a kind of syllogism or a syllogism at all but simply the reasoning or inferential process in a rhetorical context—suffers under the misfortune of being contradicted by all modern translations and many commentaries on and works about the *Rhetoric*. Jebb (1876), Freese (1982), Roberts (1924), Cooper (1932) and Kennedy (2007) all have Aristotle speaking of syllogisms and of the enthymeme as a kind (or a species) of syllogism. Cope's footnote (mentioned in chapter 1) similarly assumes the categorical syllogism (1867, 103). But none of these comments or translations can be based on the term *sullogismos*, on the context of the *Rhetoric* or the *Topics*, or on contemporaneous usage of the term. They all rest on logical developments stemming from the *Prior Analytics* and subsequent elaborations in later Peripatetic and Stoic logic, retrojected back into these earlier works. This leads to a number of translational decisions supporting 3.0. For example, in the *Rhetoric*, Aristotle is said to observe that the enthymeme is "drawn from few premises and often less than those of the primary syllogism (*protos sullogismos*), for if one of these is known, it does not have to be stated, since the hearer supplies it" (1.2.13; 41).

This passage seems to clearly indicate the brevity of the enthymeme in comparison to what Kennedy calls "the fully expressed syllogism that is logically inherent in the enthymeme" (41 n. 54). It has been an important passage in supporting 3.0. As suggested in Kennedy's translation, *protos sullogismos* has traditionally been understood here to refer to the syllogism in the first figure (as discussed in *Prior Analytics* A.4; Smith 1989, 4–6).

Speaking of the first figure implies all the other accoutrements of the categorical syllogism as laid out in the *Prior Analytics*. This is how Freese interprets it (1982, 24 n. a). If correct, this would confirm that Aristotle compares the enthymeme to the syllogism "in the figures" (and not simply to deduction more generally) and that Aristotle uses *sullogismos* here to mean the categorical syllogism. It would also confirm that the enthymeme will be shorter than the first-figure syllogism (which has two premises and a conclusion) and that it will therefore contain only two propositions, with one premise or the conclusion unstated. We really do seem here to have rather explicit support for 3.0.

Critics have often attempted to prevent 3.0 from relying too heavily on this passage. The defense rests upon the term *often* (*pollakis*). Since Aristotle says only that enthymemes are often shorter than the primary syllogism, there will be enthymemes that are not so shortened. Thus the enthymeme cannot be *defined* in terms of the missing premise that the hearer supplies even it if does typically leave one premise unstated. Abbreviation cannot be, in Aristotle's terms, an essential feature of the enthymeme; it is merely a property of some, albeit perhaps a characteristic one and an important strategic one, like the feathers on an arrow.[19] You could shoot an arrow without fletching and it would fly, so arrows do not "by definition" include fletching. In like manner, you could technically call a syllogism with all its premises made explicit an enthymeme, but in the traditional understanding (since it is the missing premise that persuades), such an enthymeme would lose much of its rhetorical function.

Thus the *often* qualification may theoretically be a legitimate line of defense, but in practical terms, it is a quibbling one, and on its own it has been an ineffectual one. No one would shoot an arrow without fletching regardless of how we might define *arrow*. And Aristotle's little *pollakis* has never prevented 2.0 from ossifying into 3.0. As we've seen, the modern upgrades by Bitzer and Barthes have ignored the *often* pretty easily, making truncation the rhetorical sine qua non of the enthymeme's effectiveness.

But there are other more important difficulties with this interpretation of the passage. The first difficulty, perhaps more of a curiosity, is that the three syllogistic figures are of equal length: all contain exactly one conclusion from two premises and three terms. The first figure contains no more and no fewer terms or propositions than the other figures. If the enthymeme often contains fewer premises than the first figure, it will contain fewer premises than the second- and third-figure syllogisms as well. There is no reason here for Aristotle to distinguish between them. And given that enthymemes apparently also occur in the other figures (since Aristotle never mentions figures in the *Rhetoric*, there is no reason to suspect that he restricts enthymemes to the first figure), his specificity makes no sense. If *sullogismos* meant syllogism "in the figures" here, he could have said simply that the enthymeme is shorter than *sullogismos*. His restriction to the first figure confuses rather than clarifies the issue.

The second difficulty, again more of a curiosity, is that when speaking of varieties of syllogistic figures in the *Prior Analytics*, Aristotle speaks not of a "first syllogism" (*sullogismos protos*) but of syllogism through or in the first figure (*proton schema*; 1.7; Tredennick 1962, 234–35; Barnes 1981, 36–37). Interpreting *protos sullogismos* as "first (figure) syllogism" requires creative liberty on the part of the translator for which there is no Aristotelian precedent. It is the schemata that are numbered, not the *sullogismoi*. If Aristotle wanted to refer to the first-figure syllogism here, it is surprising that he didn't simply say "first figure," *schema protos*, rather than "first syllogism," though this could be simply because he hasn't explained anywhere in the *Rhetoric* what he means by *schema*.

But there is another way to read this passage. For while Aristotle does use *protos* to describe the first figure in *Prior Analytics*, he uses the same term to describe demonstrative reasoning in the *Topics*, where the differences between dialectical reasoning and demonstrative reasoning are briefly explained. Whereas dialectical reasoning proceeds from reputable sayings (*endoxa*), demonstration (*apodeixis*) is reasoning (*sullogismos*) from things that are true and primary in the sense that they can't be proven from anything else (*ex alethon kai proton ho sullogismos*; *Topics* 1.1; Forster 1966, 272–73; see also *Posterior Analytics* 1.2; Tredennick 1966, 30–33).

In the *Rhetoric*, Aristotle observes that rhetoric is a "sort of demonstration" and that rhetorical demonstration (*apodeixis*) is enthymeme (1.1.11; 33). Aristotle explains the difference between rhetoric and demonstration at 1.12, where he notes that scientific discourse (*epistemen logos*) is instruction, but "teaching is impossible" (35), by which he means, presumably, that instruction is impossible for rhetorical audiences. Kennedy inserts "for some audiences" in brackets at this point as a gloss. I here take "scientific discourse" (for *epistemen logos*, Kennedy has "speech based on knowledge") to refer to demonstration (*apodeixis*) as discussed in the *Posterior Analytics* (and as briefly mentioned in the *Topics*) and as mentioned earlier in the *Rhetoric*. Demonstrations will begin from "first" things—that is, fundamental principles or axioms that are immediately persuasive and are not themselves demonstrated—and will therefore usually be longer than rhetorical deductions, which will not begin with axioms and can skip some familiar premises.[20]

Our passage at 1.2.13 looks like an extension and a clarification of this earlier comparison. I suggest that by *protos sullogismos*, Aristotle means not the "primary" or first-figure syllogism that Kennedy suggests but (demonstrative) reasoning from first principles, as explained in the *Posterior Analytics* and mentioned in the *Topics*. Compared to scientific demonstration, which aims at instruction and begins with premises that are true and primary, enthymemes are drawn not from "all the way back" but from few premises—and often less than primary deductions (in which everything has to be stated)—for if one of these premises is known, it does not have to be stated, since the hearer supplies it (*Rhetoric* 1.2.13; 41). Just as dialectical deductions often use more premises than is strictly necessary, rhetorical deductions will often use fewer premises than the "primary deductions" of scientific demonstration.[21]

Cooper comes close to this meaning in his version of the phrase: "The links in the chain must be few—seldom as many as the links in a normal chain of deductions" (1932, 12). This rendering agrees that this reference is not to syllogistic form but to a "chain of deductions." I would simply replace *normal* with *primary* and add a footnote: "That is, a deduction from primary premises or first principles, as occurs in scientific demonstrations."

Students of dialectic may not have encountered the *Prior* or *Posterior Analytics* before the *Rhetoric*, but they probably did practice dialectic and read the *Topics* before their exposure to rhetoric. A student's knowledge of dialectic and the topics would be important for his ability to understand Aristotle's comments in the *Rhetoric*. On the other hand, although Aristotle mentions the *Prior Analytics* in the *Rhetoric*, knowledge of this work is not needed to read and understand the *Rhetoric* and probably was not required of students studying rhetoric. If Aristotle relied on his students' understanding of dialectic and the *Topics* to grasp the *Rhetoric*, then the reference to the *protos sullogismos* in the *Rhetoric* would be understood to refer not to the first-figure syllogism of the *Prior Analytics* (which students had not yet encountered) but to scientific demonstrations that begin with "primary" premises, as already introduced in the *Topics*. Of course, while this reading would be clear for Aristotle's students, who were familiar with the primary deductions of demonstrative reasoning, the comparison is lost on contemporary students of rhetoric, who mistakenly hear Aristotle to be saying not that rhetorical argument is shorter than the exacting deductions of scientific demonstration but that it is shorter than the two-premise syllogism.

The pull of 3.0 appears in other places as well. For example, Kennedy has Aristotle observe that "a syllogism is wholly from propositions, and the enthymeme is a syllogism consisting of propositions expressed." Kennedy uses a footnote to pull the passage more firmly within the orbit of 3.0, explaining that "the propositions inherent in an underlying syllogism are not necessarily all expressed in the related enthymeme" (*Rhetoric* 1.3.7; 50 and n. 86). He is apparently referring to the proposition that is "suppressed" by the speaker and "assumed" by the audience.

The relevant phrase, *propositions expressed* (*ton eiremenon*), generally means "the things that have been mentioned or spoken" or "what has been said." Aristotle uses this phrase frequently not to differentiate syllogistic premises that are spoken from enthymematic premises that are suppressed and assumed by the audience but simply to refer to something that he has previously mentioned, as he does five times just in chapter 3 of book I (3.6, 3.7 twice, 3.9 twice; 49–51). For example, here is Kennedy's translation just a few lines before the passage in question: "It is evident from what has been said that . . ." (*phaneron de ek ton eiremenon hoti*; 1.3.7; 50).

If we follow this same meaning for the passage about *tekmēria* and probabilities and signs, then Aristotle would mean that the enthymeme is drawn not from "propositions expressed," as Kennedy has it, but from the propositions that he has just mentioned—that is, from *tekmēria*, signs, and probabilities, which he had just been talking about (and not from other kinds of premises). This is how Freese understands the passage: "For the syllogism universally consists of propositions, and the enthymeme is a syllogism composed of the propositions above mentioned" (1982, 37).[22] Even if Aristotle was here referring to 3.0, Kennedy would have it backward. It is the syllogism that consists solely of propositions expressed. An enthymeme consists of propositions expressed *and* the proposition unexpressed but assumed by the speaker. But this is not what Aristotle either said or meant. If we correct Freese's *syllogism*, the passage would read, "Reasoning consists wholly of propositions, and the enthymeme is reasoning composed of the kinds of propositions mentioned above." In these and other ways, the language of Aristotle is bent or stretched to accommodate and support the standard view.[23]

For Aristotle, *sullogismos* is a kind of explanatory reasoning used in both dialectic and rhetoric, whereby certain things being so, other things are shown to follow from these because they are true. This reasoning is accomplished through the invention or discovery and serial arrangement of propositions that will lead an audience to accept something else beyond what was said. This is the basis of *sullogismos* and the enthymeme: a verbal linkage designed to prompt rational inference, triggering a listener's movement from one set of "things" to something else.

Everything beyond this is strategic and contextual because of features of the agon, the kinds of premises used, or the abilities of the audience—not because of the nature of *sullogismos*. Often the propositions and the inferences from them will be true only for the most part, and typically the things that are so will be stated as signs and probabilities, and they will be stated as briefly and concisely as possible. They will tend to fall into patterns: some specific to each genre of rhetoric (legal topics, deliberative topics, ceremonial topics) and some general across the genres, the common topics.

CHAPTER 4

2.0 and Its Problems

Where other theorists defined the enthymeme as simply a "thought" or a contradiction in word or action, Aristotle saw it to be an inference and inference to be the finding and arranging of propositions (or "things that are so") that together would lead a respondent or audience to affirm something beyond what was said—through them and because they are true. Aristotle saw this process to be the basis of deliberation, of reasoning about a question or thesis (in dialectic), and also of persuasion. He saw that inferential movements fell into patterns, topoi, *koina*, or *idia*, and he thought that familiarity with these topics would be useful for speakers: those relevant to particular genres (judicial, deliberative, or ceremonial) and those applicable to any rhetorical contests. His discussion and examples of *enthumēma* and his rhetorical topoi have no regular logical form. And even though this is how they are typically understood, the rhetorical topics do not require formulation through a traditional premise-conclusion (PC) structure (Levi 1995). None of Aristotle's rhetorical "common" topics (*Rhetoric* 2.23) preclude narrative reasoning. In fact, the topics, *sullogismos*, and the enthymeme as a kind of rhetorical inference can be understood through a narrative frame and, I would argue, understood better than it can be through a formal PC frame. Many of the topics are inherently narrative in their movement and invite "fleshing out" in a narrative context.

For example, topic 1, "from opposites," says that "one should look to see if the opposite [predicate] is true of the opposite [subject], [thus] refuting the argument if not, confirming if it is" (*Rhetoric* 2.23.1; 172). The first example Aristotle offers concerns character traits: if to lack self-control is harmful, then to be temperate is a good thing. If a trait can be predicated of a subject (or character), then see if the opposite trait can be predicated of the opposite character. But these character traits clearly imply actions and the patterns of action and choice that both form and reveal a character and a moral quality. Aristotle quotes a lost play to illustrate:

> Since it is unjust to fall into anger
> at those who unwilling have done wrong,
> if someone benefits another perforce,
> it is not appropriate for thanks to be owed. (2.23.1; 172)

This example suggests more clearly the narrative basis of this and other topics. Kennedy's translation of this topic "from opposites" (2.23.1; 172, quoted above with Kennedy's brackets) suggests a PC structure, with each proposition suggesting a "predicate" and a "subject" (172). But the passage could equally well be translated like this: "See if the opposite [result or behavior] is true of the opposite [action or trait]." The invitation to a scene and act becomes palpable.

Someone inadvertently or unwillingly performed an act that benefitted someone else. Should the recipient be grateful or feel indebted to the doer? There is narrative movement here—a potential cadence in the episode, an emotional impetus—with character and moral implications. The question also betrays contention: one party expects gratitude or indebtedness; the other refuses. There is a counterfactual conditional narrative episode encoded within the "premise," which is presented as a hypothetical: If you had unavoidably harmed me, I couldn't really blame you or repay the harm with harm, so why should I be grateful or beholden to you, seeing that you never intended your action to benefit me? In a world where favors or benefits required reciprocation or incurred obligation, the question was not a trivial one.

So even though this can be represented as an atemporal PC sequence without reference to action, circumstance, or consequence, in experience and in any legal speech, it would arise and be felt as a narrative episode and a challenge: I don't owe you anything. Many other topics in book II reveal the same narrative roots.[1]

But it must be admitted that Aristotle's dialectical framing of rhetoric, his brief and isolated examples in the *Rhetoric*, the formulation of his topics, and his later work on logic all tend toward the view that a narrative analytical framework (such as is found in the *Poetics*) is irrelevant to *sullogismos* and the enthymeme, nor did either of these depend for their effect on an invoked storyworld or other features of context (e.g., the law, the issue, and the counternarrative). 2.0 was, and is, rather an isolable and independent series of propositions leading to a conclusion—looser in structure than 3.0 or the categorical syllogism, to be sure, but a PC series nonetheless. The limitations of this view become apparent only when we consider an alternative possibility: the enthymeme might be a fragment of narrative reasoning.

From this perspective, it becomes clear that although Aristotle presents *sullogismos rhetorikos* in much broader and looser terms than 3.0, his description of enthymemes implies and is generally understood to involve a few limiting assumptions. These assumptions are basic to seeing inference as *sullogismos*, explanation via a lining up of statements, and they will deter later generations from seeing the real power of enthymemes and from granting to orators their role in developing enthymematic reasoning. There are at least two such restrictions in operation that ought to be made explicit and examined.

First, the "things" (from the definition in the *Rhetoric*) that are known to the audience to be true that will lead to the audience seeing "something else" as true as well are universally understood to be propositions. For Aristotle, *logos*, *logismos*, and *sullogismos* all suggest that truths will take the form of discrete assertions that function as premises. Every relevant "thing" from which inferences are made will be a proposition of one or more terms that predicate something of something else, a subject: "Aristotle takes it for granted that in every premise . . . there is a subject (which is 'that about which' something is said) and a predicate (which is that which is 'said of,' or perhaps denied of, something)" (Smith 2003, xxix). Every proposition will assert the truth of something by predicating something of something else. For this reason, Aristotle approaches the producing of arguments through the analysis of propositions (categories and predicables) and their terms (subjects and predicates).

These propositions will take a particular form, they will be combined in particular ways, and their effect will depend on these forms and combinations. And every proposition, once lined up like so many numbers in a column or equations in a proof, will become a premise that is linked to another. Together, they lead to the conclusion. There is as yet no restriction on the number of premises in a proof, or the number of terms in a premise, or the nature of the predication. But the form of the premise as a proposition and the arrangement of propositions in serial order will be taken for granted. Focusing on topics as patterns of PC moves encourages

78 THE ENTHYMEME

seeing inference in terms of this PC framework. These restrictions already shape our understanding of what the enthymeme will look like: it will be a PC sequence.

While Aristotle's definition (*Rhetoric* 1.2.9; 40) and his discussion of categories and predicables, predicates and subjects, and propositions and topics (in the *Topics*) may not explicitly rule out the admissibility of other forms of reasoning as *sullogismos* or *enthumēma*—a slice of narrative could fit his definition and a topical pattern—his language and all of his examples work against any such understanding. Readers of the *Topics* and the *Rhetoric* will have no reason to suspect that a narrative could count as *sullogismos* even though narrative audiences do inevitably infer "something else" from the "things" that were said and understood to be true (or at least true within the frame of the narrative).

The second restriction in Aristotle's enthymeme is language. That *sullogismos* will take place through the serial assertion (externally or internally) of propositions implies that it will take place in or can be reduced to language. It will not occur to readers of Aristotle that some of the "things" known to be true and some of the other things that are accepted as true "as a result" will not exist in language at all but will occur only as an emotion, a recalled and felt sensation, an image or mental representation, a scene or model, or some other multimodal kind of awareness. Nowhere does the possibility present itself that truths might be inferred, known, and understood not through language but through perception, image, experience, or bodily awareness or memory.

For example, when in Doyle's "Silver Blaze" Sherlock Holmes learns that Hunter the stable boy had passed out on the evening of the theft and that curry was served for dinner, he suspects (i.e., he infers) that opium was introduced into the food for the purpose of incapacitating the stable boy.[2] He knows this not necessarily on the basis of propositions he has heard or posed to himself but on the basis of flavors he has tasted (including opium) and an experiential familiarity with flavor combinations: curry masks the flavor of opium.

Certainly, such knowledge can be conveyed through language, but it is not fully captured by the language. The knowledge is sensory and prelinguistic. Even if Holmes communicated this observation to another opium-and-curry taster, they would know the result not simply on the basis of the propositions but on the basis of gustatory experience.

Their knowledge would be of a different quality than that possessed by non-opium-and-curry-tasters who are told the same set of propositions. Inferences, or deductions, do not have to occur through or on account of stated premises, or propositions, or language at all. But this would not occur to a reader of the *Rhetoric* because Aristotle's discussion and examples of enthymemic reasoning are regularly guided into the channels of propositions as premises.

Given the primacy of narrative in oratory (to anticipate the argument of chapters 5 and 6), why does Aristotle restrict reasoning to propositions in this way? Surely this is partly because of his commitment to dialectic and demonstration as the two valid modes of knowledge creation. Rhetoric, like these others, tries to prove that something is so. But it is also possible that in crafting the *Rhetoric*, Aristotle did not encounter speeches as stories—that he did not rely on the study of rhetorical *speeches* at all. As will become clear to anyone who reads the *Rhetoric* with an eye to its examples and sources, Aristotle frequently uses nonrhetorical texts to illustrate his points about rhetorical artistry. He does sometimes refer to individual lines from Athenian orations, but this fact hides a deeper problem articulated clearly by Trevett: "Aristotle fails in the *Rhetoric* to quote from or allude to the text of a single deliberative or forensic speech" (1996, 371).

Five of the ten Attic orators he does not mention at all (Antiphon, Andocides, Lysias, Isaeus, and Aeschines).[3] The omission of Lysias, Trevett rightly observes, is "particularly striking" given Lysias's output and reputation (1996, 377).[4] Aristotle mentions a fallacious post hoc, propter hoc topic from Demades but refers to no particular speech (371). We need not review all mentions of judicial speeches that Trevett considers; his conclusion is that based on Aristotle's selections, wording, and the nature of the citations, not a single instance demonstrates that Aristotle actually consulted a speech rather than simply using a passage culled from a speech, either in a collection of sayings or by hearing it repeated second hand. "There is in my opinion," says Trevett, "no reason to believe that Aristotle's source in any of these [forensic or deliberative] cases is a published speech" (372). This argument from silence could be complemented by looking at the texts that he does refer to.

We can use the example of the general Iphicrates, just one of many that Trevett offers, to illustrate the point. Aristotle refers to sayings of Iphicrates on ten different occasions in the *Rhetoric*. They are listed below, with brief context in parentheses:

1. 1.7.32 (71): "Iphicrates lauded himself, speaking of his origins." (Aristotle illustrates the topic from "the more difficult and rarer is greater." Iphicrates was from low origins but became a leading general.)
2. 1.9.31 (80): "Such were the remarks of Iphicrates about his [humble] origins and success." (This illustrates the topic of praise from something that goes beyond the norm in the direction of the nobler and more honorable.)
3. 2.21.2 (165): "A maxim is an assertion—not, however, one about particulars, such as what kind of person Iphicrates is, but of a general sort."
4. 2.23.6 (175): "Another is from looking at the time, for example what Iphicrates said in the [suit] against Harmodius: 'If, before accomplishing anything, I asked to be honored with a statue if I succeeded, you would have granted it. Will you not grant it [now] that I have succeeded?'"
5. 2.23.7 (175): "And there is the argument Iphicrates used against Aristophon when he asked [the latter] if he would betray the fleet for money. After [Aristophon] denied it, [Iphicrates] said, 'If you, being Aristophon, would not play the traitor, would I, Iphicrates?'" (This illustrates the topic "from turning what is said against oneself upon the one who said it.")
6. 2.23.8 (176): "And [another example is,] as Iphicrates [argued], that the best person is the most noble; for there was no noble quality in Harmodius and Aristogeiton until they did something noble, while he himself was more like them [than his opponent was]" (This illustrates the topic "from definitions.")
7. 3.2.10 (200): "As also when Iphicrates called Callias 'a begging priest' rather than a 'torchbearer' and the latter replied that Iphicrates was not initiated into the Mysteries, or he would not have called him a begging priest but torchbearer." (This illustrates the use of metaphor to adorn.)
8. 3.10.7 (220): "And Iphicrates, when the Athenians had made a truce with Epidaurus and the neighboring coast, complained that they had deprived themselves of 'travelling expenses' for the war." (This illustrates metaphor by analogy.)
9. 3.10.7 (221): "And when Iphicrates said, 'My path of words leads through the midst of Chares' actions,' it was a metaphor by analogy and 'through the midst' is before-the-eyes."
10. 3.15.2 (237): "The question at issue concern things like this, as in the reply of Iphicrates to Nausicrates; for he admitted that he had done what the other claimed and that it caused harm but not that he had committed a crime." (This illustrates how to counteract an attack by denying what is at issue.)

Each of these examples offers short, memorable sayings of Iphicrates that could be memorized and recited or written down for reading and admiration. In none of these cases does Aristotle claim to have access to a written speech. In no case does our understanding of the saying rely upon the content of the speech, the situation, or the law or the issue: Aristotle is interested in the internal structure of the saying, in the relationships among its terms, and in its ability to illustrate a more general point, topic, or trope. For example, number 10 need not identify the opponent or his claim; the act, the harm caused, or the crime alleged; or the relationship between Iphicrates and his opponent. The point of raising Iphicrates's reply is to demonstrate the *form* of this kind of counterargument: deny that it caused harm, that it was a crime, or that it is the crime of which you are accused.

The large number of citations to Iphicrates is itself remarkable. Trevett compares it to the large number of military stratagems attributed to Iphicrates by Polyaenus, which leads him to suggest that both Polyaenus and Aristotle had access to a collection of sayings by and about Iphicrates (1996, 374). Citation number 3 in the list above suggests that there was interest in what kind of person Iphicrates was, and citations 1 and 2 suggest that this interest was connected to his rise from low beginnings to political and military prominence. A biography or collection of anecdotes and sayings about Iphicrates would satisfy that interest, revealing the quality of the man that might account for his rise. Momigliano observes the "obvious delight which Aristotle and his pupils took in anecdotes" and sayings by and about the illustrious and famous, such as might be found in collections (1993, 68). In dialectical training, Aristotle encouraged his students to gather just such collections of notable sayings as *endoxa* for their debates (*Topics* 1.14; Smith 2003, 12–13).

Citation number 7 gives further support to this notion: Aristotle not only refers to the words of Iphicrates, who called Callias a begging priest (*mētragurtai*) rather than a torchbearer (*dadouxos*), but adds the response of Callias. Aristotle would have access to sayings about or responses to Iphicrates in a collection of anecdotes and sayings but not in a speech by Iphicrates, where Callias's response would not be recorded. If the citation is from a trial, then a witness may have extracted and remembered (perhaps not word for word) both the line from Iphicrates and the response by Callias, perhaps recording them together as point and counterpoint. Kennedy too observes that "there is no reason to believe that the [speeches of Iphicrates] were published," making it unlikely that Aristotle had access to the entire speech (2007, 71).[5]

Trevett concludes from his analysis of these and similar examples that "most of the political and forensic quotations in the *Rhetoric* derive from oral tradition" (1996, 374–75), some of them collected by Aristotle and his students, and that although Aristotle refers to sayings from forensic and deliberative speeches, he nevertheless "systematically fails to cite two of three types of oratory, even though these are accorded equal treatment with epideictic in the text of the work" (376).

This is in marked contrast to Aristotle's frequent citation of Greek poetry, especially Homer and Euripides, to illustrate rhetorical moves. Aristotle demonstrates the qualities of a forensic introduction with examples from dithyrambic, epic, and tragic poetry (*Rhetoric* 3.14.5–6; 233), and although he illustrates the role of narrative in forensic speeches with references to the poets Homer, Phayllus, Euripides, and Sophocles and to Aeschines Socraticus (not the orator but the follower of Socrates), he uses nothing from Lysias or any other orator (3.16.5–8; 240; see also Trevett 1996, 376). For comparison, we might imagine Aristotle discussing the nature of dramatic plot and action in the *Poetics* with examples from Gorgias, Antiphon, and Lysias but without reference to a single work by Homer, Aeschylus, Sophocles, Euripides, or any other Greek playwright.

Aristotle does make repeated reference to epideictic speeches. He frequently refers to them by name and uses language that suggests access to the speech rather than simply to an extracted line. He gives passages from Isocrates's *Panegyricus*, *Panathenaicus*, *Philip*, *Antidosis*, and *On the Peace* (*Symmachus*), and he alludes to the *Helen* and *Evagorus*. He also refers to epideictic speeches by Pericles, Theodectes, Alcidamas, Lycophron, and Gorgias. Trevett mentions several examples of epideictic speeches being written down, copied, read, and memorized for pleasure and discussion, as Phaedrus does for the *Eroticus*, attributed to Lysias in Plato's dialogue *Phaedrus*, or the funeral speech of Aspasia in *Menexenus*. The availability of epideictic speeches in writing and their attention to literary craftsmanship and to memorable sayings specifically would have made them much more useful to Aristotle's school for collection, memorization, and analysis.

Unlike epideictic speeches, legal and deliberative speeches were not widely available. And if collections of sayings were common, Aristotle may not have had reason to seek them out or encourage his students to study them. Both factors seem to have played a role in Aristotle's failure to cite them. Deliberative speeches, notes Trevett, were not often written down and were not "objects of literary appreciation." Judicial speeches, though often written, were rarely circulated or published and were likewise viewed as ephemera, of interest only to the client and the logographer, rather than as works of lasting or more general value: "They were not widely read in educated circles, nor known by a title."[6] Epideictic speeches, on the other hand, were objects of literary admiration and "counted as serious literature" (1996, 377). Many epideictic speeches of the sophists and orators were written to be performed, admired, learned, and emulated as prose equivalents of poetry. When Phaedrus wanted to learn a speech of Lysias, he chose a display piece about love, not a murder defense.

Trevett also mentions "a certain fastidious disdain for forensic and deliberative oratory" (1996, 378) on the part of Aristotle and his students, as evidenced by his comments in the *Rhetoric* and the *Politics* on the defects of popular democracies and the democratic audience. And his metic status and his time away from Athens afforded Aristotle little opportunity to take in forensic and deliberative oratory as a spectator even if he were inclined to. He drew his examples instead from collections of sayings, probably for the most part in written form.[7] These, as we have seen, included epic and tragic poetry, Socratic dialogues, well-known epideictic speeches, and collections of anecdotes and sayings by and about well-known sages and reputable persons.

In this way, says Trevett, "Aristotle reveals a detached and somewhat unsympathetic attitude towards 'real life' oratory and its practitioners" (1996, 379). I would conclude from this not that Aristotle's discussion of the enthymeme in the *Rhetoric* was uninformed by forensic and deliberative speeches. Certainly, Aristotle does refer to court cases, such as the trial of Demosthenes (not the orator) and "those who killed Nicanor" (2.23.3; 173) and the dispute between Ismenias and Stilbon (2.23.10; 177). But his discussion of forensic and deliberative oratory in the *Rhetoric* seems not to have been based on the analysis of full speeches in the context of a legal case or political issue, what Trevett calls "real life oratory," and was not viewed through the lens of narrative development and narrative logic; rather, it was based on sayings extracted from speeches, memorized or written down for collection, and inserted into deductions as premises.

Aristotle's disinterest in forensic and deliberative oratory is unfortunate as well because these two genres are rife with a variety of interesting and effective enthymemes. Even Aristotle himself would be forced to admit that the enthymeme deserves closer attention in the original sources than he gives to it. We can make the case in deductive form. In the *Rhetoric*, he acknowledges that the rhetorical technique best suited and most important to forensic oratory is the enthymeme (1.1.3, 3.17.5; 31, 243). And in the *Athenian Constitution*, he argues that one of the most democratic features of the Athenian constitution is the law court—that is, the right of the people to appeal legal decisions to a popular jury.[8] If we were to present these assertions in the trappings of dialectical reasoning, we would have to conclude that the enthymeme was central not only to rhetoric but to democracy:

> Democracy depends upon the opportunity for legal appeals to mass juries.
> Every legal appeal to mass juries requires legal oratory.
> All legal oratory is produced by rhetorical artistry.
> The body of rhetorical artistry is the enthymeme.
> Thus democracy itself depends upon the enthymeme.

As we'll see in chapter 8, Lysias make just this kind of argument, naming the forensic enthymeme as vital to the life of ancient Greek democracy.

We've already seen that one problem with 3.0 was that it is functionally independent of the context in which it operates. We can now suggest that this problem is not a corruption of 2.0 but an exacerbation of an already existing problem with 2.0: Aristotle's particular interests—in the elements and forms of deduction, for example—encouraged a view of rhetorical reasoning that was based on finding individual propositions and arranging them according to proven forms or topics but not on actual speeches or the cases that they made and based on the stepwise progression of dialectical reasoning from premise to conclusion but not on the particular features of rhetorical interactions as they were expressed by practitioners.

PART THREE

1.0

CHAPTER 5

Enthymizing in the Orators

If 2.0 is unclear or misleading and 3.0 is incorrect, what, then, is the enthymeme? And where should we go to look for it? This is an old question. Aristotle asked it and scolded his predecessors for ignoring it (*Rhetoric* 1.1.3; 31). Quintilian asked it and offered multiple answers from multiple theorists (5.10.1–8; Russell 2001, 366–69). De Quincey was still asking it in the nineteenth century. Bitzer (1959) seemed to settle the question in favor of 3.0, but the question kept coming up. Conley (1984) put the question in an epigraph and decided that the answer (a) was more complicated than we thought and (b) might include style—something like a "finely wrought cap" to an argument. Walker (1994) asked, too, and like Conley returned to pre-Aristotelian use. Walker's lengthy definition centers on a "kairotic argumentational turn" (53) that is strategic, abrupt, and stylistic. Nemesi (2013) thought it might be like implicature but confessed that both concepts were too vague to be sure. Meanwhile, Sorensen (1988) had already proved that it wasn't an argument, though Goddu (2016) thought it still might be.

The problem of the enthymeme is like the financial problems of Gayev in Chekhov's *The Cherry Orchard*. "If a great many remedies are prescribed against an illness," Gayev says, "it means the illness is incurable. . . . I have many remedies, a great many, which in fact means none" (2015, 66). We have a great many theories of the enthymeme, which means we have none. And having no viable answers recalls the problem of knowing virtue in Plato's *Meno*. Socrates has just refuted all of Meno's opinions about virtue and suggests that because he knows no better than Meno what it is, they ought to proceed with their inquiry together. Meno is at a loss: "On what lines will you look for a thing of whose nature you know nothing at all? . . . Or even supposing, at the best, that you hit upon it, how will you know it is the thing you did not know?" (80D; Lamb 1952, 298–99). Having a great many ideas about the enthymeme, where are we to look for one?

And this is only part of the problem. For even if you find a way to recognize what you're looking for, once you've set all existing models of the enthymeme aside, all the various associated notions and assumptions attendant upon the concept continue to operate in the background. Once learned, a thing cannot be easily unlearned, and the habit of using it dies slowly. One tends to continue thinking along the same lines and looking for and finding all the old features of the model without consciously attempting to do so: deduction, truncation, the causal conjunction, audience-added premises, and the rest. Treat a model like a reality for long enough, and soon it begins to act like it.

I propose to solve these problems not with immortality, as Plato did, or with useless, decadent sentimentality, as Gayev did, but with clues, as a detective would. My clues will not be found in etymology, in the *thumos* root, or by returning to Aristotle or to treatise writers earlier than Aristotle. These lines of inquiry have all been explored by keener eyes. Rather, I will turn to practice, to the orators and their speeches. Specifically, I will be looking at how the orators used forms of the term *enthumaomai*, what I am transliterating as "enthymize." These clues will give us a place to begin thinking about the enthymeme outside the penumbra of theory, and they will offer a seawall against the surge of mental detritus that the term *enthymeme* continually throws up. The orators' use of this term ultimately reveals (to paraphrase Bennet and Feldman 2014) that the Greek rhetorical agon—rhetorical artistry and the rhetorical appeals, including logos—are all organized around storytelling (3) and that the enthymeme is a central feature of rhetorical narrative. The rest of this chapter will develop a view of enthymizing that relies solely upon its use in Attic oratory. I will refer to this oratorical technique as 1.0. Future chapters will look at some examples in further detail and explore the value of a narrative perspective on the problem of the enthymeme.

1. ENTHYMIZING AS TERM AND TECHNIQUE

The first task in this process will be to describe enthymizing generally as used by the orators, to lay out the various ways in which the term could be employed, and to separate out those uses that attempted to achieve (and name) a rhetorical effect from those that did not. After this analysis, it will be possible to clarify the use and effect of the term by seeing how they are used in orations.

I use the verb, *enthymize* (*enthumeisthai*), rather than the noun, *enthymeme* (*enthumēma*), primarily because the orators use the verb regularly. What's more, the verb will keep us off the shoals of Enthymeme, and it will remind us that enthymizing is something that speakers and audiences do—it is performed and experienced—more than it is a linguistic or logical structure on the page or in the mind.

Attending to *enthymizing* makes it less likely that we will confuse the flow of speech, thought, and response for the logical mold into which it can be poured. It will remind us that oratory is not theory, logic, or even merely an argument but is primarily a narrative contest. Determining the number, type, and order of premises in oratorical enthymizing is as relevant to its effectiveness as (to borrow a metaphor used earlier) calculating the geometrical formula that describes an arrow's flight to hitting a target. Enthymizing must be defined through practice—by its goal and its effect upon an audience.

The basic sense of *enthumaomai* is clear and easily recognized. To enthymize something is simply to think about, notice, or consider it. Liddell and Scott have "lay to heart" or "ponder," "think much or deeply of," and "notice" or "consider" (1985, 263). Additional senses include to "think out" or "form a plan" and to "infer" or "conclude." It is often rendered through metaphors, as it is itself a metaphor: to "lay" something "to heart," to have it "weigh upon" the conscience or to "hold" something "in mind." The term often does but need not involve a recognition of a thing's meaning within a situation or an inference that can be drawn from it as an induction, abduction,[1] or deduction (infer, conclude). It can indicate a perception (notice, take note of), an emotion (be concerned, be hurt or angry at, or be worried about), or a more effusive and indefinite cognitive response (ponder). It can include recalling something from the past, taking notice of something in the present, or planning something out for the future (plan, lay to heart), but universally it suggests bringing something to the foreground of consciousness. In the language of Perelman and Olbrechts-Tyteca, we might say that something enthymized gains "presence" (1971, 116–19, 142). As we'll see, however, in oratory and particularly in adversarial storytelling, enthymizing tends to gravitate toward a few more specific uses. It offers what Amsterdam and Bruner have more recently called a "consideration" (2000, 118). The term *enthumaomai*, or "enthymize," is used frequently by orators to signal to audiences a fact or narrative detail worth attending to. What is revealed through the study of this usage is the gradual formation of a regular—that is, rule-governed—technique and the development of a technical term to describe and analyze it.

Though I am relying on the orators' use of the verb as a guide, the orations include many instances of enthymizing that do not rely on the term. That is to say, the usage only indicates the rhetorical technique; it does not constitute it. It is a clue to the thing, not the thing itself. The orators can also direct the audience to "mark" a narrative detail—to consider it or "take it to heart"—with a synonym like *phrontízō* (think, consider), *katanoeō* (understand, perceive), *mnēmoneuō* (remember, call to mind), *apoblepō* (pay attention to), or *dialogizomai* (take account of, fully consider) or periphrastically in other ways. In chapter 6, we'll see Andocides repeatedly using forms of *skopeō* and *skeptomai* (behold, contemplate, consider, examine) alongside *enthumaomai*.[2] Much enthymizing occurs without being announced or linguistically marked.[3] I don't need to say *attention* to get your attention.

Everything that follows results from a study of the extant orations of the ten named Attic orators.[4] I included all speeches from the fifth and fourth centuries regardless of attribution or performance.[5] I began by locating all uses of the verb, just over two hundred instances. I looked at the context in which each instance of the verb occurred and the kind of work it was attempting to do in the speech. Not all of these uses have any clear relevance as a rhetorical technique, as will be clear in what follows. Several appearances of the term were incidental.

But in a sufficient number of cases, the term was used in a way that indicated a clear rhetorical goal, and most of these cases followed a clear and consistent pattern: they were functionally similar. After cataloging these uses, I coded them in terms of their relevance as a rhetorical "move" and the type of move initiated. This grading system is described in section 2 below. The features and patterns of its use suggest that the practice was regular and significant—that it was employed as a deliberate, standard, and repeatable technique that could be talked about and taught. 1.0 was used by orators and became known by the term with which it was most closely associated: the place where you call an audience to *enthumeisthai*, or enthymize, an important fact became an *enthumēma*, enthymeme.

2. TYPES OF ENTHYMIZING IN THE ORATORS

In what follows, I'll organize all uses of the term *enthumaomai* into twenty-six representative cases in order to demonstrate its range of use in Attic oratory. These examples will fall into four sets of variables: (A) mood (indicative/imperative), (B) mediacy (immediate/mediate), (C) stance (supportive/contradictory), and (D) novelty (mnemonic/didactic/heuristic). Of course, these are not the only ways to categorize enthymizing, but this set of variables will serve to illustrate how enthymizing came to be put to the service of oratory as a rhetorical technique. In each case, I'll boldface the word or phrase that translates some form of the Greek term *enthuméomai*. In the process of describing these different kinds of enthymizing, I'll suggest where and how enthymizing takes on a specifically persuasive function.

A. Mood: Indicative Versus Imperative

1. Indicative

It is not uncommon for speakers to simply describe (in the indicative case) something that he or someone else notices or has taken to heart. This isn't surprising, given that legal cases are built upon narratives of what the speaker did and thought, and many cases turn on the question of what can be seen and known and what can be premeditated and intended: What did the defendant realize or plan—both meanings are within the range of *enthuméomai*—and when did he realize it? What's more, Greek agonistic culture operates on the assumption that anyone facing some kind of risk (through either wrongdoing or an upcoming trial) would have to consider (to enthymize) his actions well (see "Antiphon" 5.6; 52; [c] below).[6]

Speakers will often describe their own enthymizing (a) or that of a third party (b) either about a specific fact (a and b) or as a kind of general rule (c); about a fact in the past (a and b) or in the present or future (c).

> (a) "Many times before now, by Zeus and Apollo, I have **reflected** on [*enethumēthēn*] the good luck of our city" (*Aeschines* 1.108; Carey 2000, 60).
> (b) "And the woman who was really responsible, and who **thought up** [*enthumētheisa*] the plan and carried it out, she will have her reward too, if you and the gods are willing" ("Antiphon" 20; 14).

(c) "A man who faces personal danger cannot avoid making some mistake, since he must **consider** [*enthumeisthai*] not only his arguments, but his whole future" ("Antiphon" 5.6; 52).

Typically, as here, speakers will emphasize the importance of enthymizing as an antecedent to action—often the thinking that guides their own action. Both Andocides (chapter 6) and Lysias (chapter 7) will narrate how they thought to themselves (enthymized) about the situations they were in and what they ought to do about it. In this they agree with Thucydides, who congratulates the Athenians for deliberating before they act (2.40.2–3; 1996, 113–14). This thinking, considering, or reflecting is not necessarily linked to any persuasive technique or any demonstrative or communicative process supporting an argumentative claim, but it typically works to move the plot forward and reveal a character's (or the narrator's) ends, motives, and choices.

In other cases, a speaker will want to point out that he or a third party has failed to enthymize something. This will be particularly useful when a speaker wants to convey a lack of intent to commit a crime (d) or to urge consideration of an issue that has been neglected (e).

(d) "I had no suspicions and **thought** no more of it [*enthumoumenos*], but gladly went to bed, since I had just returned from the country" (*Lysias* 1.13; Todd 2000, 18).

(e) "Personally, I am amazed if none of you, men of Athens, is **concerned** [*enthumeitai*] or angry when he considers that when the war began, our object was to punish Philip, but now that it is coming to an end, it is to avoid suffering harm at his hands" (*Demosthenes* 4.43; Trevett 2011, 84).

In (d), the speaker's wife has reluctantly gotten up in the middle of the night "to feed the baby" who had been crying. Later he wakes up again because "both the door of the house and the courtyard door had creaked" (*Lysias* 1.17; Todd 2000, 18–19). But he thought nothing of it and went straight back to sleep. Only later will he discover that a creaking door is a sign and that while "feeding the baby," his wife also received a visitor.

In (e), Demosthenes expresses amazement that his countrymen have not taken to heart their earlier resolve and their subsequent failure to hold Philip accountable for his aggressive actions. In both cases, failing to realize the significance of (i.e., to enthymize) one's own situation leads to avoidable negative consequences.

2. Imperative

More often than they describe a case of enthymizing, speakers will tell the audience to think about something (often but not necessarily in the imperative case). Sometimes a specific fact or detail is to be enthymized (a, b); at other times, a range of evidence, a scene, or an entire case (c).

(a) "**Bear in mind** [*enthumeisthe*] that none of those who will be pleading for him has done as much good for the city as the damage he has done it—so you have more right to exact vengeance than these men have to offer help" (*Lysias* 30.33; Todd 2000, 306).

(b) "We must also make it our policy and be resolved to detest those who speak to you on his behalf, **keeping in mind** [*enthumoumenous*] that it is not possible to defeat our city's enemies until you punish those in the city itself who are their servants" (*Demosthenes* 9.53; Trevett 2011, 170–71).

(c) "You must **consider** [*enthumeisthai*] these facts, gentlemen, and remember that I am the deceased's nephew, but she is only his cousin; that she is asking to possess two estates, but I claim only this one into which I was taken by adoption" (*Isaeus* 7.45; 128).[7]

It will not be surprising that this form of enthymizing is so common as to be the norm, but it is worth mentioning that even descriptive enthymizing in the indicative case will lead the audience to enthymize something. Demosthenes's chastisement in A.1.e. also serves the purpose of reminding his audience of what they ought to keep in mind during their deliberations. Similarly, in A.1.d. above, the speaker's description of his own failure to enthymize his wife's actions leads the audience to take to heart something else—namely, the wife's affair and the speaker's naivete and folly. In this sense, we might say that all enthymizing is meant not only to describe someone's thinking but also to generate or emphasize a thought (the same or different) in the audience.

But in these later examples (2a, b), what is to be enthymized is named directly. The speaker is calling attention to a fact that he wants the audience to keep in mind. In more contemporary language, we can say that this kind of enthymizing brings the fact to the foreground, giving it, in Perelman and Olbrechts-Tyteca's terms, "presence." We can take this as the first step toward a more specifically rhetorical and persuasive technique. The speaker can explicitly link the enthymized fact to its context, as Demosthenes (A.1.e) and Lysias (A.2.a) do. Doing so shapes its meaning and effect and so already has a rhetorical function. The fact that we are trying to avoid suffering at Philip's hands will feel different when we recall that at the outset, our goal was to punish Philip. Lysias unfavorably compares the damage done by the defendant to the good claimed by his witnesses, hoping to minimize the effect of those witnesses. But even in these cases, what is enthymized is not presented in deductive form or as involving any explicit inferential step. It is simply named as a fact worth attending to within the context of the case.

B. Mediacy: Immediate and Mediate

1. Immediate

Sometimes the speaker states explicitly what the audience is to realize, think about, or react to. In these cases, the thing is to be kept in mind for its own sake. What could be simpler, if you want someone to think about or consider something, than simply telling them about it?

(a) "**Consider** [*enthumeisthai*] this in particular—and don't be upset if I repeat these points several times, since I face great danger; if you decide correctly, I am saved, but if you're at all deceived by their lies, I am destroyed—so don't let anyone make you forget this" ("Antiphon" 5.46; 61).

(b) "**Bear in mind** [*enthumēthēte*], therefore, gentlemen of the jury, what sort of citizens we ourselves are, and also our ancestors. We claim the right to be pitied by you and to receive justice for the wrongs we have suffered" (*Lysias* 18.1; Todd 2000, 193).

One could argue that each of these examples is meant to lead a jury from the statement offered to another implied statement—"Acquit me" or "Punish my opponent"—but I would argue that in these and similar instances, a statement can be made simply to be kept in mind for its own sake either because it directly addresses innocence or guilt (a) or (even though it may also imply another statement) because the statement immediately evokes its own nonverbal response: an emotion, an image, a value judgment, or a character assessment. In (b), the speaker asks the audience to enthymize "what sort of citizens we ourselves are" not to lead the jurors to infer another statement (as premise to conclusion) but to invoke in them an attitude (gentleness and fairness) and an emotion (pity).

Thus not all enthymizing is inferential. But even immediate enthymizing can perform an important rhetorical function. A fact enthymized, even if it doesn't lead to an inference, will contribute to the construction of a narrative whose persuasive effect will depend partly on its arousal of emotional, aesthetic, and moral judgments; its completeness and internal coherence; its correspondence to popular understandings of how people behave and how they ought to behave and how a culture's stories are told.[8] Insofar as the enthymized fact contributes to these features of the story, we could say that it fulfills a rhetorical function independent of its inferential force.

2. Mediate

Although simple and direct, immediate enthymizing is neither as common nor as effective as another type, in which the speaker describes a thought or tells listeners to think about something so that they will also enthymize something else, creating or breaking a link between the thing asserted by the speaker and "something else" understood or felt by the listener. Aristotle fixed upon this as the essential feature of the enthymeme and the factor that made it possible to compare rhetoric to dialectic. The speaker asks the audience to consider a set of factual propositions not for their own sake but for the sake of a fact that they prove or disprove. The facts stated and inferred could in many instances be reframed as a logical deduction. In 1.0, the relationship between the presented fact and the fact to be enthymized is highly variable, from the most loosely associative, imagistic, and experiential to the strictly syllogistic. Each fact now takes on a second valence of meaning and effect given to it by the first.

The two facts (the one stated and the one inferred, felt, imagined, meant, or deduced) can be connected (or separated) by logical, visuospatial, emotional, normative, or experiential relations. And even a "logical" inference can feel as much like seeing a fact as deducing one (Pierce 1935, 112).[9] Observing a servant take a paper from a man in the marketplace and give it to a woman in her home, I see that she is delivering a message. I also might see a liaison being made.

Sherlock Holmes was famous for his ability to see. Examining a valuable old watch that has been engraved, cleaned, and badly scratched around the winding key and with multiple pawn markings, Holmes "deduces" that the owner, an oldest son and originally a person of means, fell in and out of poverty because of drink and finally succumbed to his weakness and passed away.[10] Sherlock Holmes referred to this as deduction, Pierce (1935) called it abduction, but we could also refer to it as narrative reasoning. The knowledge that it produces arrives almost immediately upon perception; it does not depend upon translation into premises arranged in proper order. When done skillfully, the inferred facts will often "strike" the audience as true in a sudden realization or aha moment of insight, abruptly increasing their adherence to it. Perelman and Olbrechts-Tyteca might refer to these as liaisons (1971, 134).

The kinds of links established or destroyed typically depend on experience with the natural and social world and not exclusively or even primarily on the correct manipulation of logical forms, on propositions, or even on language, though it can sometimes be represented (with varying adequacy) in premise-conclusion (PC) form. Deduction is the analytical afterword to the enthymized detail, but an inferential response on the part of the audience typically does not feel like a deduction so much as a perception, a moment of recognition or realization, colored by emotional responses and moral judgments. From a rhetorical perspective, the logical nature of the link matters less than its strength and its effect: What is being linked to what?

The mediated link can be deductive, inductive, abductive, analogical or paradigmatic, semiotic or indexical, imagistic or metaphoric, emotional, normative, experiential, or even physiological.[11] This is because the elements and their relationship are not encountered in isolation as premises but are situated within and known through the narrative frame and the storyworld that it evokes: motivated characters making choices and experiencing the consequences of those choices as told by a narrator, speaking for a purpose to a listening and interpreting audience who feels and responds with the actors in the narrative and their circumstances.

When most effective, mediate enthymizing bears a resemblance to the *anagnorisis* of Aristotelian poetics, introducing a rapid change from ignorance to knowledge as the audience gains awareness or recognition of (what appears to be) the true significance or meaning of a fact and thus of the episode, the characters, and the plot connected to it. As a result, the nature of the situation can be transformed or suddenly clarified as the ambiguity or dilemma is resolved, the misunderstanding is corrected, the deception or lie is found out. Mediate enthymizing done well feels like the resolution of a confusing situation and a real gain in knowledge.

This form of enthymizing can be expressed in several ways. In some cases, the speaker states explicitly both the fact (or a series of facts) and its (or their) import.

(a) "It seems to me, men of Athens, that your deliberations about the war would be improved if you were to **bear in mind** [*enthumētheiēte*] the nature of the place against which you are waging war, and observe that Philip often achieves his aims by getting a head start on us. We need to **bear** these things **in mind** [*enthumoumenous*] and to wage war not by means of relief forces—since if we do so we will be too late for everything—but by means of a permanent standing force" (*Demosthenes* 4.31–32; Trevett 2011, 80).

(b) "I ask you to convict Theomnestus, **bearing in mind** [*enthumoumenous*] that no contest could be greater for me than this one. I am prosecuting him now for defamation, but in the same vote I am also defending myself on a charge of murdering my father" (*Lysias* 10.31; Todd 2000, 110).

In (a), Demosthenes makes a point about Philip's use of season, locale, and distance to prevent an Athenian naval response in order to lead the audience to his policy recommendation. He connects the initial demonstrable fact that Philip routinely attacks cities far from Athenian forces or in bad weather to its practical significance—that is, they need to deploy more quickly by forming a standing army—and he uses the term (forms of *enthumaomai*) at each step. In (b), Lysias ties the fact that he is prosecuting Theomnestus for defamation to a series of related claims, each of which would be less evident on its own terms. Since Theomnestus accused the speaker of murdering his father, the speaker, though technically the plaintiff, is at the same time defending himself against an implicit charge of patricide by proving Theomnestus to be a liar. A jury that acquits Theomnestus will in effect be convicting the speaker of killing his father, the greatest of crimes and a capital offense. Focusing the audience's attention on the initial fact allows the speaker to establish a connection between it and subsequent facts, each of which gains salience from the one before.

In other cases, only the initial fact need be offered. Its meaning, what finally needs to be understood and believed, will be immediately clear to the audience.

(c) "**Consider** [*enthumeisthe*] this point too: the note differed from the man's testimony, and the man differed from the note, for when tortured he said he himself killed him, but the note, when opened, indicated that I was the killer. So which should we believe?" ("Antiphon" 5.54–55; 63).

The speaker, Euxitheus, is the defendant in a murder charge. A slave has confessed to committing the murder with Euxitheus, and a note has been found naming Euxitheus as the killer. Here the speaker brings together two previously established facts—what the note said and what the slave said—to form a new fact: the two statements differed. The question that follows leads the audience immediately to realize another fact: the note must be wrong. Only the context of Athenian culture, including legal culture, allows this inference to stick.

For example, the audience in this case must accept that statements made by slaves under torture or the threat of torture are reliable and that when two statements disagree, one must be wrong. The former is a fundamental feature of Athenian culture and law and is the reasoning behind the *basanos* procedure, the questioning of slaves under torture to extract evidence for use in court. The second belief is a standard presumption behind contradictory enthymizing but is also an important element in the binary forced-choice legal procedure (C.2 below), as binary opposition is a common avenue of Greek thought (see Lloyd 2014, 111–27). A third common belief, which held written documents to be open to forgery and therefore less reliable than the testimony of sworn witnesses, is also characteristic of Athenian legal culture, as is the understanding that an invalidated piece of evidence will weaken a claim that relies on it. There are probably other cultural rules at work as well. Given this newly stated fact within the context of this supporting nexus of cultural beliefs, the speaker ensures that the audience will supply the expected conclusion, which also must be enthymized: the note is false. They may also draw, or be moved toward, the further conclusion that the slave was telling the truth and the prosecution's case (insofar as it rests on the note) is false as well.

The rhetorical power of mediate enthymizing derives from the solidity of the fact mentioned, from the connection between that fact and its meaning (which may or may not be left implicit), and from the clarity and singularity of this connection; it should immediately come to mind as naturally being entailed by the stated fact. Speakers do sometimes state explicitly both the established fact and the linked conclusion and sometimes one or more (but rarely all) elements of the situation governing the interpretation of the stated fact. But the power of indirect enthymizing comes rather from so tightly connecting a known fact to a doubtful claim or story element that once the first is uttered, the second alone is immediately enthymized, and with greater confidence than it otherwise could have been. Whether it is stated explicitly or not is of little importance. In fact, proper delivery (via a well-timed pause) can allow the audience to arrive at the expected conclusion just before the speaker says it. Orators will also frequently frame the fact to be enthymized as a question that leads unavoidably to an answer (C.1.c or D.3.a below).

Mediate enthymizing is of special interest because in many cases, the goal is not simply getting the audience to attend to something but getting the audience to connect something with something else. It is by means of these links that a speaker builds a narrative and links it to reality, to a *nomos*, to the law. In traditional Aristotelian terms, inferential reasoning allows orators to connect an easily accepted fact or proposition (*A*), a fact that the audience has no reason to doubt, to another proposition (*B*) that the orator wants the audience to think about, understand, feel strongly about, and accept as true. Once fact *A* is enthymized as a sign or cause of fact *B*, the confidence afforded the former can be transferred to the latter. With Perelman and Olbrechts-Tyteca, we could say that the speaker will grant *presence* to *A* to create a *liaison* to *B* in order to enhance the audience's *adherence* to *B*. Just as a mechanic will charge a weak battery by connecting it to a strong one, mediate enthymizing transfers confidence to a posited fact (*B*) by connecting it to an accepted fact (*A*). It is in the interest of the speaker to make the cable linking the facts feel like an identity between *A* and *B*, like seeing that *B* means or simply is *A*, so that one is perceived to be the other.

But in addition to connecting a fact to a deducible conclusion or meaning, mediate enthymizing is also used to connect one part of a story to another: a scene to an act; an act to an actor; an actor to a motive; a deposition, witness testimony, or will to an event and a character; a story to an emotional response or moral judgment—and all of these to a verdict. It can also establish or destroy links between a part of one story and another story: the defendant's account to the plaintiff's account, to a hypothetical alternative or counterfactual account, to a larger cultural myth or social script that resembles the legal narrative, or to an analogous historical or fabulous story as example or precedent. Much enthymizing performs multiple tasks at once: a stated fact can establish a motive and clarify the plot as it blackens the character of the opponent, arouses the suspicion of the audience, and assimilates the speaker to the protagonist of a familiar cultural tale or myth. The goal is not simply drawing conclusions from premises but building a familiar, coherent, and believable story and setting it within a normative world, or *nomos*. Enthymizing is the "linking unit," the building block that binds narrative elements into a story and connects that story to a situation, to a *nomos*, and to the listeners' sense of injustice and harm.

The persuasive effect of this form of enthymizing relies heavily on its narrative context, which is necessary both to anchor the reliability of the stated fact and to secure its connection to the inferred one (Bennet and Feldman 2014, 108). The formal structure through which the link is made is not the PC unit in a deductive frame but a character-motive-action-circumstance unit in a normative world. Being a certain type of character from a certain family, tribe, or city, for example, he is likely (or unlikely) to have done or thought something. Having done something before, a character is likely to do something similar *again*. Having *done* something, a character is likely (or unlikely) to have *thought* something, or vice versa. Having done something in *public*, he is likely to do something in *private*. Having *thought* something, he is shown to *want* something. Having *done, thought,* or *wanted* something, he is shown to *be* something. *Being with* others of a certain sort, he is shown to *be of* the same sort. Being something, he is to be praised or censured, punished or vindicated, admired or pitied or hated. 1.0 links all of these elements together to form a story that the audience feels deeply, that disproves the opposing account, and that gains support from familiar cultural scripts and myths with which it aligns.

C. Stance: Supportive and Contradictory

1. Supportive

Some enthymizing offers the audience a fact that ultimately supports the speaker's case. Of course, insofar as speakers address the question at issue, their enthymizing will both support their case and weaken their opponent's, and a good deal of enthymizing can be read from either perspective. But some enthymizing is more clearly meant to recommend the speaker and the case to the audience not only by pointing to facts that confirm the speaker's version of events but also by mentioning past actions—such as liturgies or military service, noble ancestry, upright character, or the promise of future service—or aspects of the speaker's present action that recommend his version of events. The speaker in (a) below mentions both his liturgies and "the most difficult liturgy," a lifetime of prudence and respectability. In (b), the speaker reminds the audience that while he had every opportunity to flee Athens to avoid trial—an attractive option for those facing a capital charge—he came to court, suggesting that he was willing to face significant risks to prove his innocence.

(a) "I ask you gentlemen of the jury to have the same attitude toward me as in the past. Do not simply remember the public liturgies but **bear in mind** [*enthumeisthai*] also my private activities. You should realize the most difficult liturgy is to behave respectably and prudently at every moment, right to the end of your life" (*Lysias* 21.19; Todd 2000, 235).

(b) "I want you to **bear in mind** [*enthumēthēnai*] that I've come here today even though nothing compelled me to remain in Athens" ("Andocides" 1.2; 101).

In both of these examples, the speaker calls to the audience's attention facts ("I've come here today"; "I've lived a respectable and prudent private life") that he hopes will lead the audience to link past and current actions to the speaker's character and thus either his honesty and innocence or the mercy or pity due to him.

2. Contradictory

We would expect enthymizing to support the speaker's own argument, but at least as common and generally more effective enthymizing instead counters the opposing argument by (a) presenting to the audience a relevant and accepted fact that contradicts an opponent's claim, (b) pointing out contradictions within the opponent's speech or between the speech and other statements, or (c) demonstrating a contradiction between the opponent's claims and his own actions. Anaximenes in *Rhetoric to Alexander* emphasizes this feature of the enthymeme in part because it is so common and so effective in legal pleading.

(a) "Next, you must certainly **bear** this point **in mind** [*enthumeisthai*]: according to the laws that exist now and have been in effect for a long time (not even this man can deny that they are excellent), each man performs liturgies every other year so that he is exempt half of the time" (*Demosthenes* 20.8; Harris 2008, 24).

(b) "**Consider** [*enthumeisthe*] the impudence of what they are saying. The man who was about to give his sister in marriage to a man with an estate worth three talents, as he says, when arranging such an important matter, claimed that a single witness was present on his behalf, Pyretides, and our opponents produced his absentee deposition at that trial, a deposition Pyretides has disavowed, and he refuses even to admit that he gave any deposition or knows whether any of it is true" (*Isaeus* 3.18; 52).

(c) "I know he will try to trick you by saying he sailed as a merchant and that he went away to Rhodes for business reasons. If he says this, **look at** [*enthumeisthe*] how easily you will catch him lying. First of all, men who sail for trade do not leave by the back gate and board their ships at Akte, but inside the harbor, where they are sent off in full view of their friends" ("Lycurgus" 1.55; Harris 2001, 175).

In (c), Lycurgus points to his opponent's (Leocrates's) own actions to contradict his claims. Leocrates claims to have left the city on business (and not, as his opponents charge, in flight from military service). But those traveling on business do so publicly from the harbor in the company of their friends, not secretly at night by the "back gate," as Leocrates has done. Earlier in the speech, Lycurgus had named Akte (the spot where Leocrates was said to have boarded his ship) the "back gate" because it sits along the open ocean. Isaeus in (b) counters the opponent's claim (that his sister's marriage to a wealthy man was witnessed) by pointing out that such an important marriage was witnessed by only one man, Pyretides, and that Pyretides had subsequently disavowed the deposition (introduced at trial) and denies any knowledge of the marriage. In (a), Leptines has claimed that liturgy exemptions (which allowed wealthy citizens to avoid paying a tax) harmed the city by depleting the treasury and so ought to be eliminated. Demosthenes contradicts this claim by pointing to a kind of exemption that all (including Leptines himself) knew to be beneficial and praiseworthy.

The power of contradictory enthymizing derives from the elimination of alternatives coupled with the binary forced-choice system that was the Athenian legal trial. When only two opposed alternatives are available, you need not demonstrate the truth of your case; you merely need to show the inconsistency or implausibility of the other. If an opponent's claim is refuted as inconsistent or incredible, then the speaker's alternative version must be true. It's no wonder that contradictory enthymizing is so common, since demonstrating one clear inconsistency in an opponent's case can be significantly more effective than demonstrating consistency in one's own. The oratorical preference for contradictory enthymizing also fits within the larger general pattern of oppositional thought that is characteristic of Greek argument (Lloyd 1966, 31–41, 111–27).

D. *Novelty: Mnemonic, Didactic, Heuristic*

This axis concerns the familiarity of the material to be enthymized. Some material will be familiar to the audience: a well-known law, common experience, or an easily visible feature of the trial itself and its participants. The speaker will merely need to remind the audience of the relevance of this fact. Other material will be a new piece of information, not widely known and introduced for the first time in the speech to explain an event, motive, or opportunity. A third "intermediate" type of enthymizing between the familiar and the novel will reintroduce a fact stated earlier in the speech to demonstrate its true significance. It is not entirely new, since it was mentioned before, but it is not initially highlighted, nor its special relevance understood. I will identify this kind of enthymizing as "heuristic," and it is a particularly effective form of enthymizing.

1. Mnemonic

Sometimes the thing to be kept in mind or pondered is something that the audience (presumably) already knows but is simply being asked to recall. The speaker can remind the audience of a well-known or recently experienced fact (a) or a generally accepted (though not otherwise explicitly articulated) truth (b, c).

(a) "**Bear in mind** [*enthumeisthai*] that you have sworn to decide what is just, not to vote for whatever these men tell you" (*Lysias* 15.8; Todd 2000, 175).
(b) "**Keep in mind** [*enthumoumenous*] that justice and the oath advance your interests and those of the whole city, but partisan supporters make their entreaties and pursue their schemes for private gain" (*Demosthenes* 19.1; Yunis 2005, 121).

In (a) and (b) above, jurors are reminded of aspects of their own legal process (the jurist's oath) and its purpose, aspects that they are already familiar with (having been required to swear the oath).

The speaker may also "remind" the audience of something, sometimes flattering, that states or has the appearance of a general truth or common opinion even if the hearers have never before articulated it explicitly to themselves. Isocrates is particularly fond of this use. In (c) below, he "reminds" his audience of their willingness to face danger to preserve their reputation and avoid shame in the pursuit of wisdom and justice.

> (c) "**Consider** [*enthumoumenous*] first that it is your custom to fear not dangers but rather a bad reputation and shameful behavior, and second that those who win at war are not those who violently overthrow cities but those who manage Greece with more justice and tact" (*Isocrates II* 14.39; Papillon 2004, 237).

2. Didactic

The speaker can also present to the hearers a new fact for them to keep in mind in the mode of instruction or explanation. Any orator who had investigated a case or political situation would find it necessary to explain to the audience aspects of the case and their implications that would not be widely known. Demosthenes uses this type of enthymizing frequently to educate his audience, though its use is common and widespread.

> (a) "It is worthwhile to **consider** [*enthumēthēnai*] and evaluate how Philip's affairs now stand. His present situation is not one of readiness, even though it appears to be and a careless observer might so describe it" (*Demosthenes* 1.21; Trevett 2011, 38).
>
> (b) "**Bear in mind** [*enthumeisthe*], gentlemen of the jury, that some of the soldiers were sick, and others lacked the necessities of life. The former would gladly have remained and been treated in their communities, the latter would gladly have returned home to look after their affairs" (*Lysias* 14.14; Todd 2000, 165).

In (a), Demosthenes briefs his audience on Philip's military and diplomatic strategies and achievements (compare his assessment of Philip's strategy in the *First Philippic*, B.2.a). Similarly, in (b), the speaker informs the audience (many of whom would not have been there) about the conditions of the troops on a particular campaign.

3. Heuristic

A third, intermediate type of enthymizing we might call "heuristic" from the Greek for "discover." This kind of enthymizing will mention a detail in the narrative—often an apparently irrelevant or trivial fact—and then reintroduce and enthymize the detail later, showing it to be unexpectedly meaningful (we saw this with Lycurgus first narrating and later enthymizing the embarkation point of Leocrates at C.2.c). Since the enthymized fact has already been established earlier in the speech, the restatement acts like "reminding" the audience of what they already know. In restating it, the speaker will clarify its relevance to the case so that the audience suddenly "sees" its significance. The sudden clarity that results from this explanation makes the enthymized fact "feel" like a new discovery, much as when a detective in a mystery explains the significance of a clue that had been seen but passed over. Heuristic enthymizing can be exceptionally effective, as is this example from Lysias:

> (a) "But just **think for a moment** [*enthumēthēte*], gentlemen. If I had been laying a trap for Eratosthenes, would it not have been better for me to dine somewhere else with Sostratus, instead of bringing him home for dinner and so making the adulterer less likely to risk entering my house?" (*Lysias* 1.40; Todd 2000, 23).

The audience had already been told about the dinner with Sostratus on the evening of the murder, but as the speaker narrated the events of that day, the audience had not likely made any connection between that detail (Sostratus coming over for dinner) and the speaker's central claim that he did not premeditate the killing of Eratosthenes. In fact, much of the narrative concerns details that seem on first hearing to be irrelevant to the case at hand. Only with a subsequent moment of enthymizing in the argument portion of the speech do they discover that something they had already been told (and had no reason to question) had unanticipated relevance and meaning. No one planning to entice an adulterer over for the purpose of murdering him would dine at home with a friend; he would instead rely on the friend's return as a pretext to leave the house. The empty house would be more likely to lure the adulterer over. The fact that he had Sostratus over for dinner, once enthymized, is meant to lead the audience immediately to another: he was not plotting murder, simply entertaining a friend. This kind of move is similar to Chekhov's gun,[12] but rather than simply being a prop that must be used later in the narrative, this is a detail mentioned early and then enthymized to show what it can be linked to, or what it means.

3. FROM ENTHYMIZING TO ENTHYMEME

These uses of the term make clear how *enthymizing* as a verbal marker could come to indicate a particular kind of rhetorical move. It is even possible to posit a process of development, beginning with the casual use of the term and other synonyms to indicate a narrative detail worth attending to because it was relevant to the plot and its application to a law. This would include the speaker's description of their own enthymizing by way of explaining their state of mind, motive, or intent (or lack thereof) as important narrative details. At some point, it achieved the status of a "marked" term indicating a particular kind of rhetorical move and gained preference over synonyms. Its use could have remained fairly broad but always, I would argue, for building a story and linking it to an applicable norm or law. At some stage, it was transformed into the cognate noun familiar to theorists to describe the technique as a concept. Ultimately, it became a technical term used—independent of the speeches in which it occurred—to describe a common rhetorical technique whose features were not yet clearly articulated. Isocrates, Alcidamas, Aristotle, and others each assimilated it to their own developing models of rhetoric.

Aristotle gave it more attention than others, emphasizing it as a series of propositions lined up together (*su-*) to give an explanatory account (*logismos*). I'm suggesting that this view is misleading but not incorrect if *account* can mean "narrative" (as it can in English) as well as "calculation" or "tabulation." I will suggest in chapters 6 and 7 the work that narrative theory can do in accounting for 1.0 and will argue in chapters 8 and 9 that Lysias was pivotal in the early steps of this process and among the first to establish enthymizing as an important rhetorical, legal, and political technique.

All of this is, at this point, conjectural; my goal was not and is not to trace the history of the term and its particular rhetorical development but to nominate the term and the move that it enacted as relevant to our understanding of the early enthymeme in use. Regardless of the specifics of its development, 1.0 was employed as a move by the orators that with repeated practice became standardized as an identifiable technique long before it was transformed into theory and articulated as a static concept in rhetorical treatises.

The orators' use of the verb suggests how enthymizing operates within a narrative and how a plot might be tightened and enhanced by the highlighting of important narrative details. The features of enthymizing reviewed here also suggest how enthymizing could have been lifted out of its context and named as a nominal concept, an enthymeme. Some approaches to or features of enthymizing would be more amenable to a particular theorist's view of rhetoric and its most characteristic forms. For example, because the *Rhetoric to Alexander* fixes its attention primarily on legal trials, where direct opposition is more important than in assembly speeches, this treatise defines the enthymeme in terms of contradiction. And in fact, contradictory enthymizing is very common among the orators and can result in highly pointed and very effective rebuttals of an opponent's account.

Similarly, since Aristotle makes dialectic and deduction central to his view of rhetorical artistry and defines enthymeme as a kind of deduction, and since deduction is a statement that arises from and because of other things that are so—either necessarily or for the most part—he will naturally focus his attention on an approach to inferential enthymizing that highlights its similarity to dialectic and is amenable to his versions of deductive reasoning (*Rhetoric* 1.2.9; 40). Inferential enthymizing is very common and is, as Aristotle says, key to rhetorical speeches generally. But as I've suggested earlier, not all rhetorically effective enthymizing is inferential, and not all inferential enthymizing is best portrayed as deductive or strictly logical; there are many ways to move an audience from one statement to another.

This view of enthymizing can thus also help us test and challenge familiar theoretical dogma. For example, whereas Aristotle (usually) distinguishes induction and the example (*paradeigma*) from deduction and the enthymeme on logical grounds (*Rhetoric* 1.2.8–10, 13–19, 2.20.1–2; 40, 41–42, 161–62), he also identifies examples as enthymemes for purposes of refutation (2.25.8; 190), and he offers the example (*epagoge*) as a topos for enthymemes (2.23.11; 177).[13] The orators, on the other hand, often enthymize examples; they summarize the point of an analogous story to prompt new understanding in the audience about the current case. And whereas the syllogism, truncated or not, seems a poor device for arousing emotions or portraying character, enthymizing embedded in narratives offers clear and compelling reasons to see them as emotionally and ethically charged (1.2.2–6, 3.17.8; 38–39, 243).

Of course, these different types of enthymizing are merely illustrative and neither exhaustive nor mutually exclusive. Inferential enthymemes can be contradictory and mnemonic. The final enthymeme (D.3.a) is imperative, inferential, contradictory, and heuristic. It illustrates Aristotle's view of enthymemes as inferential movement as well as Anaximenes's emphasis on contradiction. In fact, insofar as it examines a detail from the earlier narrative of Sostratus for the purpose of refuting an opposing assertion and caps off this interrogation with a pregnant rhetorical question, it involves the very kind of exetastic movement that Anaximenes in the *Rhetoric to Alexander* counts as an important use of the enthymeme (5.1–3, 10.1; 510–11, 526–29; and see Walker 1994, 50). Indeed, it is clear from this brief review that inferential, contradictory, heuristic enthymizing drawn from the opponent's own words and actions can be especially effective and can seem practically irrefutable.

This view of the enthymeme similarly illustrates Isocrates's view that enthymemes should embellish or adorn (*katapoilikai*) a speech (13.17; Mirhady and Too, 2000, 65). If we think of enthymizing as calling attention to a few key details of the narrative to clarify the plot and its coherence, the sense of *embellish* becomes clear: as they are given presence by the orator, those details stand out and attract attention as particularly clear, and together they weave a pattern of clues that lay out the plot. The hearers cannot be expected to—nor would the orator want them to—attend to or reflect equally on every statement or every detail narrated in the speech. Enthymizing is introduced sparingly so that the pointed attention afforded to a series of significant facts in a narrative can lift out of the plot, like crumbs on a path, and trigger a final clarity, a convincing grasp of the real story.

In this way, the orators can be seen to support the accounts of different theorists even if the theorists' descriptions do not exhaust all the possible species or functions of enthymizing. The orators knew that an important aspect of rhetorical pleading involved directing the audience's attention to facts that were central to the narrative and its persuasive effect. It would not be surprising if theorists, observing the frequency with which the orators used this term and this technique, adopted the noun form to name one or another aspect of the technique that fit their theoretical schema. But even if this hypothetical development is incorrect, it is clear that the orators frequently and deliberately led their audiences to enthymize facts that were relevant to the case at hand in order to move them to a decision, displaying in the process an implicit understanding of an important rhetorical skill.

CHAPTER 6

Oratorical Enthymizing in Context

Oratorical enthymizing was a move used by the Greek orators to call attention to important facts and their significance. It will be useful at this point to see how these moments of enthymizing operate within a narrative and a trial. I'll begin with a few examples that can expand our understanding of how enthymizing can work, and then I'll discuss more generally the context that made enthymizing so valuable to ancient oratory: narrative contests.

Our first example is from a speech by Isaeus, *On the Estate of Cleonymus*.

ISAEUS 1, *ON THE ESTATE OF CLEONYMUS*

This example concerns an inheritance claim. The deceased has named in his will some relatives as heirs to his property: we will call them "the relatives." The speaker and plaintiff contesting the will is one of Cleonymus's nephews and his brothers: we will call them "the brothers." The speaker claims that the brothers are the closest surviving relatives of Cleonymus and that recently they have been his caretakers. He brings a suit to challenge the will and claim possession of Cleonymus's estate. To clarify how the brothers came to be left out of Cleonymus's will, the speaker has to tell the story.

Cleonymus had no children, but he had nephews (the brothers), the children of his sister and her husband. When the brothers' father died, the father's brother (their uncle) Deinias became their guardian. But Cleonymus and Deinias were enemies, so Cleonymus severed relations with the family while Deinias was alive. He didn't want the brothers to inherit his estate while they were minors, so he wrote a will at that time to keep the property out of Deinias's hands.

But then Deinias died, and the family was struggling. At that time, Cleonymus took them in and raised them, saved their property from creditors, and "took care of our affairs as if they were his own" (1.12; 19). The brothers were on the closest of terms with him. He was intending to alter the will and name them as his heirs. Meanwhile, the relatives had become estranged from Cleonymus over a recent quarrel. When Cleonymus became ill, he asked Poseidippus (one of the relatives) to fetch a magistrate to speak with him about the will. Poseidippus not only failed to call for one, but when the magistrate arrived, he refused to admit him. Cleonymus argued with them and asked another of his relatives, Diocles, to bring the magistrate back the next day but succumbed to his illness unexpectedly during the night and died. The opposing speaker admitted that Cleonymus called for a magistrate to visit his house the day before he died. But he claimed that he did so only to confirm the will.

As the speaker recalls this detail in his speech, he directs the audience to enthymize (translated here as "remember") what their behavior could mean: "Next, remember that they allege that Cleonymus called for a magistrate to confirm their bequest, yet being ordered [by Cleonymus to admit the magistrate] they didn't dare to bring him in, but even sent away the magistrate who came to the door. Faced with the choice either to have their bequest confirmed or to offend Cleonymus by not doing as he asked, they chose his enmity in preference to his bequest. What could be more incredible than that?" (1.22; 21). What is clear is that the magistrate was called by Cleonymus but refused entry by the relatives. The question is one of motives. Why did he call the official, and why did they turn him away? We have here a moment of inferential, heuristic, contradictory enthymizing. The action of the brothers narrated earlier seems now to contradict their claim based on what we can infer from their actions.

The full force of this passage depends upon the full narrative. Its description of animosities and severed relationships, switching allegiances, estrangements, and reconciliations raises the possibility that Cleonymus again meant to change the will. This inference is encouraged by the progressive form of the narrative's movement, its cadence, or *periodos*. Cleonymus's dispute with Deinias, which pulled him away from his nephews (the brothers, through no fault of their own) early in the story, would be answered by a movement back in their favor at the end of his life. The recent quarrel with the relatives would negate their earlier closeness to Cleonymus.

The "proper" inference also receives support from cultural norms of behavior and expected actions of character types: the elderly want to put their affairs in order before they die, to right wrongs and "settle their accounts." Closure includes giving people "their due." Actions taken in anger can be righted when the anger has passed. If Cleonymus had written the brothers out of the will because of Deinias and had intended to change his will, as the brothers claim, his sudden illness might have prompted him to take action. Then again, people who change their minds and take action out of anger often reverse course and return to their original thinking when the anger has cleared.

In this context, the answer to our question becomes clearer: Cleonymus did want to change the will back to what it previously stipulated. If this is right, then another inference is possible: the relatives must have known that was his intent. This would explain why they refused the magistrate entry to prevent that from happening. Given the volatility of this family patriarch, the relatives would refuse admission to a magistrate only if they already knew he was called to reverse the will in favor of the brothers.

As in the examples we saw earlier (chapter 5, B.2), this passage is mediate or inferential: it uses one fact—the magistrate was turned away by one of the heirs—to lead the audience to another. Insofar as the detail of the magistrate's visit was mentioned in the narrative portion of the speech, this enthymizing functions as a heuristic, and since it contradicts the brothers' claims that Cleonymus had called the magistrate only to confirm the will, this enthymizing is contradictory. But I want to shift here more explicitly away from an understanding of inference as tied to deduction and traditional premise-conclusion (PC) scaffolding and toward a narrative framework.

This enthymizing could be reproduced in traditional PC form, as a kind of deduction, but attempting to do so proves unsatisfying. The "premises" that guide the inference are not easily separated out to be numbered: the entire narrative sways the conclusion based on the history of the family, the character of Cleonymus, and the shape of his story. If we think of this inference in terms of propositions, we could easily multiply the premises and the conclusions that the audience might arrive at: the heirs didn't want the magistrate to complete his business there, his business wasn't to their benefit, Cleonymus probably meant to change the will, Cleonymus is a capricious and stubborn old man, the nephew's claims about their closeness to Cleonymus were probably accurate, the intended change to the will was detrimental to the heirs and beneficial to the brothers, the heirs must have known about this intended change, and so on. But listing them in this way misrepresents *how* they are known; it distorts how they are felt and judged and why they are believable. They all work together as parts of a convincing storyworld.

A review of the many instances of 1.0 like this one reveals a pattern—but a pattern based on narrative function, not logical structure. This kind of enthymizing works in four complementary ways: (1) It asserts and invites the audience to attend to or "take to heart" a credible fact, a fact that listeners can be relied on to accept as true, because it fits within and is supported by the surrounding narrative and its characteristic movement, because it is commonly known and believed, because the opponent has not disputed it, or because the opponent has explicitly admitted it. (2) This fact is linked to other facts to form a narrative and, ultimately, a story. It acquires most of its significance and effect from this context. The inferential threads stretch not from a few premises to their conclusion but across the story to the laws, the case, and the *nomos* in which they are situated. Inferences can also lead from this story to other similar stories that clarify and support it. (3) The fact is shown to be central to the narrative's plot and theme as it helps frame and answer the legal question at issue. It helps determine not only the plot (what really happened) but also the proper application of the law. That is, the fact is seen to be situated at the nexus of narrative and legal meaning. (4) At the same time (because there can only be one such nexus), it shows the opponent's argument (perhaps even based on his own words or actions or drawn from his own narrative) to be irrelevant, incredible, shameful, unjust, or impossible. In this way, the enthymized fact resolves an ambiguous situation in favor of one reading of the events and the law over against the other. The contrast between the speaker's account and the opponent's is often revealed through a comparison of what did happen (Cleonymus changed his mind again) to what couldn't (the relatives refused entry to a magistrate who had been called simply to confirm the will).

1.0 is named for both the statement that triggers this moment of enthymizing and the effect that it has on the recipient. As a piece of strategic communication, it is in equal parts a textual marker and an interactional and psychological process—eliciting attention and creating meaning. It is often given a stylistic form to maximize its effect through the use of a rhetorical question, isocolon, or some other rhetorical trope or figure.

In these ways, 1.0 helps crystallize the speaker's case and the verdict to which all the evidence points, comprehending the general thrust of the relevant facts, their coherence in a familiar narrative, their fit with the cited laws, and the point of conflict between the speaker and the opponent. When set up properly, the meaning of the fact will seem clear, unavoidable, and inevitable. Not all enthymemes achieve all four goals, but the better a statement accomplishes these four goals, the more enthymematic it is.

1. Isaeus's enthymeme begins with a simple fact that is already admitted by the opponents: when the magistrate arrived, they refused to admit him. By itself, this fact is ambiguous. Perhaps out of concern for Cleonymus's dire condition, they didn't want to bother him with any business. Perhaps they deemed him too ill or too confused to make any rational decisions about his estate. Perhaps Cleonymus was asleep, in pain, or otherwise occupied. But by asking the audience to enthymize this detail, the speaker nominates it as a relevant fact—a plot kernel and a key to the proper understanding of the case.

2. This fact clings to other narrative details accumulated along the way to form a simple plot and a complete story: After their father's death, the brothers were adopted by Deinias. Cleonymus hated their adoptive father and kept the boys out of his will for fear that Deinias would get his hands on the property. After Deinias died, the uncle brought the nephews into his house, saw to their affairs, and protected their property from creditors. They were his closest relatives. The boys became so close to Cleonymus that even their opponent's friends admitted that they merited a portion of the estate. Seeing this reversal, the relatives plotted to keep the old man from changing the will. What will happen to the brothers?

    The enthymized fact reinforces these other narrative details that together form a familiar and satisfying story arc that echoes a fundamental cultural mythos: the faithful son, orphaned and rejected, overcomes scheming relations to reunite with the aging family patriarch, who seeks to reward the son's filial piety and restore his position before the patriarch dies.[1] Like most good legal narratives, this one remains incomplete: only the jury will determine whether the deceased's final wishes will be fulfilled or thwarted by a group of opportunistic pretenders.

    The narrative scene, its details, and the inferences drawn from them are comprehended by the audience not as discreet items but as a single familiar "line" of motivated action and result, a line whose plot trajectory can finally be grasped in one view as a *periodos*—Cleonymus moves emotionally away from and then back toward the brothers—forming a story with thematic and experiential unity. This movement is powered in part by its assimilation to a recognizable narrative frame or script. Based on this story, the audience can see the capricious and tempestuous Cleonymus, the innocence of the young brothers, the deathbed repentance of the old man, and the relatives conspiring to block Cleonymus's desire to finally honor the brothers, his nephews. The detail takes its place in completing the rhetorical form set up across the narrative and assimilating it to its guiding *muthos*. The audience is led to arrive at the "correct" inference through the constellation of individual and concrete details linked to each other and to the law. Some of the details are narrated, some are enthymized, while others are inferred or imagined as part of a complete storyworld informed by familiar plot and character archetypes, scenes, traits, motives, and actions.

3. This clue and the narrative situation that it clarifies in turn frame the legal issue in a way favorable to the brothers. The real question, argues the plaintiff, is not the authorship or language of the will. They admit that it was written by Cleonymus. The question is its current validity in honoring the feelings and intentions of Cleonymus: What is Cleonymus's will? Who was he closest to in blood and affection, and who did he really want to inherit his property? The written will is only a text, a temporary and imperfect record of that intention. If it was made in a state of anger and with a purpose that is no longer relevant—if it no longer reflects the wishes of Cleonymus—then it ought not to be applied. The enthymized fact in the context of the plot becomes a central clue to supporting and answering this legal question and thus to comprehending the case. This fact suggests that "will" as intention is of more importance than as testamentary document. The defendants' own words and actions not only prove Cleonymus's intent; they also prove that they knew about it and understood its importance. That's why they turned the magistrate away at the door.

The enthymeme does not merely shape the details of a recognizable plot; it shapes the legal issue so that it asks a question that the plot can answer, triggering in the audience a clear grasp of the fact's relevance to the question, the law, and argument as a whole. When imbued with meaning by the narrative context and the proper legal question, the fact increases the audience's adherence to a controversial claim by tying it to their felt sense of what is probable, appropriate, just, honorable, or expedient (and what is incredible, inappropriate, unjust, or shameful).

4. All of this is accomplished more easily and irrefutably through antithesis. The enthymeme does not directly demonstrate that Cleonymus wanted the brothers to inherit; it rather shows something that the opponents did *not* want, and it shows a contradiction between their words and their actions, demonstrating the opposing speaker's account to be incredible. By focusing on the last wishes of a dying man concerning the boys he loved best, this enthymeme helps upend the opposing argument, which will focus on the written will. It helps us see what this case is "really about." This is the move and the point that the opponents will not easily refute or answer, as it is based on their own admitted actions. It is the opportunity as *kairos*, the opponent's misstep that the speaker takes advantage of: if the magistrate had been called simply to confirm the will, the relatives would have been eager to admit him, but they refused him, so. . . . The same result can be achieved with a rhetorical question. Contradictory or antithetical enthymizing is important because of the two-sided nature of the legal agon; the side shown to be incredible cannot be the true one, so the other side must be. This is why orators particularly look for irrefutable, contradictory enthymizing.

Of course, the opponent might see an opportunity for himself in this narrative episode, a detail worth enthymizing: Cleonymus asked a relative (not one of the brothers) about the magistrate. If the brothers were "closer to him than anybody," as they say (1.4; 17), then why did Cleonymus ask the relatives, and not one of them, to fetch a magistrate, and why were the relatives, and not the brothers, there with Cleonymus to receive the magistrate (or turn him away)?

It is also worth noting another feature raised by contradictory enthymizing: the narrative context is never singular. Because the legal or political speech is always contested, adversarial narratives are always plural, and so the effect of enthymizing is always refracted by the multiple narrative "layers." The speaker's account of what happened is always juxtaposed with and attempts to counter the opponent's narrative. These two narratives are not entirely different but will overlap in places and differ in others: a common set of characters enacting two versions of the events. The relatives who refused the magistrate admission to the home of Cleonymus are the same as the group defending Cleonymus's will and the protagonists of their story, so a detail that casts doubt on their account will simultaneously assist the brothers' own account and discredit the relatives' characters, arousing pity for the brothers and animosity against the relatives.

There are other narrative layers at work as well. At least one of these accounts, in this case the speaker's, will arouse and be implicitly measured against an imagined sense of what is socially expected, how things likely went, and what should happen. This we could call the probable (*eikos*) narrative.[2] The brothers' story will be weighed against the audience's knowledge of family dynamics, irascible patriarchs, and grasping relatives. This story is not told but imagined, and unlike the brother's narrative, it will have a fitting ending—an ending against which the spoken narrative will be measured and that (the speaker hopes that) the audience will want to honor. If successful, the narrative told by the plaintiff will feel incomplete until the jurors enact the *eikos* script, honoring Cleonymus's wishes and granting them his estate.

And each account (those told, those felt, and those imagined as social norms and completed by corrective actions) will also explicitly or implicitly call upon a larger cultural *nomos* and its myths or "archetypal story forms" (White 1978, 58).[3] The foundational myths and archetypal storyforms support and give credence to legal accounts that rely on them; they provide so many potential maps to the open terrain of a legal case. The relatives rely on a mythos of Athenian respect for the law and for the right of childless testators to bequeath their estates to whomever they wish through a written will. The brothers rely upon a more emotionally satisfying story of paternal estrangement and reunion. The enthymized detail about calling the magistrate and having him turned away is the penultimate delaying episode in a plot that bends the legal case to this larger pattern (the final episode is the trial itself).

The relationship of the cultural mythos to the *eikos* narrative and to the speaker's account can be left implicit or it can be emphasized through an explicit appeal to a familiar tale as a historical or mythic example (as illustrative case or precedent) that clarifies the plot and illustrates its moral force. In his speech *Against Timarchos*, Aeschines distinguishes proper homosocial love from shameful prostitution through reference to Achilles and Patroclus and the nature of their friendship as recounted in the *Iliad* (1.141–51; Carey 2000, 70–73). By adapting the language and narrative details of their account to a familiar myth or archetypal storyform, speakers can strongly evoke those narratives and the emotional and moral responses they trigger without ever naming them explicitly. Enthymizing helps establish a web of links or relationships among these narratives, each of which helps guide the interpretation and completion of the narrated account.

LYSIAS 6 AND ANDOCIDES 1

The following two examples address the same set of events and are drawn from speeches on opposing sides of a single case. Both speakers use the term and the technique; the defendant, Andocides, makes enthymizing central to his case. The first speech, *Against Andocides*, is a supporting speech prosecuting Andocides for impiety. It is included in the corpus of Lysias but was probably not written by him. The second, *On the Mysteries*, was Andocides's own defense speech in the same trial.

The full story is complex, and there is much that is not well understood.[4] But the events leading up to this case are worth summarizing because both speeches use versions of *enthumaomai* repeatedly and in various ways. We can limit ourselves to details that are important for this case. Andocides was from an old aristocratic family (perhaps from the clan Kerykes, from which the Eleusinian priests were drawn)[5] and a member of a private club, or *hetaireia*, probably with oligarchic leanings.[6] These clubs met in the men's quarters of private homes for drinking and conversation and political organization, typically among men of similar status and political affiliation. Such fraternities were often seen as hotbeds for oligarchic sympathizers.

The case begins with a pair of incidents that occurred in 415 during the Peloponnesian War—just prior to a planned invasion of Syracuse on the island of Sicily. This invasion was led by the popular leader Alcibiades along with two other generals. On the eve of this large military offensive, most of the herms in the city were defaced.[7] A herm was a partially iconic public statue of Hermes, a messenger god of travel and communication. It consisted of a carved head in the likeness of Hermes on top of a rectangular base on which was carved an erect phallus. Herms were common at the doorways of temples and private homes and in the agora, and they could be seen on roads between cities. This vandalism was, says Thucydides, "thought to be ominous for the expedition, and part of a conspiracy to bring about a revolution" (6.27.3; 376). Anyone with knowledge about the event was invited to come forward and offered immunity from prosecution in return for useful information.

As this crisis was unfolding, a popular leader named Pythonicus produced a servant of Alcibiades who had illegally learned the Eleusinian mysteries, a secret fertility cult conducted twice a year at the city of Eleusis (a part of the Athenian polis) in honor of the Two Goddesses, Demeter and her daughter, Kore Persephone.[8] Pythonicus charged that Alcibiades and others were privately parodying the sacred ritual in their homes. This was another serious offense, a sacrilege, or *asebeia*. In exchange for immunity, the servant (Andromachus) named the persons involved, and soon others also came forward with names—first about the mysteries and then also about the herms. The illegal performances and public defacings were understood to be linked to an antidemocratic agenda. Fear of an oligarchic coup was widespread.[9]

Alcibiades was named and indicted, and he requested a trial before his departure, but he was thwarted by his political opponents. Only after he had sailed was he recalled for trial, but he fled into exile, as did many others. Andocides was also named in connection with the herms and also possibly in connection with the mysteries (MacDowell 1962, 167–71, 173–76; but see also Marr 1971). Some of his club members and relatives were also named. He was arrested, and facing execution, he agreed to give information in exchange for immunity. On the basis of his information, he and a number of others, including some of his family members, were released, while others were charged.

Soon after, the decree of Isotimides was passed, making it illegal for anyone guilty of impiety (*asebeia*) to enter any sacred or public place. This decree would have applied to—and might even have been written to target—Andocides. Unable to move about, Andocides had no choice but to leave the city. While he was in exile, several oligarchic coups took place, first under the 400 (in 411) and later under the Thirty Tyrants (404–403). The latter executed or exiled many leading democratic citizens. In each case, democrats regrouped, defeated the oligarchs, and recovered control of the city, and the democracy was restored in 403. During the political turmoil of this period, a decree was passed (in 405) by Patrokleides restoring citizenship to all those who had been exiled, except for those guilty of homicide or those attempting to overthrow the democracy.[10] After the fall of the Thirty and under Spartan supervision, a general amnesty was declared (403), enjoining all Athenians to "refrain from vengeful action provoked by the memory of past wrongdoing" (Joyce 2008, 507; and see Carawan 2002), specifically wrongdoing between democrats and oligarchs stemming from the recent civil uprisings.

After the decree of Patrokleides was passed and amnesty declared, Andocides judged it safe to return to Athens and his old life. He again became politically active, not only participating in public life but initiating citizens into the Eleusinian mysteries (1.132; 135–36). But a few years later (in 400 or 399), Callias (with whom Andocides had a history of hostility) convinced another initiate (Cephisius) to denounce Andocides for attending a sacred ceremony contrary to the decree of Isotimides. Callias further accused Andocides of illegally placing an olive branch on the altar at Eleusis, also a punishable offence. Andocides was charged and brought to trial.

The question, then, is whether Andocides is immune from prosecution based on the amnesty law and decree of Patrokleides or whether he can be prosecuted because of his earlier confession and his continued presence in temples in violation of the decree of Isotimides.

Lysias 6, Against Andocides

The primary prosecution speech is not extant. Lysias 6 is the text of a speech from a supporting speaker. It spends little time narrating the events or parsing the conflicting decrees and the relevance of each to the case. Most of this would have been handled by the main prosecution speech. Rather, it amplifies the religious implications of sacrilege and the dangers to the city of harboring such an individual. In the speech, the speaker introduces a rather blunt but exceptionally clear instance of enthymizing, asking the jury to keep in mind not so much a narrative detail as a scene.

The enthymized scene is held up as important to the narrative and the case but is more importantly recommended as an important context for voting:

> Men of Athens, remember what Andocides has done. Bear in mind [*enthymize*] also the festival for which you have been specially honored by many people. Because you have often seen and heard them, you are by now so numbed by my opponent's offenses that even what is terrible no longer seems terrible to you. But focus your attention, let your minds imagine they are seeing what my opponent has done, and you will come to a better decision. This man put on a ceremonial robe. He mimicked the sacred rites and revealed them to

those who were not initiates. He gave voice to words that must not be spoken. He mutilated the gods whom we worship and to whom we sacrifice and pray, honoring them and purifying ourselves. This is why priests and priestesses stood facing the west and cursed him. (6.50–51; Todd 2000, 75)

The "festival for which you have been specially honored" is the Eleusinian ritual that Andocides was said to have parodied, and the "mutilated" gods are the herms that were disfigured (i.e., this speaker accuses Andocides of both crimes). Pseudo-Lysias is unusually explicit here about what he is asking his audience to enthymize because, as he says, they have become so inured to Andocides's offenses (now over a decade old) that his actions no longer appear as outrageous as they should. Though it might be said to prompt a kind of inference, this example has very little of the feeling of logical deduction. It establishes a link between the crimes themselves, the character Andocides in the narrative who did all those horrible things, and the defendant Andocides, who was attending religious rites and sitting right there in the courtroom.

This narrative marker occurs near the end of the speech and so seems designed to provoke immediate emotional and character effects: shock, indignation, and antipathy against Andocides, who by requesting immunity seemed to have confessed to making a mockery of rites respected throughout Greece even as he maintained the privilege of attending them. It also seems designed to influence the decision-making process. It is an emotional enthymeme and a characterological one but also a normative one, evoking as it does a strong sense of irreverence and wrongdoing and a desire for punishment. By prompting the imaginative reconstruction of an august normative storyworld and its parodic perversion, this example provokes a strong desire to restore order and piety to Athens regardless of the status of this or that legal decree. Other orators like Isaeus used 1.0 to emphasize and interpret an important narrative detail to shape the plot, but the speaker here asks the audience to imagine a full scene or episode to shape their perception of Andocides and their desire to see him punished. It seems clearly to be aimed at coloring the jurors' deliberations as they vote. We could call it perorational enthymizing.

But we should not imagine that Lysias here is simply making an emotional and imagistic appeal; this enthymeme also implicitly contributes to his legal argument. This argument emphasizes the decree of Isotimides and its interpretation but does so by linking it to unwritten law and the *nomos* of the city. By calling up this scene, Lysias wants us to see what matters: the same Andocides who now frequents public places and attends the sacred mysteries has offended the gods (Demeter, Kore, and Hermes in particular) and polluted the city by smashing them in public and mocking them in private. The real question at issue is whether the city should harbor and protect someone who is guilty of such an offense.

For the speaker, Andocides's continued participation in sacred rituals constitutes an ongoing offense against the Two Goddesses and everything that the city holds sacred. By encouraging the listeners to *feel* that offense, the speaker's enthymeme tacitly contributes to the argument that the decree of Patrokleides and the ensuing general amnesty were meant to apply to public debtors and political opponents but never to acts of sacrilege like this.[11] Legal decrees about the recall of exiles and political amnesty resulting from an oligarchic coup and democratic restoration cannot erase an offence against the gods. The orators were generally reluctant to forward arguments about pollution, but the speaker comes close here. "You know," he says, "how actively these two goddesses punish wrongdoers. Everybody should expect that the same will happen to himself and other people" (6.3; 65). The ancestral and unwritten laws of the gods are laws that "nobody has ever had the authority to abolish or speak against" (6.10; 66). They are immutable, and their abrogation is dangerous and polluting not just for the guilty but for the city that harbors him. Andocides will argue that "the law referring to him has been annulled" (6.9; 66), but the speaker counters that impiety laws cannot be annulled, and Andocides must not be allowed to pollute the city and its sacred spaces. The speaker instructs the audience to focus their attention on what Andocides did and on what it means. Then, he says, the audience will come to the proper decision to punish Andocides and rid themselves of an accursed pollution that threatens the entire city.

Andocides 1, On the Mysteries

Andocides himself, of course, tells a different story and calls other details and episodes to the attention of the jurors, including a private dispute between himself and his enemy Callias, who drives the prosecution from behind the scenes.[12] He uses the verb *enthumaomai* several times in the speech, including at the very outset, to bolster his character in the face of prejudicial arguments like the one above. This enthymeme was mentioned earlier (chapter 5, C.1.b) as an example of supportive enthymizing: "Keep in mind," says Andocides, "that I didn't have to come here today. I did because I trust in justice and I trust in you, that you will make the right decision" (1.2; 101–2).[13] Self-imposed exile was always an option for defendants; they escape the risk of a trial and a guilty verdict but at the same time virtually declare their own guilt. If Pseudo-Lysias's was a perorational enthymeme appealing to emotion, this is a proemial one appealing to character. It aims to color the jury's reception of the speaker and the speech more than to shape the jury's deliberation afterward. It too is a slice of narrative about Andocides's decision to go to court instead of fleeing into exile, and it also leads to a kind of inference about his confidence in the legal process, his trust in the jury, and his belief in his own innocence.

A bit later, but still in the introduction of the speech, Andocides enthymizes another kind of episode to remove prejudice and create doubt in the minds of the jurors about his guilt: "You should also bear in mind (*enthymize*) that often before now people have made serious accusations and then have immediately been proven to be lying so plainly that you'd have been much more pleased to punish the accusers than the accused" (1.7; 103). This enthymeme works as a generalized example, offering a common kind of legal episode as an interpretative model for Andocides's plight: accusers in the past have brought grave charges, telling lurid stories of shocking crimes, and were then shown to have been lying, so you should realize that my accusers could also be lying. This kind of enthymizing seeks not only to forge a link to a certain kind of case but also to break one: you know how people lie, how malicious gossip can transform an innocent event into a scandal, so don't infer guilt from the severity of the charge.

This, in brief, is Andocides's defense. The crime was horrible, he says, but he is not guilty of it. He confesses that defacing the herms was discussed in his club, and he discloses that at his immunity hearing, he named four members of his club as participants, but he did not name other family members or confess to the act himself (he was, he claims, injured on the night it happened), and he never confessed to, participated in, or said anything about privately performing the mysteries or seeing them illegally performed. *How* Andocides tells this story reveals how "enthymizing" a crucial fact and its meaning—first as indicative to the speaker and then as an imperative for the audience—can play an integral role in a story, altering the shape of the plot.

Andocides's narrative is spotty. He understandably skips over many of the episodes that his accusers embellished (the crimes themselves). The first task of an orator is not deciding which narrative facts to enthymize, what emotions to arouse, or how to present himself but deciding what the law means and what the narrative facts are, or what the legal story is. Knowing where to start will help shape what the center of the story will be. Andocides focuses on the aftermath of the affair, taking us directly to the call for information about the crimes, the series of informants who came forward, and what these informants said. Four individuals offered information about the Eleusinian mysteries (Andromachus; Teucrus; Agariste, the wife of Alcmeonides; and Lydus). Andocides lists the men named by these informants: he was not among those named. About the mysteries, he says, "the speeches of the prosecution wailed on about those grisly horrors," but "what do those stories have to do with me?" None of the informants named him, he says, nor did he cause any of these men to be indicted, nor is he "guilty of a single offense, great or small, concerning the Two Goddesses" (1.29; 109). He calls witnesses to support this account. Then he moves to the affair of the herms. Teucrus also gave information about the herms. Andocides lists those named. Here again, he points out, he was not among those accused.

Having skipped over much of the early part of the story, Andocides now slows his narrative down. Narrative pacing is another important rhetorical skill. He invokes the unrest and confusion of the time, adding more intimate visual details to aid the jury's imagination, and (as Pseudo-Lysias did) he explicitly calls upon them to remember what happened. After the commission of inquiry began its work, two of its democratic members, Peisander and Charicles, announced one of their findings: this wasn't the act of a few men but was rather a calculated attempt to overthrow the democracy (1.36; 111). The city was in such a state of panic, says Andocides, that people fled the agora whenever the council went into session. Everyone was afraid they would be secretly named and arrested.

He slows down a bit more to focus on an important scene. The panic encouraged Diocleides; this was when he came forward with his information. "Please pay close attention, gentlemen" says Andocides, "and recollect whether I am telling the truth" (1.37; 111–12).[14] Diocleides claimed to have been out late walking by himself on the night of the crime. He said he saw around three hundred men gathered together by the theater of Dionysus. The next day, when he heard about the smashed herms, he realized that those men were the culprits. He said he recognized about forty of them in the moonlight. And then he named names.

First of all, says Andocides, notice how conveniently this alleged sighting allows Diocleides to name whoever he wished and to exonerate whoever he wished (1.39; 112).[15] Diocleides claimed that Andocides and his friends tried to bribe him, but when they failed to turn over the money, Diocleides came forward with his information. He named not only Andocides but many of Andocides's friends and relatives as well. Some of those named fled the city. The rest of them were thrown in the stocks. The generals were summoned, and troops were mobilized. The council slept in the acropolis, and the Boeotians (a people north of Athens) marched to the border. During all of this panic, Diocleides was crowned and hailed as the savior of the city (1.43–45; 113–14).

Andocides then slows down even more, to dialogue and monologue pace: dialogue is sparsely used in oratory, but it is uniquely effective in bringing the storyworld to life and in transforming story time into real time. Andocides also introduces an abrupt change in tone. While the city panicked, he sat in the jail cell with his father, several cousins, a brother-in-law, friends, and other citizens. Things looked dark for all of them, he says. At night, the prison closed. One man had his mother there, another his sister, another his wife and children. The men were moaning and weeping over their desperate situation. Then Charmides, Andocides's cousin of the same age who had been brought up with him in his household since childhood, confronted him:

> Andocides, you see how serious the situation is. Up till now I didn't want to say anything to annoy you, but now I'm forced to by the trouble we're in. Some of your friends and companions outside our family have already been put to death on the same charges that we're facing, and others have gone into exile, condemning themselves as guilty. So if you've heard anything about this business, say so, and save yourself first, and your father, whom you naturally love most, and next your brother-in-law, husband of your only sister, and then all these other relatives and members of the family, and also me. I've

never given you any trouble in my whole life and I've always been ready to support you and your family interests. (1.49–51; 115–16)

Others, says Andocides, began to entreat him in the same way.

Here, at the emotional "bottom" of his tale, in jail and hearing a touching plea for help, Andocides thinks. The turning point in the story will be triggered by Andocides's thinking, and in this story it will be highlighted through pacing, in dialogue, and with terms for enthymizing. He thought (*enthumēthēn*) to himself, "Am I to do nothing while my own relatives are unjustly destroyed ... and while three hundred other Athenians are going to be put to death unjustly and the city is in the greatest trouble and mutual suspicion?" (1.51; 116). In this moment, Andocides realizes that he does have something to say. Because of Charmides's prompting, Andocides enthymizes something that will save himself, all his relatives, and the rest of the three hundred innocent Athenians named—something that will protect his integrity and at the same time prove that Diocleides was lying. What he realizes will become a turning point or "node" in the plot—not only an important narrative detail but a central and a crucial one. It was his club, says Andocides, and his club mates who talked about defacing the herms. "I thought [*enthumēthēn*] to myself and calculated [*elogizomēn*] that ... there were four left of those who took part against whom Teucrus didn't inform" (1.52; 116).

The difficulty for Andocides was that one should help but never hurt friends. It is an unwritten rule of Athenian life, like honoring the gods and one's parents, and so Andocides has been reluctant to inform on his club mates, particularly when doing so meant his release in exchange for their imprisonment. Indeed, he admits he has kept silent about the guilt of his friends until now. But then he thinks to himself: Diocleides had named most of Andocides's friends and relatives, who were either sitting in jail or had already fled the country or been executed. Isn't it likely that Diocleides had already named these other four as well? If Andocides came forward with what he knew and with these four names, he would harm four of his club mates, but they were in fact guilty men who probably already had been identified. And he would save himself, his father, his relatives, his friends, and many other innocent Athenians besides, and his information would restore calm to Athens. Wasn't his duty to help these greater than his obligation not to hurt those four men?

What Andocides is asking here is whether his duty to the polis and its law isn't greater than the duty to his friends: "Considering [*skopon*] all this, gentlemen, I found that the least of the evils was to state the facts at once" (1.60; 117).[16] He does offer his information; the council and the commission of inquiry question Diocleides. Diocleides confesses that his information was false, and he is executed. Andocides and his relatives are freed, the panic that gripped the city dissipates, and life returns to normal.

Andocides frames and describes this eureka moment—imprisonment, emotional despair, inner struggle, sudden realization, and decisive act—with multiple instances of *enthumēthēn* and its synonyms. Our categorization here breaks down a bit: since everyone already knows that Andocides will offer information, get immunity, and be freed, the result is not surprising, and in that way, this is like mnemonic enthymizing. But by taking us through the event in this way—in jail, speaking to Charmides and thinking to himself—Andocides gives us a new perspective on it so that it takes on new significance, much like heuristic enthymizing. This is not the story, says Andocides, of a man guilty of sacrilege who went free by implicating his friends and who now wants to return to normal life under an amnesty struck between oligarchs and democrats. This is the story of an innocent man with guilty friends who had to choose between his reluctance to destroy them and his duty to save his city.

We can also see that Andocides is not wed to this term. He uses several synonyms as well. But here at the center of the story he repeats the term and links it to the technique, realizing the crucial detail or node that will turn the plot and then revealing it to the audience to help them see what is important and what it means: Andocides did not admit to any crime, he did not participate with his friends in the mutilation but opposed it—even if he knew about it and kept quiet so as not to betray his friends. And he betrayed his friends not in exchange for freedom but in an attempt to save his family. He only gave his information under the direst circumstances and only after hearing and suffering from Diocleides's lies and inferring from Diocleides's accusations and the ensuing arrests that his four associates had already been named. Andocides did not "buy" his immunity with their imprisonment; he was released with the others who were innocent. To enthymize is to see clearly what happened and what it means and to act on it. Of course, it would be difficult to verify most of this and impossible to recover what was said in the jail cell, what Andocides's motives really were, or whether he told the truth, but it is a powerful story that centers on a plausible rationalization that seems to align with the facts.

Andocides also uses *enthumaomai* to inform the jurors' understanding of the laws and what they mean: "Now, gentlemen, consider the laws and the prosecutors" (1.92; 125). And later (at the end of the speech), he uses it to praise Athenians and their prudent laws: "And you should also bear in mind [*enthumēthēnai*], gentlemen, that at present the whole of Greece regards you as very generous and sensible men, because you didn't devote yourselves to revenge for the past, but to the preservation of the city and the unity of the citizens" (1.140; 137).

Just as Isaeus did in our first example, Andocides asks the audience to "enthymize" details that are favorable to his case, and he draws links among them and to other elements (laws, witness statements, examples) to craft a satisfying *periodos* that centers upon a moment of moral clarity that spurs action. He uses the technique to temper hostility, to enhance his ethos and praise the ethos of the city, to define the legal issue, to frame his case, and to transform the plot from apparent guilt and mercenary betrayal to wrongful accusation, deep moral struggle, bold assertion, family liberation, and civic-mindedness.[17]

Because the stories are so different, the usage across these examples and those listed in chapter 5 is varied. Enthymizing appears in the proemium, in the peroration, and at the very center of the narrative. Sometimes it is directed at the audience in the imperative mood outside the narrative; other times it is part of the narrative, describing the thinking of the narrator or a character that is then reported to the audience as inner monologue. Sometimes it calls attention to a fact to establish a logical inference that can be drawn from it; other times it calls up an entire narrative episode and a scene. It can evoke emotional responses and character assessments as well as moral judgments and logical deductions. Sometimes it is pointedly oppositional—but not always. The terminology is not consistent. At best, we could say that we have here a "family" of rhetorical techniques that are loosely related to a set of synonymous terms. At the most important points of the story, Andocides seems to prefer *enthumaomai* to other terms, but he is happy to use other words as well or to achieve the effect without a marking verb. But all these various uses derive from and contribute to their common source: the needs of adversarial storytelling to tell a concise but complete narrative and to highlight and interpret facts that are important to the plot, the law, and the verdict.

CHAPTER 7

Enthymizing and Adversarial Narratives

Despite their variety, each of the previous examples of enthymizing operates within a narrative and one or more legal texts and cultural norms. Each of these examples is part of a narrative and a *nomos*—and not simply a narrative but multiple narratives offered in a narrative contest. Enthymizing's function is intimately connected to the oppositional stance of the narratives in legal trials. As a term and a rhetorical technique, it works differently in adversarial storytelling than it might in other kinds of discourse. It could be said to have genre- and situation-specific functions. So it makes sense to approach enthymizing through the lens of narrative theory and especially work on adversarial or what Lucaites and Condit (1985) call "rhetorical" narratives.

Rhetoric and its definitions have broadened considerably since Lucaites and Condit's essay appeared, and it is now commonplace to say that literature, science, history, and all other texts, acts, places, structures, beings, objects, and things are "rhetorical."[1] One frequent consequence of the "everything is rhetoric" stance is the presumed universality of constituent rhetorical elements. Alongside Schiappa's syllogism,[2] I offer this deduction: If Aristotle found enthymemes, ethos, and topoi in ancient oratory, then these are parts of rhetoric, and if everything is rhetoric, then its constituent parts are in everything. Everything is rhetoric, so everything will include enthymemes, ethos, and topoi.

But persuasion in a legal case does not work, look, or feel the same as persuasion in television ads, photographs, civic monuments, sports performances, actantial models, or object relations. I am arguing for a special view of rhetoric that allows us to focus on a narrower set of abilities required of the *logographos* or rhetor. 1.0 is specifically relevant to Lucaites and Condit's "rhetorical function" of narrative (1985, 93). It may be absent from or look different in other kinds of narratives, discourses, or artifacts because it will be less important or irrelevant to their generic features and their rhetorical purpose.

In the same way, narratives can be defined broadly and in broadly rhetorical terms, and narrative can be "big" similar to how rhetoric is "big"—defined so as to include a wide range of disparate kinds of texts.[3] But not all kinds of narratives are the same. Here, too, I am arguing for the value of narrowing the focus on narrative to speak of rhetorical narratives of a rather specific sort and in a particular context: listeners who witness contrasting accounts of the same set of recent and ongoing human events from participants in those events are required to vote for one account and one speaker and against the other promptly after hearing the speeches.[4] Persuading in this context means, in practical terms, winning a contest. Narrative in this context involves human conflict in a normative storyworld and a plot arc that can move listeners away from and back toward a sense of what is just or right. Enthymizing is a kind of scoring move in that contest—an attempt to score a "point."

Other kinds of persuasion and other kinds of narratives will display a wide range of features, to be sure, but in only a narrow subset will the author or narrator have to perform the task of creating a story and fixing it to a law or norm so that he or she can overcome an opposing normative/legal story to win over a majority of listeners who are required to choose one or the other. It is within this narrower understanding of rhetoric and of narrative that enthymizing was developed and that it performs its characteristic function. The adversarial narrative within the legal trail stands as the paradigmatic or prototypical framework for this rhetorical technique and for much of ancient rhetorical artistry.

How does 1.0 operate within rhetorical or adversarial narratives, or what feature of these narratives make enthymizing a particularly relevant and effective move? I'll begin by reviewing some of the features of rhetorical narrative and how enthymizing contributes to it and then move on to a brief discussion of the contest. The rhetorical or adversarial narrative has several interrelated features.[5]

1. Complete
    a. The rhetorical story (except the ending, which the jury provides) needs to be complete, particularly in terms of its emotional and normative movement. The story will thus need a believable initiating event and a series of linked consequences and accompanying states in subsequent episodes, each of which follows and is explained by the preceding event, the final of which will initiate the suit that the jurors are there to adjudicate. The result should feel like a smooth arc moving toward emotional resolution and retributive justice that matches the initial wrong (including perhaps the suit itself as a wrong) to the fitting punishment or exoneration that the jury will carry out.

        All the parts of a story must be present: Characters need motivation and opportunity. Scenes and circumstances need to support the action. Not all the parts of the story need to be in the narrative, but any piece not explicitly proven or at least asserted will need to be inferred or imagined as part of the story by the audience, with sufficient assurance to overcome the opposing account. The audience should be left with no questions about what happened or why or how it happened. 1.0 will help audiences infer pieces of the story that are not stated and highlight the required pieces, thus contributing to the feeling of completeness even in a narrative that leaves some elements unstated. For example, having denied guilt for either defacing the herms or profaning the mysteries, Andocides needs to establish a plausible reason for his immunity and a motive for his prosecutor's actions.

    b. But rhetorical narratives are also incomplete in the sense that the story and its movement are unfinished. The narrative ends, but the story does not yet have an ending; it enlists the audience as participants in carrying out its final episode by voting against one litigant and for the other. The audience is required to complete the narrative arc—the return swing of the pendulum—repaying the litigants in the case for the acts of the characters in the narrative. In this way, the story advocates for something beyond itself. The movement from the narrative's final sentence to the story's end is driven by the listener's experience of the story's beginning and middle, the first "movement" of the *periodos*. If enthymizing is what places in the mind of the listener the factors that are important to his or her decision, then we could say that enthymizing prompts the completion of the story. Audiences well established in a rhythm of inferring, experiencing, and judging the story as it unfolds

from the pieces stated in the narrative will feel confident in carrying the story that they now inhabit to its proper conclusion.
2. Plausible
   a. Coherence (probability): The story must be univocal and unambiguous. All the pieces must "hang together" to agree with, complement, and reinforce each other. Any internal thematic tension or inconsistency, any ambiguity or lack of clarity must be eliminated or minimized. By clarifying what details mean and where they fit in the story, enthymizing can help highlight the coherence of a story and prevent the interpretation of details that might compromise that coherence. For example, enthymizing the relatives' refusal of the magistrate (in Isaeus 1) was shown to be inconsistent with the claim (that Cleonymus simply wanted to confirm his will). Andocides (in Andocides 1) will need to eliminate the ambiguity surrounding his immunity by drawing attention to important details: he informed on some club mates but not on family members, and he did not confess to any crime himself.
   b. Correspondence (fidelity): All parts of the story must agree with what the audience knows to be true.
       i. Every detail of the story should be confirmed by the things that are admittedly or observably true, including the inartistic proofs (testimony, witnesses, oaths, wills, etc.) and (since the trial itself will become part of the story) known features of the judicial procedure, the trial, the litigants, the court scene, and so on. Enthymizing is particularly useful here and in the next point to highlight inconsistencies in an opponent's account or to refute charges. Accused of informing on his own father, Andocides points out that if that were true, either his father would have been executed (for impiety) or he would (for false denunciation), but since everyone knows that both he and his father survived the whole affair, this allegation cannot be true.
       ii. The narrative must also be consistent with the everyday life of the audience—with how things are done and how people behave or are expected to behave. This is the realm of not only objective reality but also social convention and expectation. These kinds of details will be mentioned to heighten the realism but will not often be enthymized unless there is a reason for them to stand out (e.g., to contradict an opposing claim), but they will form an important backdrop to those narrative facts that have special significance as departures from the everyday. The orator Aeschines (in *Against*

Timarchos) builds his entire prosecution speech upon "what everybody knows" to be true of that effeminate prostitute Timarchos.

    iii. Similarly, narrated facts should find confirmation in the normative cultural framework of the audience, in the collective *nomos*—its values and norms as expressed in its myths, its archetypal storyforms, and its tellable-tale structures. This is less about social conventions and realities than it is about cultural ideals and attitudes, narrative scripts and genres. The narrative should be made to look like the kinds of stories that are told—the familiar initiating events and complications (desires that people pursue, wrongs they perpetrate, problems they face) and resolutions that reveal how a culture thinks. 1.0 can help highlight details in a story that have corresponding parallels in familiar cultural tales, scripts, and character types. The familiar tale evoked by the enthymized details will add support, credibility, and clarity to the story and to the interpretation given to it by the speaker. Andocides invokes the "help friends, hurt enemies" norm to explain his difficulty informing on his club mates and evokes the tension between hurting friends and helping the city in his final decision to come forward.

3. Brief
    a. Rhetorical narratives should have no extraneous details, characters, episodes, or subplots. This is often expressed as a call for brevity (Lucaites and Condit 1985, 96, quoting Quintilian), but it is more appropriately understood as a need for efficiency and simplicity. Every detail should contribute to one strong plotline, and the plotline should be clear and linear. The speaker does not offer the audience a tantalizing puzzle to solve, detailed descriptive scenes to get lost in, the excavation of a unique inner or outer world, or multiple overlapping plotlines to untangle. A legal story should focus only on the issue before it and include only explanatory episodes and details that advance the plot, enhance its clarity and plausibility, and fit with the relevant law. Despite this call for brevity, legal cases can be complex, involving a large number of scenes, characters, and episodes—too many for an audience to retain. Enthymizing helps tie plot threads and episodes together into a coherent whole, maintaining a feeling of brevity and simplicity even amid a complex case and narrative by highlighting crucial character traits, scenic elements, and plot points around which other details can cluster, gaining clarity and meaning through their orchestration into familiar storyforms.

For example, Demosthenes 59, *Against Neaera*, runs to forty-one typescript pages and 126 sections and includes many characters and episodes and a long-running hostility between two characters, Apollodorus and Stephanus, in addition to the courtesan Neaera. In his introduction to the speech, Bers admits that the speech is "repetitious and sprawling" and therefore probably not by Demosthenes (2003, 151). It struggles amid the long and winding narrative to keep in view the simple plot: Stephanus is illegally living with a foreign prostitute as though married to her and repeatedly passes her foreign children off as his own native citizens.

4. Unique
   a. Rhetorical narratives seek to be the only credible account of events. They must demonstrate their own plausibility and completeness, but they can establish their uniqueness more effectively by also invalidating the opposing account—contradicting what is said with something else that was said, something else that is manifestly untrue, or something manifestly true but inconsistent with what was said—or by otherwise contradicting something else implied by or dependent upon what was said. This of course is contradictory enthymizing. Enthymizing contributes to the certainty achieved by bringing the audience to believe that the opposing account is incredible or impossible, leaving the speaker's narrative the only viable account: "If there are multiple coherent explanations for the available evidence, belief in any one of them over the others will be lessened" (Pennington and Hastie 1991, 528). We've seen several examples of this in chapter 5 (section 2.C).

As I suggested in the introduction, narrative theory can be a useful resource for exploring early rhetorical artistry, including rhetorical logos and the enthymeme. I would like here briefly to offer a few aspects of narrative theory that support and clarify rhetorical enthymizing: gaps, kernels or nodes, marking, and disnarration.

GAPS

I have mentioned the minority view that Aristotle never defined the enthymeme in terms of the missing piece of argument and have argued further that filling in logical gaps in an argument (like 3.0) is difficult and counterproductive. But following a narrative is not like following a chain of deductive reasoning. Filling in imaginative gaps in a narrative to fully experience a developing story is natural and is indeed an important element in any narrative's effectiveness. All narratives have missing pieces that separate what is said (what I am calling the narrative) from what audiences infer, imagine, and experience as the story.[6] Narrative theory speaks of these missing pieces in several ways: the "unwritten" (Iser 1972, 280), the "ellipses" or "paralipses" (Genette 1980, 51–52), or the narrative "gaps" (Gerrig 2010, 20). A narrative, says Iser (1972, paraphrasing Sterne), is "something like an arena in which reader and author participate in a game of the imagination. If the reader were given the whole story, and there were nothing left for him to do, then his imagination would never enter the field, the result would be the boredom which inevitably arises when everything is laid out" (280).

Barthes (2002) found enthymemes in the narrative *Sarrasine* but restricted their operation only to logical deduction and only to deductions that drew upon unstated and faulty cultural knowledge. But such restrictions are unnecessary if we think of narrative inference more generally as "gap-filling" of all sorts: drawing conclusions as well as fleshing out characters, inferring traits, imagining scenes, and judging decisions and actions in situations based on what was known or said.

Bitzer (1959) saw the need for audiences to contribute to a discursive exchange, and he argued that this participation was necessary for understanding and persuasion. Audiences are persuaded when they participate in the argument. I would say rather that audiences believe what they can "see for themselves"—even if it is internal seeing through narrative description and audience gap-filling. Like Barthes, Bitzer similarly restricted the narrator-audience interaction to the terms of 3.0: supplying a premise. Here, too, the restriction is unnecessary. If all interpretation requires and rewards interpretative input on the part of the reader or listener, then Bitzer's "missing piece" will apply to narrative as well as (I would argue, far better than) it does to the syllogism, which is not, after all, a genre of real social interaction, as storytelling is.

Different genres of narrative will evince different levels of "gappiness." Herman speaks in this regard of "action specification," which refers to the "number and kinds of slots for action description left open in a story" (2002, 64). "Fully open" texts, like stream-of-consciousness or avant-garde fiction, are very gappy. They require so much filling in on the part of readers that they can short-circuit attempts to follow what is happening and what the rules of "tellability" are. Toward the other end of the spectrum are "predominantly closed" texts, such as police and administrative reports. Highly closed texts can violate conventions of tellability by reporting apparently insignificant actions in more detail than readers need or want (65).

A narrative can also vary internally in gappiness, slowing down to supply more detail at decisive, climatic, or revelatory moments. Rhetorical narratives sustain completeness and plausibility while maintaining their brevity by loosely sketching some parts of the story (leaving the narrative rather "open") while important episodes, scenes, and details and their meaning are specified much more fully.

We might say that the imaginative and experiential task of filling in the gaps of an unfolding story is contiguous with and inseparable from the inferences that this work requires and includes. Facts that are deduced, understood, and comprehended in a story are also always felt, imagined, seen, and judged. Separating one particular cognitive layer of this "gap-filling" as logic or logos to the exclusion of everything else seriously distorts how cases are heard, understood, and judged. It is the imaginative and inferential work of readers and listeners that allow them to inhabit a storyworld in which only some of the elements are narrated. And it is enthymizing that helps audiences fill in story gaps correctly and completely, converting a narrative into a story and a plot with a thematic, sensory, emotional, aesthetic, and normative unity that complete a full cadence, or *periodos*.

The gaps to be filled in a story do not always occur as propositions or in language. Earlier I mentioned curried mutton and what Sherlock Holmes deduced from it. The orators also called to mind (or enthymized) visual scenes—full of pathos, characters, dialogue, and action. In each case, the facts presented lead the audience to imagine others. Imagined spatial details can lead to further inferences through mental models or images.[7] For example, suppose that a defendant presents you with a scene: "My house has two stories, and in the part with the women's rooms and the men's rooms, the upper floor is the same size as the floor below. When our baby was born, his mother nursed him. To avoid her risking an accident coming down the stairs whenever he needed washing, I took over the upstairs rooms, and the women moved downstairs" (*Lysias* 1.9; Todd 2000, 17).

Already we may have inferred that the speaker is the husband communicating in the first person, and already we have begun to form an opinion of him: he is considerate of his wife's safety. We have a character and an incipient moral judgment, and we form spatial inferences as well. Based on his description, we can form an incipient model of the house, a task made easier by the fact that his listeners, for the most part, had similar housing arrangements.

We are not told but we might infer and imagine that the furnishings in the men's quarters downstairs—the couches, musical instruments, and drinking bowls, for example—were also probably moved upstairs and that the loom, the bed, the crib, and the baby's things from the women's rooms were moved down into the (former) men's quarters. And when further actions occur later in the story, we will have to recall this inverted domestic space and adjust how we imagine the actions taking place accordingly. For example, when the man invites a friend over, we would have to remember the new arrangement and infer that they are now meeting upstairs, not down on the ground floor as they normally would, and that the wife is downstairs just off the courtyard, not upstairs as she typically would be.

Similarly, when the man later tells us that he was sleeping with his wife upstairs (in the new men's quarters), that the baby then began to cry, and that he told his wife to go and feed the infant, we have to infer (i.e., to see) that she will have to go downstairs to do so. We may or may not notice (enthymize) that, having told us earlier he moved the wife downstairs so that she wouldn't risk an accident coming down the stairs whenever the baby needed washing, we can imaginatively see that his wife *still has to go downstairs* to care for the baby.

This realization could trouble his whole account, and an opposing speaker, if he noticed it, could take advantage of this inconsistency: keep in mind (enthymize), gentlemen of the jury, that this man told us he moved the women's quarters to the ground floor for his wife's safety—so she wouldn't have to go downstairs to change the baby's diaper—but he now tells us that on that night, when it was hard to see and the baby began to fuss, he told her to go downstairs to see to the baby. What could be more incredible than this? For what reason did he really move her downstairs? The defendant in the trial spoke second, but in capital trials, each speaker had an opportunity to respond to the opponent's speech, so the prosecutor could raise this problem in his second speech if he noticed it and saw what it meant.

There are many such gaps and possible inferences in most stories— many that aren't noticed or followed, many that are irrelevant to the plot, many that are seen or felt but never put into language. Because the facts necessary for important inferential moves are part of the larger stream of narrative, audiences can have difficulty noticing that some details or sets of details are meant to prompt inferences or imagined scenes, difficulty bringing together separate pieces of the narrative to see new aspects of the story, and difficulty knowing exactly which inference or feeling could or should be drawn from any particular set of facts. But seeing or finding the narrative details capable of crafting a unique, complete, and plausible story; arranging those moves so that they initiate, amplify, and then resolve a full *periodos*; and marking these particulars to show what they mean and how they fill in a story's openness—all of these would be important skills for a speechwriter to learn.

KERNELS

If it is generally true that narratives contain gaps and that audiences fill in some of them through inference and imagination to form stories, it is also true that most stories will involve more details and more gap-filling than the audience can retain or consciously focus on. Not all of these details or inferences will be equally significant: what the prisoners sat on or how many children were there. Few listeners could be expected to retain all the details of even a simple case or to reliably draw from a narrative—in fact, a set of competing narratives—the necessary inferences or contradictions to grasp the overall thematic unity that each speaker intends.

For these reasons, the marshaling of attention is especially important in agonistic discourse to help the audience know which details are central to the plot and the case and which are not and which details rise to the level of significant facts.[8] Some details are "actual hinges of the narrative" (nuclei), and others (catalyses) "do no more than 'fill in the narrative' space" (Barthes 1975, 247–48). Chatman calls them "kernels" and "satellites" (1978, 53–56). Kernels can also function as story "nodes," moments of contingency or choice that will move the plot irreversibly in one direction rather than another (Barthes 1975, 248; see also Beatty 2017): Charmides decides at last to confront Andocides. Each of these nodes can be marked for enthymizing by characters or the speaker or narrator for the audience, for what they mean, for the plot paths that they open and those that they close.

Some crucial details will not seem important, so they will not be noticed unless they are marked for attention: Holmes's "curious incident of the dog in the night time" (mentioned in the introduction) was not obviously nodal in terms of the action but was shown to be so in terms of the plot. It generated an inference that closed off one possible sequence of events (that the stranger Simpson, or any stranger, took the horse) and left open only one other (that Straker did). In the example above, the wife's movement downstairs to care for the baby could be "marked" or turned into a node by the prosecutor to call into question the motive behind moving the wife downstairs in the first place. Marking this detail would compromise the consistency and plausibility of the defendant's story and open the possibility of a different motive on the part of the husband and thus a different plotline.

MARKERS

The speaker will not want the audience to miss important narrative kernels that are central to the plot or its connection to the law. So the speaker will mark for notice and interpretation probative details upon which the narrative and the legal case can be made to turn. "Marking" advertises a detail as nodal or important and often explains why it is so, helping the audience comprehend at a glance the story, the law, and the case and to appreciate possible plotlines that are closed off by nodal events and decisions. A marked set of facts will selectively differentiate the speaker's version of events—his understanding of the facts, the law, and the question at issue—from the version posed by the opponent. By marking nodal details and guiding audiences on what to infer from them or link them to, speakers can keep their narratives brief, plausible, and consistent and ensure that the story will be complete and unique.

Tools for directing attention and conveying significance are ubiquitous in narrative; they are tools of selection and arrangement, of emplotment and emphasis. All narratives have to rely upon techniques for separating facts that need to be noticed and kept in mind from those that don't. Rabinowitz describes a number of conventional techniques of reading and writing used by authors and known to readers "before reading" to signal important elements of a narrative. He calls them "rules of notice," of "signification," of "coherence," and of "configuration," and he uses the analogy of an unassembled swing set with imperfect instructions to illustrate the problem of story construction (1987, 37–38).

We can imagine a legal case as having two overlapping but different sets of instructions for one swing set. Each author will know that another set of instructions is being prepared, and each would be advised to simplify their instructions as much as possible, focusing on important steps and warning against the recommendations of that other set of instructions by highlighting where it will go wrong. Marking can emphasize the simplicity and coherence of a narrative while maintaining its completeness.

Some important details can be highlighted within the narrative itself through how or where they are told, through a character's comment, or through their own intrinsic qualities. In legal cases, an orator will often mark important narrative elements by stepping out of the ongoing account to comment on them, momentarily pausing to call the audience's attention to a detail and its significance and implications before moving on. In this case, the marking will be "extradiegetic" (Genette 1980, 228–29), creating two levels or sections of the speech: the narrative and the commentary upon it or, we could say, the *diegesis* and the "proofs," where story kernels are given their proper meaning and can be linked to each other, to the laws, and to reputable cultural myths and norms.

DISNARRATION

Rabinowitz's swing set analogy helps us appreciate the speaker's need to not only clarify through markers the steps in story construction but also explain why the opposing steps cannot work. They would need to be disqualified as unworkable. Prince uses the term *disnarration* to refer to a narrator's mentioning of things that will not or cannot be told, that could have happened but didn't, or that couldn't have happened because of some other earlier choice or node that foreclosed the possibility. In fiction, the disnarrated can perform many functions, expressing "purely imagined worlds, desired worlds, or intended worlds, unfulfilled expectations, unwarranted beliefs, failed attempts, crushed hopes, suppositions and false calculations, errors and lies and so forth" (1988, 3). Its most important function is to demonstrate tellability: "This narrative is worth telling because *it* could have been otherwise, because *it* usually is otherwise, because *it* is *not* otherwise" (5; italics in original).

In adversarial narratives, enthymizing often works to disnarrate what cannot be otherwise or to indicate "alethic expressions of impossibility" (Prince 1988, 3). It expresses what could not have happened in order to invalidate what the opponent says did happen. Like a fork in a path, a narrative node closes off one set of future possible actions by taking up another. At a narrative node, I can say, "Since this happened, that was likely to occur as a matter of course, and since that did not happen, this cannot have been a result," or "If this had happened, that would have been the result, but since (as we can all see) that did not occur, this could not have been the case." This latter form, suggesting something that might have happened (was possible at the time) but did not happen or, given what resulted, showing that something *could not* have happened, we can refer to as disnarrating. Some narrative nodes provide opportunities for disnarrating one or another aspect of an opponent's account as impossible by giving what was known to have happened. This can be rendered in the form of *modus tollens* (if A, then B; but not-B, therefore not-A), and Sherlock Holmes refers to this simply as eliminating possibilities.[9] But these forms of reasoning typically occur in and through narrative, as they do for Holmes himself, and it is important to see that the operation need not be reduced to logical formulae in order to describe and understand it.

Antiphon 6, *On the Chorus Boy*, like Andocides 1, involves a defendant who is forbidden from entering public or sacred spaces or performing ceremonies. In the latter case, this is because of a charge of impiety (*asebeia*); in the former, this is because of a charge of murder. Both defendants disnarrate a possible course of events to support their claims of innocence—what should have happened (if their opponents' charges are true) but did not. Before now, Andocides says, he has initiated people into the mysteries and has "entered the Eleusinian and made sacrifices" (1.132; 135). Antiphon similarly observes that "[my opponents and I] talked in shrines, in the Agora, at my house... and everywhere else," and "to top it all off, in the Council-house and in front of the Council, Philocrates here joined me on the podium, and with his hand on my arm he talked with me, calling me by name" (6.40; 86).

Each defendant has entered public spaces and shrines, sacrificed, served in office, and participated in rites prior to his arrest and was never prevented from doing so by his opponents. Andocides asks, "Why is it that I've been in town for three years since my return from Cyprus without their thinking me guilty of impiety?" (1.132; 135). "These men were in town and present at these events," says Antiphon, and "they could have registered the case and banned me from all events" (6.46; 88). But instead, they "proposed me for liturgies" ("Andocides" 1.132; 135) and "joined me on the podium" ("Antiphon" 6.40; 86). "So far from thinking me impious," says Andocides, "they've proposed me for liturgies.... I was also a treasurer for the sacred money on the Acropolis. And now I'm guilty of impiety, am I, and am guilty of an offence by entering the holy place?" (1.132; 135–36). If he was guilty of profaning a holy place, Antiphon points out, "Why didn't they register it?" (6.46; 88).

In both cases, the prosecutor's claims are disnarrated by revealing what should and would have happened had these accusations been true: if the prosecutors really thought Andocides and Antiphon were guilty, they would have banned those men from sacred shrines, rites, and public offices long ago and prevented them from taking part in any public proceedings, but instead, the prosecutors not only allowed it but participated with the accused in these events, proving that the charges are slander and that even their opponents don't believe them. These decisions and these actions—proposing, joining, participating, allowing—are shown to be nodes in which one set of actions belies the possibility of another, which are disnarrated through counterfactual conditionals. The significance of a narrative detail can be marked as nodal to disnarrate the opposing account. In these and other ways, the language of narrative theory can help us discuss and understand the various manifestations and functions of enthymizing.

CONTESTS

Just as Greek oratory can be profitably viewed in terms of narrative, so is it also a kind of contest or consequential game, and the features of the enthymeme respond to the rhetorical agon in which it occurs. *Enthymizing* will name the move or play that attempts to score a point.[10] When a speaker interprets a narrative element that helps the reader or listener grasp how the details fit together (or could not fit together) into a convincing plot and story, the speaker can be said to have scored a point. A point moves the listener in the direction of the speaker, and by accruing "points," the speaker can move ahead of the opponent.

Not unlike a play in a game, enthymizing works (when it works) more because of how it is set up and executed within the context of the agon than because of its logical or linguistic form. Like a move in any game or contest—basketball or soccer, for example—enthymizing needs to be planned out (in advance), set up, and executed on (or in) the court. In the same way that a rhetorical argument or narrative "line" might be punctuated with an enthymematic "cap" (with a nod to Walker 1994), a drive in basketball culminates in a shot on goal that attempts to score a point, but the players and the coach must attend to more than just the point and more than just the shot on goal.

Every shot must be set up through the unfolding of a play or series of plays, such as the moves and reactions Andocides describes in *On the Mysteries*. In many games and sports, the boundary around the play that results in scoring a point is fluid. In the same way, the line between a moment of enthymizing and the story and case that it builds upon is fluid and open to interpretation. Still, it will be important for the speechwriter to discover the facts or details that will make up his own and his opponent's narrative and, since not everything will be attended to equally, to determine which of these details might be missed or misinterpreted and which will be most effective in differentiating his story from that of his opponent. These will have to be stated and enthymized for maximal effect.

Of course, the purpose of the game (and the setup) is to score points, and the speaker's goal is in some sense the same. I'll shift to a boxing metaphor here. Enthymizing, like the punch, must strike with force: an objectively sound setup with an otherwise perfectly executed jab that arrives late or lands only a glancing blow is wasted effort. The point is measured by its effect, but it is influenced by its form. Whereas the observer (particularly an untrained observer) attends to the glove and its target, the boxer must utilize the ring and the floor, the foot and leg, the hip and core, the shoulder and arm to execute the jab. In the same way, enthymizing is often simply the striking effect of a portion of the narrative (an episode) and the law that it stands upon. A detail takes on its meaning and force only in this context. The difference between "sleeping in" and "desecrating the fast of Yom Kippur" (Cover 1983, 8) and between watching over the sheep and fattening them for slaughter lie in the narratives and normative storyworlds within which those activities take place (Burke 1969, 27).[11]

On the other hand, the variables of setup and execution in spectator games and sports also reveal the desire for a rapid score—the quick uppercut that catches the opponent off guard or the breakaway and slam dunk.

A quickly executed and unanticipated move followed by a score that seems sudden and effortless can be more effective than one that is advertised or requires a long setup. The sudden point attracts attention, exaggerates the ability of the player, exhilarates fans, deflates opponents, and shifts momentum. In the same way, a sudden, quick, and unexpected moment of enthymizing will energize supporters of a litigant and demoralize opponents. The best enthymemes will strike the audience clearly and suddenly so that they see the meaning of the enthymized detail as one integral component of the narrative whole.[12] This is part of the value of heuristic enthymizing, which can surprise listeners with the sudden relevance of a small detail, especially when it is a detail mentioned by the opponent.

Of course, the proper execution of a thrilling play, especially a surprising and rapid one, may seem sudden, effortless, or lucky to the untrained audience and yet require the long development of unique skills, the careful preparation and execution of a complex game plan, and dexterous capitalizing on fleeting opportunities for advantage (or *kairos*), most of which goes unnoticed. A simple and rapid effect does not imply simple, easy, or spontaneous execution.

The question of effectiveness and spectatorship highlights a difference between some sporting or gaming contests and rhetorical contests. Many games and sports rely on an unambiguous and objective scoring system: the arrow's placement on a target is verifiable, as is the passing of a ball over a goal line. Rhetorical contests—somewhat like boxing or figure skating—have no similar features of game play. Points are not objectively determined with the help of game implements (a target) or features of the field of play (a net or goal line); they are awarded by observant judges. A move that is not noticed by the judge—however technically difficult, meticulously timed, or flawlessly executed—is no point at all.

This is a particularly relevant factor when the judges are not themselves experts. A trained and experienced boxer or ice-skater will see and appreciate subtle or fleeting but technically proficient moves that a popular audience fails to appreciate, while they may downplay flashy moves that seem more difficult than they really are. Before a popular or untrained audience, though, it will be important not only to score points but to advertise them, directing the attention of the audience to the scoring move so that it has maximal effect. Getting the audience to see and acknowledge a move as worthy of a point will be the only way of gaining one. Given the range of details spoken in a narrative or experienced as part of the story by the audience, it is almost inevitable that audience members will fail to appreciate the proper significance of some details, fail to see how they contradict the opposing account, or simply draw the wrong inference from them.

Another similarity with sport or game is that while a player or speaker will plan and attempt to execute their plays with the anticipation of scoring points, some of these plays will be thwarted by the opponent even as unexpected opportunities for scoring present themselves through the opponent's errors. The winner is not just the team with the superior game plan but the one that best carries through with their plan while taking advantage of opportunities that present themselves during play to block the opponent's strategy.

So a team will need to develop skills in recognition and adaptation that allow them to exploit their opponents' weaknesses and disrupt their plays. Since no game plan will exactly match the game itself, every team and player will be advised to anticipate, watch for, notice, and capitalize on opportunities presented by the opponent in the unfolding contest. This is one meaning of *kairos*—not just timing or opportunity but opportunities presented by an opponent's lapses or by unexpected features of game play that temporarily favor one side and that a prepared player can take advantage of. A play that disrupts an opponent's drive can be as valuable as one that scores.

In these and other ways, we can understand enthymizing, the enthymeme, and rhetorical logos better if we see them as features of a narrative contest.

PART FOUR

Lysias and the Enthymeme

CHAPTER 8

Enthymizing in Lysias 1, *On the Death of Eratosthenes*

I have argued that 1.0 was developed in and for legal trials and that 1.0 is best understood as a technique of attention management and story construction in the performance of competing legal narratives. I prefer this model because it makes sense of a common and important oratorical term and technique, and it honors the subjective experience of following a legal speech. Hearing an enthymeme feels like following a story, discovering a pattern in a set of narrative clues. Ancient legal reasoning was the reasoning of an untrained lay audience, and story is an "everyday judgment practice" that "enables a diverse cast of courtroom characters to follow the development of a case and reason about the issues in it" (Bennett and Feldman 2014, 4).

I want to argue now more directly that 1.0 was neither an accident nor a natural or inevitable quality of Greek literature, the "Greek mind," or democratic oratory. Least of all was it simply the execution of a traditional practice codified and made explicit by Aristotelian theory, as it has often been portrayed. Historically, searching for enthymemes has meant looking for the textual structure mentioned in chapter 1: two statements as premise and conclusion—what I have been referring to (after Levi) as a premise-conclusion (PC) sequence—joined by a "because clause" (Levi 1995, 70). Most recently, this was the approach of Knudsen (2014), who found many instances of 3.0 in speeches in the *Iliad*. Her conclusion was that Homer knew rhetoric and that the rhetoric Homer knew was Aristotelian. Bourdieu calls this mistaking the model of reality for the reality of the model (1977, 29). I want to challenge this account by arguing that early enthymemes did not look like 3.0 or 2.0; they looked like "nodal markers" linking narrative details to each other and to other supporting elements, including laws, archetypal storyforms, inartistic proofs, and common experience. They were developed by orators through practice and technical refinement.

It is possible to see Andocides's use of enthymizing at the center of his *On the Mysteries* as a demonstration of the rhetorical possibilities of this technique and as forging a loose association with the term, which Andocides uses, though not exclusively. Here, I want to focus on Lysias 1, *On the Death of Eratosthenes*, to demonstrate the role of this text in articulating more clearly the rhetorical value of enthymizing. Lysias, and Lysias 1 in particular, was of some importance in the development of oratorical enthymizing and the enthymeme. In what follows, I will argue that Lysias can be shown to have isolated and refined this technique. He used it, promoted it, argued for its importance and proper use, and taught this understanding to his readers and students, in the process offering his students an opportunity to learn the technique as well.

As a logographer and teacher, Lysias conceptualizes and models enthymizing for his students not in the form of a treatise but through this exemplary speech. In *On the Death of Eratosthenes*, Lysias rather explicitly asserts the central place of enthymizing not only in rhetorical practice but in oratorical display, in household management, and in the political life of the democratic city. Understanding the centrality of Lysian enthymizing will in turn shed light on the functioning of ancient Athenian rhetorical, legal, and political performance. And examining this orator and this speech will, I hope, alter both our estimation of Lysias and our understanding of the enthymeme.

LYSIAS (~445–380 B.C.E.)

Lysias was born into money. Cephalus, Lysias's father, was a wealthy native of Syracuse in Sicily. Syracuse was in the fifth century a vibrant but politically volatile city; it enjoyed periods of democracy but succumbed to tyrants repeatedly in its history, including the Deinomenids Gelon, Hieron, and Thrasybulus through the first half of the fifth century and then Dionysius I at the end of the century, when Lysias was in his forties. Cephalus left Syracuse with his family after being encouraged by Pericles to move to Athens sometime before Lysias was born.[1]

Lysias was raised in Athens as a *metic*, or resident alien, and he was educated among the sons of Athenian elites. When he was fifteen, Lysias went with a contingent of colonists to the city of Sybaris, or Thurii, in Syracuse with his brother, Polemarchus. There he received his portion of the estate of his father (who had since died). He remained in Thurii and continued his education with Nicias and Tisias. After the Peloponnesian War and the disastrous Athenian attack on Syracuse, Lysias was accused of being pro-Athenian and fled to Athens. He remained there until the coup of the Thirty Tyrants, when he and Polemarchus were arrested and his goods were confiscated. Polemarchus was executed, but Lysias escaped and fled the city for Megara.

Lysias participated in the democratic revolution that ousted the Thirty, and he contributed two thousand drachmas to this cause. A general grant of citizenship to democratic supporters promised to make him a citizen of Athens, but the proposal was attacked as contrary to the laws and was never carried through. Lysias allegedly gave or wrote (since he was not a citizen) a speech against Archinus, the person who indicted the grant of citizenship, and he also prosecuted Eratosthenes, a member of the Thirty, for the death of Polemarchus (more on this episode below).

Having lost his business and wealth, Lysias became, for a while, a teacher of rhetoric and then a prolific and highly admired logographer for native Athenians—perhaps due in part to his prosecution of Eratosthenes. Dionysius of Halicarnassus knew of 425 speeches attributed to Lysias, and he counted 223 as genuine. They covered a range of genres: "speeches for the law courts, and for debates in the Council and Assembly . . . also panegyric and amatory discourses and discourses in the epistolary style" ("Lysias" §1; Usher 1974, 20–23). "With these," says Dionysius, "he eclipsed the fame of his predecessors and of contemporary orators" (§1; 22–23). The high esteem in which Lysias was held is indicated by the fact that Plato chose him as Socrates's target and foil in the *Phaedrus* and possibly the *Republic* as well (Howland 2004).

Thanks to both his fictional portrayal in Plato's *Phaedrus* (where he serves as a disingenuous, disreputable, and disorganized foil to Socrates) and the reputation bestowed upon him by Dionysius (with his emphasis on Lysias's skill at portrayal of character, or *ethopoiia*; his compelling and entertaining narratives; and his plain Attic style), Lysias is well known for a set of decidedly alogical rhetorical virtues and some disqualifying sophistic vices. He has never been accused of being a rhetorical theorist.[2]

LYSIAS 1, *ON THE DEATH OF ERATOSTHENES*

Lysias 1 is a good place to begin looking for enthymemes; it is also an excellent teaching text. As I've suggested above and will demonstrate below, it is at once a legal speech, a political speech, a display piece, and a teaching text comprising all three of Aristotle's genres, though it is traditionally understood to be a homicide speech. Its richness is easy to miss. Compared to many other legal (especially homicide) cases from ancient Greek oratory, this speech is relatively simple and straightforward, short, lively, and entertaining. Unlike most legal trials in ancient Athens, in which litigants and their associates pursued complex and long-standing feuds through suit and countersuit, this case presents itself as a one-off between the two participants and requires little legal, social, or political backstory.[3] The authenticity of the speech has never been seriously questioned, and it illustrates well the range of rhetorical techniques for which Lysias is known, including his narrative technique (*diegesis*), his portrayal of character (*ethopoiia*), the traditional divisions of a speech (*taxis*), and his Atticism and associated plain style.[4] This speech thus offers a particularly clear example of classical Greek rhetorical artistry. Here, as with Andocides, enthymizing turns out to be central to Lysias's narrative and argument.

Lysias 1 is a case of murder in retaliation for adultery.[5] Euphiletus, the speaker, defendant, and husband, is on trial for having killed the alleged adulterer, Eratosthenes.[6] The speech tells a tale of seduction, humiliation, and vindication involving a small cast of characters: a naive husband, a deceptive wife, a cunning adulterer, an old "busybody," a pliant slave girl, and a set of trusted friends and neighbors. Euphiletus does not dispute having killed Eratosthenes but claims that the killing was legal.[7] His argument rests on a pair of laws that bear on the case. One law addressing justifiable homicide states that "if anyone kills in athletic games involuntarily, or taking him on the road, or during war in ignorance, or with his wife, or with his mother, or with his sister, or with his daughter, or with his concubine whom he keeps for purposes of free children, one is not to go into exile because he has killed for one of these reasons" (*Demosthenes* 23.53; Harris 2018, 47–48).[8] The language of this law was interpreted to sanction killing in cases where the husband discovers the pair in flagrante delicto. But if the husband could be shown to have premeditated his response, perhaps even contriving to entice the man into his home and bed (this would be a convenient way to eliminate an enemy with impunity), he could be convicted of murder.

The text of the other law, an *apagoge* (summary arrest by the plaintiff) against "wrongdoers" (*kakourgoi*), is not available but can be reconstructed in rough from texts that allude to it: if a man takes a thief, or adulterer, or killer in the act (*ep' autophōrō*), if the wrongdoer admits his guilt, let the man do whatever he pleases with him, but if the offender denies the charge, let him be brought into court (or to the Eleven) and if he is acquitted, released, but if convicted, executed. If Demosthenes 59.66 is relevant here, the law may have read, "[Let him] in a lawcourt, do to the debaucher whatever he wishes, provided he does not use a weapon [i.e., without killing him]" (Bers 2003, 174–75).[9]

Though the law permits killing an adulterer when he is caught "red-handed" (*ep' autophōrō*),[10] other adultery cases suggest that killing was not the typical response: the husband could accept financial compensation from the adulterer (Eratosthenes made such an offer), he could hold him ransom until his family paid, or he could take him to court and, if victorious, punish him physically but perhaps not fatally.[11] Against this expected response, Euphiletus's reaction might seem excessive to the audience, so Euphiletus's goal will be to demonstrate that his response was not only technically legal but fair. He will need to show that he neither enticed nor forced Eratosthenes to his house or bed, that he did not plan the killing, and that he killed Eratosthenes for no ulterior motives—only for his adulterous act.

The case will have been brought by a male relative of Eratosthenes, and his central claim seems to have been that Euphiletus planned the murder, that he enticed Eratosthenes to the house with the aid of the slave girl and perhaps forced the man inside either to avenge a previous insult or injury or in retaliation for his known prior adultery, and that he forcibly removed Eratosthenes from the hearth where he took refuge before killing him (1.4, 27, 37; 16, 20, 22).[12] In chapter 9, I'll outline an alternative line for the plaintiff that Lysias makes possible.

It isn't simply a matter of Euphiletus denying that he had any prior knowledge of the affair, for he admits—perhaps because it was established by the opposing speaker—that an elderly woman had informed him about the affair on an earlier occasion, and her account was confirmed by Euphiletus's slave (1.15–20; 18–19). Further, even according to his own account, Euphiletus entered his own home surrounded by friends bearing torches, suggesting that he had been forewarned and was already prepared to confront Eratosthenes (1.23–24; 20). He must show that despite having been told about the affair on two separate occasions beforehand, and despite having arrived on the scene prepared to do violence, and despite his refusal to accept payment or ransom as was customary, his killing was not premeditated or excessive but legal and just.

To this end, Lysias begins his narrative by showing Euphiletus to be a simple and naive husband, credulous to the point of folly. The details in the first half of this narrative are not always clearly connected to his larger argument; he recounts his marriage to his wife, the birth of their first baby, and the configuration of rooms in his house. These and other details seem out of place in a defense speech on a charge of murder, but they fit Lysias's rhetorical strategy. The wandering account and the colloquial style leave the impression of both personal simplicity and simple artlessness: Euphiletus, it seems, is simply telling us everything about his marriage from the beginning. Yet the narrative forms a tightly woven, entertaining, and credible story of a trusting husband done wrong. That is, Euphiletus presents himself as the duped victim of Eratosthenes's adultery rather than the defendant and perpetrator of murder.

When Euphiletus married, he says, he thought it best neither to "trouble [his wife] too much" nor to "let her do whatever she wanted" but rather to give her the "proper amount of attention" (1.6; 17).[13] We will see that the economy of attention, where and how carefully to attend to the details of a marriage, will be central to the speech. After the birth of his first baby, he says, he "began to have full confidence in her" (1.6; 17). Out of concern for her safety, he inverted the living arrangements in his house: "To avoid her risking an accident coming down the stairs whenever [the baby] needed washing," he turned the "men's room" (*andrōn*) downstairs into the woman's quarters, and he moved into the women's quarters upstairs (1.9–10; 17).[14] His wife would go downstairs at night to nurse the baby and often as not end up sleeping down there while he remained upstairs.[15]

Euphiletus's troubles began, he says, with the death of his mother. Eratosthenes (the adulterer) first saw Euphiletus's wife at the funeral and began to make advances to her through the slave girl (1.7–8; 17). He recalls one evening when, having just returned home from the country, he was woken up by the baby, who was crying. "The serving girl was deliberately teasing it," he says, "as I found out later" (1.11; 17). His wife at first says that she doesn't want to go down to calm the baby, but he pesters her about it until she finally gets up. She jokes that he only wants to get rid of her so that he can "have a go at the slave girl" (1.12; 17–18) and she leaves, teasingly (or so he thought) locking him in the room (as was possible for the women's quarters), and he laughs about it.

ENTHYMIZING (ONE OF THREE): "I THOUGHT NOTHING OF IT"

At this point, Euphiletus claims, he had no suspicions, and thinking (literally, *enthymizing*) "no more of it," he went to sleep (1.12; 18). This will be the first of three uses of this term in the speech. It is not simply that he does not think something but that he does not attend to the details of a situation that he ought to notice, recognize, and respond to—a situation that bears directly on his well-being and that he can alter if he understands it properly and acts upon this understanding, just as Andocides enthymized his plight and found a way out in *On the Mysteries* (chapter 6). In this case, Euphiletus's failure to enthymize is a failure to read a situation that calls for action, to read it in a way that others would (i.e., as the audience is meant to) and in the way that he should, the way that is most advantageous—most fitting, just, honorable, and beneficial—for him.

We can gauge the significance of his *enthymizing* in this section by the dramatic irony that is established through its absence: when Euphiletus declares that he had no suspicions and "thought nothing of it," he indirectly hints to the audience (if they haven't already caught on) that there is something to be suspicious about. The audience is meant to see this as the kind of situation that should alert Euphiletus and arouse his suspicion. They begin to realize, or enthymize, what he does not—namely, that the wife and slave girl are engaged in what Goffman calls "covering moves" here (1971, 14–19).

The misreading and the dramatic irony increases. In the morning, he says, his wife unlocked the door, and he noticed that she had makeup on despite being in mourning (her mother had died recently). He asked her why both the room door and courtyard door had creaked during the night, "and she claimed that the baby's lamp had gone out, so she had to get it relit at the neighbors'" (1.14; 18). "I believed this account," he says, "and said no more." If to enthymize means to attend to telling details in a situation and to interpret them correctly or in a way that allows one to respond advantageously, then the audience should now enthymize Euphiletus's plight pretty clearly, even if he does not. Alert audience members will fill the gap in the story.

ENTHYMIZING (TWO OF THREE): "EVERYTHING CAME BACK TO MY MIND"

Several days later, an old woman approaches Euphiletus. She asks him not to think her a "busybody" (*polupragmosunē*)[16] for speaking to him: "The man who is humiliating (*hubrizein*) you and your wife is an enemy of ours as well," she warned. "Get ahold of your slave girl, the one who does the shopping, and torture (*basanisēs*) her . . . you will discover everything." The man has, she says, corrupted many other wives, for "he makes a hobby (*technēn*) of it" (1.15–16; 18). Only then, Euphiletus says, does he realize what had truly been happening: "At once I became alarmed. Everything came back into my mind, and I was filled with suspicion. I remembered (literally, *enthymizing*) how I had been locked in my room, and how that night both the door of the house and the courtyard door had creaked . . . and how I noticed that my wife used makeup. All these things flashed into my mind and I was full of suspicion" (1.16–17; 18–19).

He at once understands the true meaning of all these facts and his own dire situation. This second use of the term marks, as it had for Andocides, an emotional, psychological, and attitudinal response crystallized into a moment of recognition in which everything falls into place. Euphiletus's enthymizing leads to alarm, suspicion, and active remembering—the rapid searching of the memory to recall and reassess earlier events that confirm the suspicion and realign one's "sizing up" of the situation. At once, an unremarkable situation becomes something other than what it was. This enthymizing marks an abrupt shift in perspective involving the whole person. If Euphiletus was at first limited to naive moves (Goffman 1971, 11), he is now capable of "uncovering moves" (17–19). He no longer simply accepts things as they seem on the surface; he now anticipates subterfuge, doubts appearances, and is anxious to get to the bottom of the situation.

The old woman's revelation and Euphiletus's moment of enthymizing thus marks a pivotal moment in the plot and in his development as a character; it catalyzes his transformation from a trusting, foolish, passive, and isolated husband to an active, vigilant, and engaged citizen. He takes the slave girl to the house of a friend and interrogates her under threat of torture (a staple uncovering move). She accuses (*kategorei*) Eratosthenes, reveals how Euphiletus's wife was contacted by Eratosthenes, and admits that she became their messenger and helped Eratosthenes gain access to the wife (1.18–20; 19). As this aspect of her confession is mentioned, the audience has an opportunity to recall and interpret (enthymize) a detail they have already heard (at 1.11): the girl used to tease the baby to make him cry when Eratosthenes arrived (and thus bring the wife downstairs). By mentioning this detail early in the speech so that he can set up its recall later, Lysias invites a response on the part of the audience that qualifies as enthymizing and that echoes the sudden recognition of Euphiletus. With the husband, they too can suddenly remember and attend to a detail (the crying baby, the creaking door) that gains its full significance only in the context of the situation (the affair and the slave girl's confession). When an unremarkable detail is seen to confirm the larger account, the whole narrative becomes more convincing. The disparate parts cohere so well together that they must be true.

Confronted with the serving girl's confession, Euphiletus shows admirable and deliberate restraint, introducing a familiar "words/actions" binary to assert that he will not rely on her testimony alone. "I don't want words," he says, "I want you to show me them in the act [*ep' autophōrō*]," and the girl agrees to help him (1.21; 19). He tells us that after some time had passed, his friend Sostratus returned from the country, and since it was already late, Euphiletus invited Sostratus over for dinner.[17] After dinner, Sostratus went home, and Euphiletus went to bed. Later that evening, he is awakened by the slave girl, who tells him that Eratosthenes is downstairs in the men's quarters with his wife. Euphiletus instructs the girl to keep the doors unlocked and runs out to the home of "various friends" to gather witnesses, though many were not at home, and he grabs some torches along the way. Euphiletus returns and, he claims, catches the man in bed with his wife. Eratosthenes confesses and offers to pay compensation, but Euphiletus refuses, saying, "It is not I who will kill you, but the law of the city," referring to the *apagoge* for summary arrest, the justifiable homicide law, or both (1.24–26; 20). "So it was, gentlemen," he concludes, "that this man met the fate which the laws prescribe for those who behave like that" (1.26). Thus ends the day and the narrative of Euphiletus and the life of Eratosthenes.

ENTHYMIZING (THREE OF THREE): "JUST THINK FOR A MOMENT, GENTLEMEN..."

In the remainder of the speech, Euphiletus comments on both his and his opponent's stories. He presents laws, witnesses, and arguments demonstrating that this account is fundamentally correct and that his actions were permitted (and in fact, he says, required) by the law. In the process of refuting the opposing speaker, Euphiletus comes to the prosecutor's claim that he planned the murder and (with the slave girl's help) enticed Eratosthenes to the house. As we have seen, this claim and this question are central to the case: if he did entice Eratosthenes to the house (via a message brought by the slave girl made to look like it was from the wife), he could be found guilty of murder. He asks his audience to "consider how they are lying about this as well" (1.39; 23), after which he reminds his audience about his dinner with Sostratus: "As I told you before, gentlemen, Sostratus is a close friend of mine. He met me around sunset on his way home from the country, he had dinner with me, and when he had eaten well he left. But just think (*enthymize*) for a moment, gentlemen. If I had been laying a trap that night for Eratosthenes, would it not have been better for me to dine somewhere else with Sostratus, instead of bringing him back home for dinner and so making the adulterer less likely to enter my house?" (1.39–40; 23).

This marks Lysias's third use of the verb—not to describe what he himself did or did not realize (indicative enthymizing) but addressed to the audience in the second person (imperative enthymizing), directing them to attend to a fact (dining at home) in such a way that they understand its relevance to the question at issue and the law. This was the example of heuristic enthymizing offered in chapter 5. By directing the audience to focus their attention on the dinner and by demonstrating the relevance of this detail to their understanding of the unfolding course of events—and especially to Euphiletus's state of mind—the detail is made meaningful, and its meaning is made clear. It is shown to be a preferential indicator, supporting one account of the situation and contradicting (or disnarrating) the opposing view and thus resolving an otherwise ambiguous or misleading situation. Euphiletus could now say, "If I had wanted to entice Eratosthenes over, I would do so by leaving the house on the pretense of dining at the home of a friend. Instead, I invited Sostratus over to my house, making it less likely that Eratosthenes would risk coming over. Therefore, I must not have been trying to lure him to the house, and my killing of him remains legal."

When attending to the meaning of a narrative detail clarifies one's understanding of a rhetorical situation and generates a feeling of greater confidence about what "really happened" (or is happening or will happen) and what should be done about it, one can be said to have enthymized both the detail and the resulting assessment of the situation, including any preferred response. Once properly set up, the process can happen rapidly, producing a sudden aha moment of clarity and understanding. Enthymizing can produce a striking shift or alteration in understanding, emotion, attitude, and inclination—from confusion to clarity or from one perspective to another—and thus it lends itself to being expressed in terms of contrast or opposition: "I thought . . . but then I realized . . ." or "He claims . . . but in fact . . ." It can be compared to the recognition (*anagnorisis*) described in Aristotle's *Poetics*.

At this point, we can take note of a pattern in the enthymizing that Lysias has orchestrated on the part of both himself (as a character in his narrative) and his audience.

1. Enthymizing as a reaction in an audience or spectator can occur in several ways. It can happen immediately upon perceiving a situation and without being narrated. If the old woman perceived the serving girl speaking to Eratosthenes in the marketplace and then returning to Euphiletus's house with a note that she gave to the wife (perhaps the old woman's suspicions were aroused, and she followed the girl), she could "see" that the serving girl was acting as the conduit for an illicit affair. Especially in the context of her awareness about Eratosthenes's prior adultery, the woman would enthymize that he has used the girl to seduce Euphiletus's wife. Some enthymizing is perceptual; no direct communication is needed.

2. Enthymizing can be aided with indirect statements in a narrative from one character to another or from the narrator or a character to her- or himself or to the audience. A detail mentioned by the narrator or observed by a character in the narrative can trigger a moment of realization in a character and, ultimately, in the audience. As Euphiletus recounts how the serving girl admitted to assisting his wife, the audience is invited to enthymize (fill in) a different but confirming detail: she was teasing the baby to make him cry. Similarly, as Euphiletus talks about his confidence in his wife, his helpful domestic rearrangements, and his lack of suspicion over her use of

makeup, he inadvertently triggers in the audience the opposite view: they realize that his wife is cheating on him. His statements of trust and domestic tranquility inadvertently lead the audience to enthymize the opposite.

3. Enthymizing can also be triggered directly by statements made for that reason. This is the case when the old woman accosts Euphiletus, and it is the case when Euphiletus explicitly tells the audience to enthymize the dinner with Sostratus and explains its meaning via a rhetorical question that compares the prosecutor's accusation with the implications of Euphiletus's own actions.

From the perspective of the audience, these examples of enthymizing are arranged from the most indirect to the most direct and explicit, as though Lysias were charting varieties of its use. Early in the speech, the audience is left to puzzle out Euphiletus's plight and to recall the slave girl's role in the affair on their own. Then they "overhear" the old woman reveal to Euphiletus the truth of his situation. Finally, Euphiletus tells them explicitly how to enthymize the dinner with Sostratus.

By arranging the variations on this technique in an increasingly explicit order and by repeating the verb that describes its effect, Lysias encourages attentive readers to focus their attention on the term and to recognize the significance of this technique and its role in the speech. His attention to both the term and the technique seems clearly designed to highlight its value as a principle of rhetorical skill that can be taught. That is, Lysias's careful arrangement of the uses of this term encourages readers to recognize and appreciate the meaning of—to enthymize—the importance of enthymizing. This view will gain support when we examine the place of enthymizing in the narrative and speech as a whole.

4. As with the examples in chapter 6, enthymizing derives much of its meaning and effectiveness from the context in which it is set. The context will involve a consequential situation that is misleading, ambiguous, or confusing—that is, one whose proper interpretation matters and is open to question. Future decisions or actions and outcomes will depend on how the situation is understood. Situations that are inconsequential or that are easily and clearly understood and are just what they seem to be will be less open to enthymizing.[18] Enthymizing is especially valuable in adversarial narratives because these accounts' interpretations are contested, inherently ambiguous, and highly consequential. Both sides have a stake in how the events and motives are understood.

Within this framework, Lysias selects details whose significance becomes clear only after the narrative context and its ambiguous or contested elements have been spelled out. The less significant the enthymized detail seems to be on its own (the baby was crying, Euphiletus had Sostratus for dinner) and the more it recedes into the background of its narrative context, the more powerful it will prove once the detail's significance is shown to be relevant to the issue. A trivial detail conveys the "reality effect" described by Barthes (1989, 141–48); its veracity is enhanced by seeming to have no dramatic role to play in the unfolding plot.[19] This truth effect affords the detail a high level of veracity so that it can later support a new realization that will resolve the central question posed by the plot. A small detail will also escape the detection of the opposing speaker, who will not bother to challenge or refute it, thus allowing it to remain unrefuted and apparently (not logically but psychologically and rhetorically) irrefutable.

We can note the work Lysias does to set up important moments of contradictory, heuristic enthymizing through the temporal structuring and pacing of the narrative and argument and the placement of its details. Lysias plants small details in the narrative (the teased baby, the dinner with Sostratus) and allows them to fade into the background. The unremarkable and apparently irrelevant detail can then be recalled and enthymized later to support a larger shift in perspective.

RING STRUCTURE AND THE CENTRALITY OF ENTHYMIZING

It isn't simply the ordered repetition of the term *enthymizing* but its place in the whole speech that enable Lysias to make enthymizing central to the rhetorical effectiveness of the case. I have noted that Euphiletus's encounter with the old "busybody" and subsequent moment of enthymizing occurs at 1.16–17. This is roughly the midpoint of the narrative (§§6–26). At this point, "a brusque change of tone sets in" (Herman 1993, 409). The entire course of action reverses itself, and the character of Euphiletus changes abruptly from passive householder to vigilant citizen.

Prior to 1.17, Euphiletus's narrative focuses primarily on his home, his confidence in his wife, and her duplicity. This section ends with his wife unlocking the women's room, where Euphiletus had been held during the evening of her tryst. He remains passive and deceived, thinks and says nothing, spends his time indoors, and has no contact with friends. After 17, having enthymized what has happened, he springs into action, travels outdoors, relies on his friends for help and helps them in turn, gets the truth from his serving girl and relies on her help to catch the lovers in the act, hears Eratosthenes's confession, and in his view, exacts the legal punishment.

Herman (1993) has argued that the abrupt change in tone and cultural framework occurring at 1.17 marks a shift from a tribal norm of private vengeance through self-help to a civic ethic of codified law and publicly enacted justice. I won't dispute this argument and will have more to say about the legal language of the speech in what follows. But I will note that this shift in tone and direction occurs at the center of the narrative action and is catalyzed by Euphiletus's enthymizing. More, the narrative as a whole follows a chiastic structure that turns upon this sudden moment of recognition. Like most symmetrical or "ring" narratives structured chiastically, this one places its most important "thematic" moment in the middle, enacting one—and the most important—of the three "basic principles" of ring composition: the loading of the primary meaning into the center of the text (Douglas 2007, 7). So not only does Euphiletus's enthymizing mark the center of the story; it acts as the hinge upon which the entire narrative turns and conveys its principle message (see table 1).[20]

Prior to 1.17, Euphiletus has "no suspicions" (13); after, he is "full of suspicion" (17). When the old woman approaches Euphiletus to inform him about the affair (16), she instructs him to threaten the slave girl with torture and predicts what he will learn: Eratosthenes has been sleeping with his wife. Immediately after 17, Euphiletus takes the slave girl to a friend's house and threatens her with torture, and once he names Eratosthenes, she confesses that Eratosthenes has been sleeping with Euphiletus's wife (18–19). Prior to the old woman's revelation, there is an interval of "some time" (15). After the confession of the slave girl, there is an interval of four or five days (22). Prior to the first interval, Euphiletus returns from the country, goes to bed, and finds himself locked in the woman's quarters to "keep him from having a go at the slave girl." His wife has sex with Eratosthenes and then lets him out under the pretense of having to relight the baby's lamp at the neighbor's house. After the latter interval, Sostratus returns from the country and Euphiletus goes to bed, and when Euphiletus is informed about Eratosthenes's presence, Euphiletus instructs the slave girl to leave the doors unlocked and gathers torches from his neighbors. The story begins with a scene of domestic trust and tranquility and ends with a scene of wrongdoing punished and order restored.

Though the opening order of events does not precisely mirror the final half of the narrative, each feature of the story's unfolding finds its counterpart in the resolution.[21]

TABLE 1: Chiastic structure of the Lysias 1 narrative

    A. (§11–14) Euphiletus returns from the country, and that evening,
        1. the wife locks Euphiletus in, away from slave girl;
        2. she slips out, creaking the door;
        3. and she "lights the lamp at neighbor's."
        B. (§13) No suspicions
            C. (§14) Wife had put on makeup
                D. (§15) Interval of some time
                      E. (§16) Old woman: threaten your slave girl with torture and you will discover everything
                          F. (§17) Everything came back into my mind
                              G. (§17) I enthymized how I had been locked in my house, the door had creaked, and my wife had put on makeup
                          F. (§17) All these things flashed into my mind
                      E. (§18–20) Slave girl threatened with torture gives a full account of everything
                D. (§22) Interval of four or five days
            C. (§17) Euphiletus recalls makeup
        B. (§17) Full of suspicion
    A. (§22–23) Sostratus returns from the country, and that evening,
        1. Euphiletus instructs slave girl to leave doors unlocked,
        2. he slips out silently,
        3. and he gathers torches from neighbors.

Euphiletus's unexpected return from the country matches Sostratus's return from the country, the wife's pretended need to light the lamp at the neighbor is answered by Euphiletus gathering torches at the neighbor's, and Euphiletus being locked in the bedroom is reversed when Euphiletus orders the slave girl to keep the doors unlocked and ready for his return. The funeral for Euphiletus's mother early in the speech corresponds to his wife attending the Thesmophoria with Eratosthenes's mother later on. The ring structure thus not only heightens the role of enthymizing; it also explains much of the repetition in the speech (Todd 2007, 52).

Euphiletus's failure to grasp the meaning of his wife's actions early in the narrative will mirror his sudden recollection and understanding of those details after his encounter with the old woman. In the same way, the audience's failure to enthymize the meaning of Euphiletus's dinner with Sostratus early in the narrative is resolved with their sudden recollection and understanding of that detail after Euphiletus enthymizes it for them.

In the first half of the speech, Eratosthenes must be shown the truth that the audience sees well: Euphiletus is being cuckolded. In the second half of the speech, the audience must be shown the truth that Euphiletus sees well: Euphiletus was not planning murder. Thus in the second half of the speech, Euphiletus takes over the role of the meddlesome old woman, searching out and explaining the meaning of prior events, and the audience takes over the role of Euphiletus: they experience the same kind of sudden realization he had experienced earlier. Because the busybody has helped Euphiletus enthymize earlier, he is equipped to help his audience enthymize later. It isn't just that Lysias includes enthymizing in his speech; he makes the speech turn on enthymizing. He wants us to attend to it and take to heart its importance.

CHAPTER 9

A Many-Layered Tale

The arrangement or placement and ordering of our term in Lysias 1 seems deliberate, aimed at highlighting the variety of applications of the technique and tying each to the term accompanying it. Lysias also crafts his speech so that it works at several different levels and in several different ways. Each new reading and each new layer of meaning magnifies the central role played by enthymizing not only in legal speeches but in domestic life, civic participation, and rhetorical training. In what follows, I'd like to suggest alternative readings of Lysias 1, each of which expands the role of enthymizing in Athenian social life.

PARTS 1 AND 2: COURT SPEECH AS DOMESTIC
COMEDY AND DISPLAY PIECE

Lysias 1 has recently become "one of the most widely read of the orators works" (Porter 2007, 60) and one that "perhaps more than any other speech... provides important information on a range of topics in Athenian social history" (Todd 2007, 54). This is in part because of the historical light the speech seems to shed on (for example) the Athenian household, the status of Athenian women and wives, adultery, domestic life, the treatment of slaves, and nursing and childrearing—all topics of importance in contemporary scholarship.[1] It has long been taken for granted that this speech is historically significant because it conveys reliable information about Athenian culture and domestic life. This assumption relies on the notion that it is meant to be taken seriously as a homicide speech that was perhaps adapted for print but originally delivered in court.

But a speech that is so apparently artless, so colloquial in style and wandering in its narrative, portraying a naive fool who simply tells the truth, yet so balanced in structure, so selective in focus and careful in timing, so deliberate in its shifts in characterization, and so striking in effect—all of this suggests that this apparently straightforward tale owes at least as much to the rhetorical abilities of the author as it does to the course of events it describes. If the speech has been understood quite simply to recount historical and social facts, it is only achieving the effect for which it was designed. But it may be a less straightforward source for Athenian law and history and a more interesting example of rhetorical ability than it appears.

For example, many of its elements bear a striking similarity to standard features of the comic adultery scenario familiar to later Greek and Roman mimes, comedies, and novels: the irresistible young seducer; the fortuitous meeting at a public rite or festival; the slave who functions as intermediary for the lovers; the elderly bawd; the rejected former mistress; the brazen, ingenious wife; the gender role reversal; and of course, the absent, benighted, bumbling cuckold (Trenker 1958, 80–84; Porter 2007, 61). This could be the artistic shaping of a true event to follow a common storyform: there is no reason to think that Athenian husbands wouldn't seek revenge on an adulterer in his house or that such an event did not populate the Athenian imagination. Trenker attributes the similarities between Lysias's characters and plot and those of the comic cuckold tale to his selection and shaping of details. He "chose from among the details provided by his client those that fitted the type best; probably he omitted certain more peculiar traits, and here and there he added a small conventional detail to round out the whole picture" (1958, 159–60).

But as Porter notes, this view "takes little account of the deeper structure of Euphiletus' tale" and all the ways in which this narrative develops according to the ironic, gender-reversing conventions of the adultery tale. The trusting husband believes his wife to be the most chaste of any in the city and takes on the role of the woman locked in her room. The wife finds an excuse to go outside at night and meets her lover in the "men's quarters" while the husband is confined upstairs. The husband has business away and returns suddenly to find the couple together (2007, 65–72). These are all staple features of the comic genre.

And, says Porter, Trenker's suggestion doesn't account for all the ways in which the speech departs from the genre of the homicide defense speech

(2007, 74–82). Not only is it half the length of other homicide speeches, but it lacks the topoi most common to a homicide case: Euphiletus doesn't mention his inexperience at speaking in court or the risks he faces in this trial, he doesn't recount the liturgies donated or any other services he has performed for the city or the wickedness of his opponent, he mentions but doesn't elaborate on the absence of any prior enmity between the two. He calls few witnesses and has no depositions read—from neither Sostratus, nor the old women, nor the friend who witnessed the interrogation of the serving girl, nor the serving girl herself. In short, the speech omits any argument that does not advance the adultery plot and makes use of any detail that does.

What's more, the names of the litigants align suspiciously with the character types they display. Eratosthenes, the cunning serial adulterer, is "strong" or "powerful" (*sthenēs*) in love (*eratos*), an irresistible charmer. Euphiletus, the thoughtful husband who relies on his friends for help, is literally "beloved," or "well loved." Sostratus is the fellow (*sō-*) soldier or campaigner (*stratos*), a comrade or mate of Euphiletus. Read in the light of the other notable features of the speech, the names suggest that we are dealing here not with historical individuals but with character types.

This constellation of elements leads Porter (2007) to suggest that Lysias 1 is not a homicide defense speech at all but a fiction borrowed from familiar satire and composed as a demonstration piece to entertain, to display, and to teach Lysias's rhetorical skills.[2] Porter notes the care with which Lysias handles a number of techniques, including the slowly building comic narrative (*diegesis*), the recognizable characters (*ēthopoiia*), and the deft amplification and diminution of pathos. We should also note the clear and well-defined parts of the speech (introduction, narration, argument and counterargument, conclusion) and the clean Attic style for which Lysias is famous. And to that list we can now add his facility with ring structure and his central attention to enthymizing. We need not accept Porter's dichotomy: the speech may have indeed been inspired by or adapted from an adultery case to maximize its literary and comic effect and highlight its rhetorical appeal as a teaching and display piece.[3]

If Porter is right and this is a display piece for study, then enthymizing would be for Lysias central not simply to Euphiletus's murder defense; it would become central to the whole range of rhetorical skills that Lysias crafted this speech to demonstrate and display. In this speech at least, the ability to enthymize—to find or "invent" and incorporate the details that will allow the listener (or reader) to appropriately size up a situation—would literally be the central rhetorical skill for both the audience and the speaker. It is the technique upon which the whole speech turns.

And why shouldn't we have from Lysias at least one display piece that highlights the rhetorical techniques that he excelled at and found important? He was, according to Dionysius, the premier logographer of his day, "[eclipsing] the fame of his predecessors and of contemporary orators" (Usher 1974, 22–23). Those predecessors and contemporaries would include the likes of Antiphon, Antisthenes, Gorgias, Protagoras, and Plato. All of them wrote speeches based on familiar myths, and all of them used narrative to display their skills and to interpose implicit arguments about the nature and power of an art of words and its importance in the life of the polis.[4] It would be surprising if Lysias's successful career did not result in at least one attempt at a similarly rhetorical display piece, albeit one drawn not from epic but from domestic comedy. It is also worth noting that Lysias was earlier in his career a teacher of rhetoric.[5] Even if he later abandoned that activity, his experience as a teacher would encourage him to develop and showcase that "rhetorical consciousness" that Kennedy says characterizes the rise of theory (1963, 30–35).

PART 3: LYSIAS 1 AS POLITICAL PARABLE

But the speech may also have a third layer of significance: Though the name is uncommon in late fifth-century Athens, Eratosthenes *was* a historical figure known to Lysias—and not as an adulterer. Eratosthenes was a member of the Thirty, the band of pro-Spartan oligarchs (or tyrants) installed at Athens at the end of the Peloponnesian War. The Thirty abolished the democracy and killed or exiled many citizens and resident aliens (metics), including most of the wealthy and notable democrats in the city. They seized the property of these men and others and abrogated the citizenship rights of the majority, drastically restricting the right to jury trials and in other ways revising or nullifying democratically established laws. In fact, Eratosthenes was named in another Lysian speech as the conspirator who killed Lysias's brother, Polemarchus. Lysias 12, *Against Eratosthenes*, recounts this killing and other actions of the Thirty. According to this account, the Thirty were determined to arrest and execute a number of wealthy metics as a pretext for seizing their assets to fund their oppressive rule. Lysias reports his own arrest as a metic by Peison (another member of the Thirty) and his subsequent escape as well as the arrest of his own brother, Polemarchus, by none other than Eratosthenes. Polemarchus was ordered to drink hemlock and died. After the restoration of the democracy, Lysias prosecuted Eratosthenes for the death of Polemarchus in, apparently, the only speech delivered by Lysias himself.

A number of scholars have argued about whether this Eratosthenes might be the same as or a relative of the Eratosthenes of Lysias 1 (since names were often reused within families by nephews or grandsons). The rarity of the name suggests that they might at least be members of the same family, and this episode with the Thirty would seem to provide Lysias with a motive for assisting a defendant who wanted to prosecute Eratosthenes but who otherwise may have been unable to afford Lysias's expertise (see Avery 1991; Kapparis 1993).

Porter's (2007) reading would temper the question of the "real" relationship between these two by making Lysias 1 a fictional case that was never really tried, and thus its Eratosthenes is a fictional character, a type, given a name appropriate to the seducer role he plays in the story.[6] But there is a third possibility and a third layer of meaning that we might see in this simple narrative. In addition to its being a compelling homicide case and an entertaining adaptation of a traditional adultery tale, Perotti (1989/90) suggests that this story may also reflect the political threat posed to a democracy by oligarchs and tyrants, an especially relevant theme during and after the reign of the Thirty Tyrants and the restoration of democracy.

That is, the story could function as a political parable about the dangers of cunning sycophants and incipient tyrants who would subvert the legitimate constitution of the city for their own pleasure and gain.[7] In this reading, the name Eratosthenes might well be used for its political overtones—as a thinly veiled reference to the hated antidemocratic oligarch. This story tells of a woman (the Athenian polis) who is loyal to her husband (the democratic constitution, or *politeia*) but is corrupted by a usurper (Eratosthenes the seducer qua oligarch or tyrant) who attempts to win over the polis as its leader and guardian, replacing the legal constitution with his own personal rule. Through the political echoes of the name, the danger posed to a household by a cunning adulterer bent on seducing a wife would also call to mind the threat posed by oligarchic elites bent on overthrowing the democracy and gaining control of the city.

One could go further with the comparison. The seductive techne of Eratosthenes the adulterer would refer to the cunning rhetoric of Eratosthenes the oligarch and the rest of the Thirty, who used persuasion to secure their hold on the city (see, e.g., *Lysias* 12.65; Todd 2000, 68–76).[8] Eratothenes's prior affairs would point to other democratic cities overthrown by tyrants, such as Lysias's native Syracuse (Perotti 1989/90, 47–48). A parabolic reading would also make sense of Euphiletus's reluctance to condemn the wife, which represents the Athenian polis, as well as his repeated insistence that killing the adulterer was not only permitted but *required* by the law (*Lysias* 1.26, 29, 34–35, 50; Todd 2000, 20, 22, 24). The sentence for attempting a tyranny was death, and tyrannicides were not only exonerated in Athens but honored. Statues of Harmodius and Aristogeiton, the tyrannicides named as fathers of the democracy, graced the agora, and their descendants dined at state expense for life.[9] This reading would also explain the legal language embedded within the speech (*polypragmosunē, hubrizein, basanisēs, kategorei, ep' autophōrō*; chapter 8). In the parable, Euphiletus would embody the very laws upon which the security of the city depends, so his behavior in the second half of the narrative will naturally follow political and legal procedures and categories.[10] It is himself (the *politeia*, i.e., the laws), says Euphiletus, who must save the city from tyrants.

But one can also press the details too far; this is not an allegory, with every aspect of the narrative determined solely by a corresponding detail in the political arena. A parable will suggest an alternate reading, but it must also work as a story on its own terms; it is not bound to render within its narrative frame all the particulars specified by its referent.[11] Above all, its most important details must work together to suggest a larger theme. For our interests, the parabolic reading suggests that enthymizing the details of an unfolding scene to accurately perceive a growing danger is central not simply to Euphiletus's household management and murder trial but to the democratic city as a whole.

Interestingly, the hero in this story is not only Euphiletus but also the old woman who keeps her eyes open and speaks out. She refers to her actions in politically loaded language, the *polupragmosune*, or "busybody," typically a term of abuse to indicate someone who is politically active, "officious," "meddlesome," or "nosy." As a term of abuse, *polupragmosune* was easily applied by elites and oligarchs to their inferiors and to democrats generally who were deemed too active legally and politically (i.e., rhetorically) for their own good, with the hint that they were active to pursue not justice but their own gain as sycophants.[12] Its opposite is *apragmosune*, the "private" citizen or "quiet Athenian" who prides himself on having never darkened the doors of a courtroom (see Carter 1986).

Lysias here revalues the term, or at least (since the old woman asks *not* to be thought a busybody) he identifies an important civic function within the term's semantic range. It can now indicate a valuable and necessary quality for even the most marginal of characters—outsiders who don't belong to the "household" (the city) but who have experience with seducers (or tyrants) and who have the best interests of the household (or city) at heart. In this story, it is the outsider who is sufficiently "nosy" and sufficiently experienced with seducers to save the household from disaster at the hands of wicked citizens.[13] She recognizes what is happening, and by speaking to Euphiletus, she saves the family.

It's worth recalling that Lysias himself was an outsider, a noncitizen metic, a Syracusan by birth, and someone like the old woman whose home city had been overthrown by tyrannical seducers—men who "made a techne" of illegitimately seizing control. It would be incredible if Lysias failed to see in the character of the busybody the central importance of his own rhetorical activity, his own enthymizing of and "taking to heart" the dangers to the democracy posed by oligarchs and tyrants and proclaiming them in the courts. Lysias's argument, then, is just this: the best safeguard possessed by a democratic city against the threat of tyrants is the rule of law, which is zealously guarded by vigilant and attentive (enthymizing) inhabitants—not only citizens but especially those loyal metics who often love and watch out for their adopted *politeia* with more zeal than citizens do themselves. In short, if you love your city, thank a meddlesome metic and his or her enthymizing rhetoric.

PART 4: LYSIAS 1', *AGAINST EUPHILETUS*

Lysias 1 has long been admired and taught as an exemplary capital defense speech that demonstrates Lysias's rhetorical skill while providing important evidence for ancient Athenian domestic life. I've argued that the speech also works as a comic domestic farce and as a serious political parable and thus that Lysias 1 is a rhetorical exercise or display speech and a teaching text. It imitates a legal speech but may never have been intended to be delivered in the courts or assembly. I've already mentioned a few of the many features of this speech that would make it useful for instruction and display to advertise Lysias's skills: it is short and entertaining, it works on a variety of levels, and it clearly displays a wide range of standard rhetorical tools, including arrangement, characterization, style, and the central role of the enthymeme. But its real value as a teaching text has not yet been touched upon.

As a teaching or sample text, Lysias 1 joins a long and illustrious tradition of rhetorical exercises or set speeches. They function not only to instruct but to advertise the author's skill, build a reputation, and gain students, followers, or clients. Examples include Gorgias's *Defense of Palamedes* and *Encomium of Helen*; many of Isocrates's speeches, such as *Busiris* and *Defense of Helen*; and probably Lysias 2, a funeral oration. The genre also includes set speeches embedded within plays, dialogues, and histories, such as the funeral oration in Plato's *Menexenus* or any of the many speeches spoken by characters in Herodotus or Thucydides.

A more complex version of the genre is the pair of counterarguments, sample texts that present speeches on both sides of an issue or case. Antisthenes's trial between Odysseus and Ajax for the possession of Achilles's armor is early; better known are Antiphon's *Tetralogies* and the anonymous *Dissoi logoi*. The advantage of this framework is that students can see how litigants anticipate and respond to opposing narratives and claims. Counterarguments were a necessary feature of legal trials and other forms of debate, and they were a central aspect of sophistic thought, so their existence in teaching texts makes sense.

Lysias's *On the Death of Eratosthenes* is virtually unique in rhetorical history in that it combines the set speech and the pair of counterspeeches by including within the frame of one oration both a defense speech and clues toward an opposing prosecution speech within the same text. Lysias does not write out the homicide case brought *against* Euphiletus; he does something more useful. He embeds within Euphiletus's speech details that students could and were meant to find and draw upon to compose an answering prosecution speech that I will call Lysias 1'.[14] This is in keeping with the need for students to find enthymemes, to find contradictory enthymemes, and to find contradictory enthymemes that are irrefutable because they draw upon details admitted by the opponent. Lysias 1 defends

Euphiletus, while Lysias 1' supplies the reader with the narrative details necessary to craft a response, *Against Euphiletus*, that includes irrefutable, contradictory enthymemes. With these, they make Eratosthenes's apparently weak case much stronger.

Lysias could, and I would suggest that he did, require students to compose such a speech on the basis of his text. In the process of producing this speech, the student would have to analyze the narrative for details that would lead to inferences supporting the prosecutor's case and to generate a counternarrative and arguments from that narrative that best utilize those details. That is, the task would include the finding and crafting of enthymemes from Euphiletus's own words and actions in order to counter his argument. As I have argued earlier, this is a basic oratorical technique and a very effective strategy. It is, in fact, very close to the definition of *enthymeme* offered by the *Rhetoric to Alexander*, where the enthymeme is simply a "contrary"—"not only in word or action but in all other ways" (10.1; 526–27).

The strength of this technique is that like a great deal of inferential, heuristic, and oppositional enthymizing, the opponent cannot very easily refute a fact that he himself admits to be true in his own speech. For example, Euphiletus claims that he threatened his serving girl with torture, after which she told him the whole truth. In doing so, he echoes a standard legal procedure in Athens and thus suggests the proper legal instincts of Euphiletus. His intelligence and self-restraint achieve only what the law itself requires. I'll suggest below a different way to read this detail as evidence that would support the prosecutor's case.

I won't here produce a version of the full speech that Lysias 1 makes possible. Instead, I'll compile a few of the arguments that I believe a student cum opponent could include in a counterspeech against Euphiletus, composed only from the facts included or implied in the text of Lysias 1.

1. Euphiletus says that he would like you to judge him just as you would judge yourselves if you had suffered what he had and to hold the same opinion about others as you do about yourselves. But he does things that none of you have ever done or dreamed of doing, and he takes actions that no one has ever heard of. He moves his wife downstairs to the men's quarters, where she could come and go as she liked and where she could let people in and out without his knowledge, and he not only moved the men's room upstairs but allowed himself to be locked in to this room so that he could

not keep track of anything going on in the house at all. What would we say about such a person? Is this what we would call giving our wives the "proper amount of attention" in order to keep the household secure?

2. Euphiletus says that he gave his wife the proper amount of attention, but even after the old woman warned him about Eratosthenes, and even after his slave confirmed these accusations under threat of torture—and, as he says, he believed her to be telling the truth—notice (enthymize) that he still neglected to move his wife back upstairs or in any way protect his family. He continued to sleep upstairs himself and continued to allow his wife to live downstairs to care for the baby. What could be more incredible than that?

3. Euphiletus contradicts himself when he says he was watching out for the welfare of his wife by moving the women's quarters downstairs so that she would not have to go down to wash the baby.[15] Remember (enthymize) he later said that she was often with him upstairs at night and would have to go downstairs to tend to the baby. Is it credible that he would protect his wife from having to go downstairs to tend to the baby in a way that requires her to go downstairs to tend to the baby at night? Which of us could possibly believe that? Did he really turn his house upside down to protect his wife from acts that she was then required to undertake precisely because he turned his house upside down, or did he make his wife available to strangers for some other reason? Is it the act of an innocent or sensible man to protect his wife in this way by exposing her to the same dangers—and to even much greater dangers than these?

4. Euphiletus relies on the law that says, "If someone kills a man caught on top of his wife or concubine or sister or daughter, he shall not be exiled as a killer on account of this." If he had wanted to, the lawmaker could have simply said, "If someone kills someone who has slept with his wife, he shall not be exiled as a killer," but he did not do this. He specified that the adulterer should be "caught on top of." The lawgiver wisely stated this to indicate a lack of any prior awareness on the part of the husband. Surely my opponent knew what we all recognize: the lawmaker intended not to enable murder or protect killers but to prevent adultery in the first place. The law was written to protect families, not to encourage a man to allow another to sleep with his wife or to give protection to a man who, having knowledge of such an act in his house, nevertheless allows it to happen so that he could extort money from the adulterer or kill an enemy. None of you, I am sure, would imagine that the lawmaker meant for such a one to receive the protection of the laws. No, by giving it the ultimate penalty,

the lawmaker meant to prevent adultery, to punish the seducer, and to protect the one who, because he discovers the pair only in the act, has no way to prevent it. But remember (enthymize), gentlemen of the jury, that Euphiletus here was informed of the affair not once but three times before he finally acted.

He was told first by the old woman, who seemed to have good knowledge of the affair. Perhaps someone might be suspicious about such an accusation, although many of you, I am sure, would not hesitate to take care to secure your household even on the accusation of one such informant, since such a thing is easily done and prudent. Who knows? Perhaps at that point, the affair had only reached the stage of notes and plans and had not yet even been consummated. Even if you were foolish enough to allow your wife to sleep downstairs, after receiving such a warning, I'm sure all of you would quickly move her back upstairs, and you would ensure that your servants were well aware of the danger posed by such an evil man, instructing them to watch out for him and to inform you of any suspicious activity. A man intent on protecting his wife might confront the accused adulterer and warn him to stay away.

But after this man was approached by the servant of a former lover, he left his housing arrangement intact. He says that he questioned his own slave girl, threatened her with torture, and conveyed to her that he knew about the affair in order to compel her to tell the truth, and she, in his own words, told him everything truthfully. Yet incredibly, he still did not act but allowed the affair to continue and kept things in his house arranged just as they had been. By the gods, what man in such a situation would behave in this way? He did not confront his wife, warning her that he knew about Eratosthenes's designs so that she might come to her senses, nor did he confront Eratosthenes. He did not alert his servant to keep the door locked in his absence to prevent any men under any circumstances from entering the house. He did not restore the proper living arrangements in his house so that at least his wife would be less accessible to strangers. Who knows but that Euphiletus told his serving girl to let it be known that his wife was on the ground floor and himself locked upstairs, letting rumor do its work, to attract men whom he might profit from or act against as he wished? I won't demean this trial by suggesting to you what we call a house where women are made available in this way, as you all already know what it is called.

If your friend—after being informed of his wife's infidelity by an old woman and a serving girl who confessed—told you a similar tale of misfortune and asked you for advice, who among you would counsel him to say nothing, do nothing, keep his wife on the ground floor, and go about his business as though nothing had happened, as my opponent here has done? Who among you would not believe that anyone who took such action was less interested in protecting his wife and his household from intruders than he was in catching someone from whom he could easily profit if such a one were wealthy or, if he were not or if he were an enemy, could be killed with impunity? He says that Eratosthenes made a hobby of his adultery, but isn't it more likely that Euphiletus made a habit of keeping his wife downstairs and available to neighbors while he slept soundly, as he says, locked in his room upstairs?

And keep this in mind (enthymize) as well, gentlemen, that when the slave girl informed this man that the intruder was in the house, he didn't rush to the bedroom to catch and confront the man who had wronged and humiliated him, or shout for help, or summarily arrest him for adultery and for hubris, hoping perhaps to interrupt him before anything happened. Instead, this man admits that he actually ran out of the house and away, as he says, to gather his friends and some torches. He didn't even know who might be at home or how long it might take to secure even a few helpers and witnesses. Consider carefully (enthymize), men of Athens: Is this the action of a man who wants to keep an adulterer away from his wife and so protect the integrity of his household as the lawmaker intended and as all of us would do, or are these the actions of a man who wants to catch someone and with the help of his friends overpower him and extort money from him, if possible, or if not, safely exact his revenge?

5. Remember (enthymize), gentlemen of the jury, that you are to judge based on the truth when the truth is available and on probability when it is not. You have seen that probability favors the prosecution. His story of trying to keep his wife safe by moving her downstairs and then keeping her there and staying silent to wait for proof is plainly incredible. But the truth is also on our side, for there was a witness to all these events: the slave girl, who was involved in the affair from the very beginning and who knew all the details. Even our opponent has admitted that she told the truth under the threat of torture. Keep in mind that Euphiletus threatened to torture his slave girl to extract the truth from her and that she did indeed tell the truth. It is for this reason that the procedure exists. If he had been willing to do such a thing simply to confirm what he already knew about the affair, and since she truthfully revealed to him everything she knew about it and held nothing back, he should have been willing to threaten her with torture in

our presence in response to our questions in order to discover the truth concerning something as important as a capital trial like this one if it could save his life. But when we challenged him legally to question the slave under torture, he refused and says nothing about it now.

Just think, gentlemen, if Euphiletus had offered to have the slave girl tortured in our presence, which he was earlier willing to do on his own, and if we had refused the challenge, he would certainly have emphasized this in his speech as evidence that we are lying. But since he refused to allow the challenge that we requested and that he himself threatened his slave with, this should count as the strongest proof that he is not telling you the truth.

Other features of the speech would obviously be necessary, including an introduction that attempted to allay the audience's hostility against adulterers, a brief narrative that emphasized the long-term value to Euphiletus of rearranging his house and the obvious convenience of such an arrangement for houses of prostitution and for entrapment, and an emotional conclusion against those who manipulate the laws for their own gain. An inventive and aggressive line of argument could draw out in detail what was only hinted at here: through this permanent housing arrangement, Euphiletus made his wife (or a concubine posing as his wife) available on the first floor as bait, either for a flat fee or for future blackmail. Once a man was lured in and caught in apparent adultery, the woman could be revealed to be a citizen and wife, and the unwitting victim could be threatened with serious criminal charges and extorted for money or dealt with as Euphiletus saw fit. That Euphiletus had to gather friends to slay a difficult "customer," one who was threatening to prosecute Euphiletus or advertise his scam, would not be surprising or at odds with the other facts of the case.

In fact, this is exactly the situation that we face in the conflict between Epaenetus and Stephanus in the speech *Against Neaera* (*Demosthenes* 59; Bers 2003, 151–94): Stephanus invited Epaenetus to his house under the pretense of offering a sacrifice but absented himself when Epaenetus arrived, while his daughter, Phano, was at home and available. Arriving home, Stephanus surprised Epaenetus in bed with Phano, threatened him with criminal charges, and demanded from him thirty minae (59.65; 174). Unfortunately for Stephanus, Epaenetus filed a suit alleging that the woman was not Stephanus's daughter at all but a prostitute and the daughter of the infamous courtesan Neaera. He admitted having intercourse with her but denied that it was adultery.[16] To support his claim, he cited a law that stated that someone cannot be taken as an adulterer who has slept with a woman lodged professionally within a brothel or who openly offered herself for hire. This, said Epaenetus, describes Phano and Stephanus's house exactly: it is not a home but a brothel. Phano was used to corrupt and defraud unwitting men who were receptive to her advances, and she posed as a citizen only to extract money or concessions from the victims (59.66–69; 174–75).

Interestingly, Lysias was himself an acquaintance of Neaera (*Demosthenes* 59.21–22; Bers 2003, 160–61). He was a patron of an elite brothel where she used to work, and he brought her; a coworker, Metaneira; and the madam, Nicarete, to visit Athens. Since Lysias was married, he put them all up at the house of his friend Philostratus. Nicarete, we are told, made a techne of sizing up girls for the trade and then teaching it to them (59.18; 159–60). Lysias promised to get them all initiated into the mystery cult at Eleusis. This is not to say that Lysias borrowed the scenario for Lysias 1 from Epaenetus's quarrel with Stephanus or his arrangement with Philostratus, but the kind of situation laid out by Epaenetus in *Against Neaera* does suggest the possibility of reading Lysias 1 in an analogous way. Whether the allegations of Epaenetus are true or not, it seems that trapping men in sexual dalliances for the purpose of blackmail or extortion was an available literary trope and legal accusation in ancient Athens. It would not be surprising if Lysias, understanding the place this kind of plot held in the cultural imagination, wrote his speech with an eye toward the availability of just this kind of stock counternarrative. The task for the student would be to find and shape this opposing plot by selecting and framing those details available in Lysias 1 that are most favorable to making that case. A teacher could also expose students to a case similar to *Against Neaera* before requiring them to respond to *On the Death of Eratosthenes* so that they were familiar with the kind of arguments that could be used in *Against Euphiletus*.

If we read the text with an eye toward crafting such an opposing speech, it becomes noticeable not only how many details avail themselves of alternative interpretation but also how well they congeal to form an alternative story of seduction and entrapment for blackmail or extortion. And this alternate reading derives completely from the very details of Lysias's narrative that evoked so successfully a set of cultural and political myths and reading conventions predisposed to generate animosity against Eratosthenes the tyrant-seducer and pity and admiration for the heroic democrat Euphiletus.

So the familiar narrative plots that reinforce each other—the domestic comedy of a cuckolded husband who gets his revenge and the political parable of a vigilant democrat who thwarts the hated tyrant—and that together make it difficult for listeners not to identify with Euphiletus and hate Eratosthenes are built from the very details capable of evoking a familiar and credible counternarrative. Lysias presents a plot that has been weighted against the prosecution by overlapping cultural stock narratives and the values and emotions that these narratives evoke, and he asks his students to use this speech to build an opposing but equally familiar counternarrative that creates sympathy for Eratosthenes and outrage against Euphiletus and a desire to punish him. In other words, he asks them to make the weaker case the stronger. This is stock sophistic practice: first stack the deck in one direction and then demonstrate—and teach your students—how to overcome it.

This example of Lysias 1', then, is another kind of reading—across or against the grain, as it were—of a story that contains within itself the seeds of its own undoing. These seeds are never planted or allowed to grow, but they are strewn plainly and clearly enough in the path of students that they could easily be gathered, lined up, and cultivated. The student would have to find the appropriate details, arrange them in a fleshed-out counternarrative, and then enthymize them for maximum effect, engaging the student in a wide range of standard rhetorical tropes and techniques, including several of the topics noted by Aristotle and several of the themes that would become standard lines of argument for many speeches.[17] In this way, Lysias could produce a strong speech for his students to learn and imitate and at the same time offer them an opportunity to produce another speech that was stronger than his.

We may not be justified in saying that in *On the Murder of Eratosthenes*, Lysias invents the enthymeme—much less that he anticipates or employs the enthymeme of later theory. He never uses the noun and betrays no interest in Aristotle's logical structure. But Lysias 1 does demonstrate interest in naming and exploring what we are calling enthymizing as a central element of rhetorical skill. Through his attention to enthymizing, he displays and calls attention to a textual, inferential, narrative, and psychological process that will later be nominalized as the enthymeme.

We might not even be justified in classifying Lysias as an important figure in the development of rhetorical theory, but the rhetorical enthymizing that he demonstrates, argues for, and teaches in Lysias 1 is a legitimate form of rhetorical knowledge—a kind of knowledge central to ancient legal rhetoric and one that establishes a regular and teachable practice and that makes later theorizing possible.

And so Lysias is a useful example of how practitioners advanced rhetorical knowledge and how knowledge that was largely tacit, embodied, and performance based could come to be regularized, highlighted, and conceptualized as an isolable technique. And it suggests how a regular practice could later be explicitly articulated and transformed into a concept of theory situated not in legal and pedagogical speeches but in a larger theoretical system made up of related concepts and terms.

In his attention to enthymizing, Lysias moves beyond simply engaging in rhetorical practice as a means to an end. He begins to explore rhetorical practice itself, the knowledge that it engages, and the value of this knowledge to rhetoric, to legal trials, to entertainment, and to the life of the polis. Lysias identifies a technique, demonstrates its centrality to rhetorical skill and to oratory, displays the variety of its forms, and gives it a name, enthymizing—a term that may inform the decision of early theorists, including Aristotle, to select this term to name an important rhetorical technique.

Conclusion

I began this project with a sense of dissatisfaction. In undergraduate and graduate courses in composition and rhetoric, I was taught and then taught others the standard view of logos: that it was inductive and deductive, that induction was example and deduction was enthymeme, and that enthymeme was a syllogism with a missing premise. I dutifully learned these terms, internalized them, filed them away in my mental catalog of rhetorical concepts, and then ignored them. Outside of teaching, not only did I not refer to them or find them either necessary or useful for rhetorical criticism or theorizing, but it did not even strike me as odd that the theoretical framework declared by Aristotle to be the "body" of persuasion seemed to be so peripheral and unimportant.

I spent no time in my own work or with students analyzing or demonstrating the persuasive power of enthymemes in rhetorical texts—in part, perhaps, because I considered them so uninteresting and unpersuasive and in part because I had no experiential familiarity with this technique: no text I wrote, read, or analyzed ever generated the feeling of processing syllogisms, of taking out a premise or piece of argument, or of adding one back in. While other aspects of rhetorical theory—such as ethos, genre, persona, and metaphor—helped my students and me talk about rhetorical interactions in interesting and productive ways, my understanding of logos and/as the enthymeme did not. I taught it but I didn't use it and I didn't miss it.

In fact, it was the process of having to add pieces to an argument that led to me becoming aware of my dissatisfaction with the traditional enthymeme. Sitting at a conference where Judith Butler was the keynote speaker, I remember struggling to connect the links between one part of her argument and the next, as though I were missing some pieces of background knowledge that I needed to link her statements. I recall frantically attempting to "fill in" these "gaps" in her argument so that I could keep up with the talk (though I felt them to be gaps in my knowledge, the result of a lack of theoretical fluency, not gaps in Butler's talk). It was a difficult and tiring experience. Later I wondered whether and how, even for arguments that were rather simpler and better adapted to an audience (arguments in which listeners would know which premises to "fill in"), listeners could mentally fill in gaps in an argument while they were listening to it and whether this could really make the argument more persuasive. I had no recollection of any such experience listening to any rhetorical speech.

I assumed that given the generations of theoretical elaboration and scholarly agreement that enthymemes were arguments with gaps, something like this must happen even if I had no familiarity with it and, in fact, had experienced the opposite. What else to do but trust the authority of Aristotle and the history of Aristotelian criticism? I continued to teach and talk about logos in the same way. But at least now I was aware that an apparently central piece of the traditional model of rhetorical argument did not fit my experience and was not relevant to my work as a scholar of rhetoric. It sat there, like a splinter, for years.

Then while working to better understand arguments from "likelihood" (*eikos*) in Greek oratory, I began rereading Antiphon, Lysias, Isaeus, and the other orators more systematically. I was looking for arguments that relied on this concept. But because I was at the same time teaching a class on legal argumentation and reading scholarship on legal rhetoric, I noticed three things that did not initially seem related. First, I was struck by the degree to which the orators were telling legal stories. Over the past forty years, legal scholarship has increasingly turned its attention to subfields dealing with narrative—subfields with titles like law and literature, legal sociology, law and narrative, and legal storytelling. In this work, I saw the observation being made over and over again that the law operates through narrative, that legal participants tell stories, and that narrative reasoning is essential to legal argument. I realized that this insight applied to ancient Greek rhetoric as well. In fact, it seemed to me that early rhetoric was even more dependent on narrative reasoning than was contemporary legal argument, as it had fewer procedural constraints on how narratives could be used. Several early and influential texts—Bennett and Feldman's *Reconstructing Reality in the Courtroom* (first published in 1981), Cover's

"Nomos and Narrative" (1983), and James Boyd White's *Heracles' Bow* (1985), among others—were central in what now looks like a paradigm shift in legal studies.

Bennet and Feldman's work in particular is perhaps one of the best introductions to ancient rhetorical artistry currently available and certainly a useful counterpoint to Aristotle. Because of these works and the growing wave of legal scholarship that followed, I began looking at the rhetoric of ancient oratory (especially legal oratory) from the perspective of popular adversarial storytelling and its requirements. How much of ancient rhetorical skill was oriented around learning to tell a moving, coherent, complete, and concise story, a story that answered the law, the evidence, and probability? I came to accept the argument among legal and narrative studies scholars that legal argument depended upon (or, in its strongest expression, was coextensive with) narrative reasoning, and I began to think about what this meant for rhetorical history, theory, and criticism.

The second thing I noticed came from work on nonverbal reasoning: Langer on visual symbols (1948), Eleanor Rosch on categorization and prototypes (1978), Lakoff and Johnson on conceptual metaphors (1980), and Johnson-Laird on spatial reasoning and mental models (2006), among others. This work suggested that human reasoning was based less on formal manipulation of propositions than on experience with social worlds, less on abstractions than on familiar images and prototypes, less on explicitly framed logical steps than on mental models and analogs.

The final piece: while reading the orators, I noticed that while they almost never referred to enthymemes, they did use the verbal form *enthumaomai* regularly. What, I wondered, did this verb *enthumaomai* have to do with the enthymeme, if anything? At first, this was just a curiosity. I did not see these phenomena as related—the paradigm shift in legal studies toward narrative, the shift in cognition research away from formal logics, my frustration with rhetorical logos and enthymeme, and the curious use of the verb *enthymize* in orations. As I read and thought further about ancient legal arguments, the path of these threads began to merge. This appears to me now to have been inevitable: if the enthymeme is a unit or form of rhetorical reasoning, and if legal reasoning is based in narrative reasoning, and if reasoning generally is immersed in sensual experience, then it would not be surprising that the standard view of the enthymeme might itself be ready for rethinking.

I decided that the process of pursuing these threads should proceed independent of anything I already thought I knew about ancient rhetorical theory or the enthymeme, and I made a conscious decision not to consult works on the enthymeme, including especially Aristotle, or to connect my thinking about enthymizing to the enthymeme until I was sure I knew what I was looking at. This process was more difficult than I had anticipated. Things learned, assimilated, and taught cannot be easily unlearned. I found myself repeatedly taking for granted various features of syllogistic or deductive reasoning and various traditional features of the enthymeme in my study of enthymizing. I repeatedly assumed that it referred to a sort of logical structure or a kind of deduction, that I should be looking for premises drawn from probabilities and signs or syllogisms shortened or truncated from its "regular" form.

For example, while I began to see that enthymizing was less like deduction or induction than like what C. S. Pierce called "abduction," I was still thinking of logos only as a three-proposition logical form—though in this case, a Piercean form rather than an Aristotelian one. I continued to think about logos and the enthymeme in terms of formal structures, logical steps, propositions, and linguistic units. Only gradually was I able to think about the verb without importing assumptions based on the technical noun, to think more of "liaisons" or experiential links than logical "steps," to see the enthymeme as a narrative marker rather than a deductive unit—a move in a rhetorical contest rather than a logical structure.

But eventually, a long process of disengaging from traditional scholarship on the enthymeme and immersion in the orators and their moves culminated in a rather wholesale recalibration of my understanding of enthymizing and the enthymeme not as a kind of syllogism but as a feature of or a kind of commentary on adversarial narrative. This shift in perspective led me back into narrative theory, to see how and whether the kind of move I wanted to talk about could be explained or had already been explained from within that framework. Thinking about adversarial storytelling and narrative reasoning rather than deductions and syllogisms allowed me to replace traditional logical terms with a richer set of narrative concepts, such as satellites and kernels, nodes and diverging paths, extradiegetic levels, disnarration, and storyworlds. I consider the concept offered here—what I have provisionally called 1.0 and variously "oratorical enthymizing," the "narrative enthymeme," and the "(dis)narrated, extradiegetic nodal inference marker"—to be a tentative and exploratory contribution to a narrative approach to rhetorical logos.

This process finally led me back to Aristotle, who is universally credited with having developed the theory of the enthymeme. It seemed to me that he neither invented the technique nor accurately described its features. The essay by Trevett (1996) suggested why this might have been so: Aristotle had been looking at reputable sayings, their combination as propositions into strings, and the patterns (or topoi) into which they could be grouped. He hadn't been looking at whole speeches and the stories they told. But going back to his evolving notion of "topics" led me to think that Aristotle was less wrong than I initially supposed. First, his enthymeme was not a syllogism, so those strictures could not apply. Second, his definition of *sullogismos* in the *Rhetoric* was surprisingly broad: unlike in the *Topics* and the *Prior Analytics*, he speaks not of "premises laid down" but simply of "things that are so."

Finally, his rhetorical topics lacked the regular logical form that dialectical topics fell into. The *Rhetoric* had no comparable examination of subjects, predicates, and their relationships: accident, attribute, genus, differentia. Rhetorical topics, I discovered, were often slices of narrative. The "if... then" structure of many topics oftener than not seemed to describe a temporal and experiential—that is to say, a narrative movement rather than a strictly logical one. Or rather, it seemed impossible to separate the experiential and narrative aspects of rhetorical reasoning from the formal and logical. This led me to suspect that though Aristotle did not explicitly describe reasoning from within narrative or poetic frameworks, he left his definition of enthymeme sufficiently loose to accommodate a narrative approach to the term.

These considerations lent additional confidence to my new understanding, leading me to propose a revision of the traditional concept. And although I have some confidence in the usefulness of this approach, I consider this "narrative enthymeme" a tentative and exploratory proposal. But the concept itself is based upon a set of more solid commitments.

RHETORIC AS NARRATIVE

First is a commitment to narrative theory as a valuable resource for thinking about ancient rhetoric, including especially ancient logos and the enthymeme. I consider narrative to be the primary framework for understanding, teaching, and analyzing ancient rhetorical artistry and practice. Because his experience is so applicable to rhetorical history and theory, and because his experience so resonates with mine, I quote Rideout here at some length:

> I have long been interested in persuasion, and for many years I have included theories of persuasion in an advanced legal writing seminar that I teach. I always ask my students the same question—"what persuades in the law?" . . . When I first taught the course, I had in mind rhetoricians like Aristotle and Cicero and moving toward more contemporary rhetorical work. Very quickly, however, I had to add narrative models of persuasion, plus a second question—"what is it about narratives that makes them persuasive in the law?" This second question has increasingly consumed the majority of our class time on theories of persuasion. (2008, 55)

I have moved from seeing *diegesis* as the part that leads to the argument to seeing narrative as the framework for all ancient rhetorical artistry, including the proofs, logos, and the enthymeme. Scholars have traditionally understood narrative (*diegesis*) as distinct from rational argument (logos or *pistis*): they are two different modes of discourse and two different parts of a speech (Bruner 1991). Narratives prepare the audience for arguments. Lucaites and Condit observe that the function of rhetorical narratives is "to prepare an audience . . . for the proof of an argument" (1985, 94). A later view saw narrative not simply as preparation for argument but as an alternate kind of argument. This was the thesis of Fisher (1984): the narrative paradigm was a kind of reasoning different from the rational world paradigm.

This division appears in legal scholarship as well. Edwards (1996) distinguishes narrative persuasion in the law from legal argument (rule based, analogical, policy based, and consensual-normative reasoning). This division has softened recently, but it remains the orthodox view (see Chestek 2008, 2010). The binary is employed in scholarship on ancient rhetoric as well. Gagarin has argued that "in practice, a narrative account is not completely separate from the argument of a case, and the two are often intermingled," but "this is not to say that narrative is a form of rational argument" (2007, 17).[1] Rather, stories present the facts that can then be put into the form of arguments to construct proofs. In legal studies, narrative has often been referred to as the persuasive part of the law, useful before juries and in popular media and literature, and rational argument as the rational part, required by judges and their opinions and legal scholars and their articles and necessary for disinterested justice. A hierarchical distinction is inevitable.

But more recently, legal and other scholars have begun to question this division, suggesting not that narrative reasoning and rule-based (or deductive or analogical) reasoning are two different forms of legal rationality but rather that narrative underlies all forms of legal reasoning and argument (DeSanctis 2012). DeSanctis uses the example of the toy gun in the bank robbery. A statute provides that "whoever in committing, or attempting to commit, any offense defined in subsections (a) and (b) of this section, assaults any person, or puts in jeopardy the life of any person by the use of a dangerous weapon or device, shall be fined under this title or imprisoned not more than twenty-five years, or both" (160).

Reasoning about and applying this law, says DeSanctis, requires narrative reasoning and not simply the application of a rule (or major premise) to a case (or minor premise) in syllogistic fashion. The question has to be answered whether or not a toy gun is a "dangerous weapon or device." But this question must also be responsive to the history of decisions based upon this law, a history that is itself also narrative. Prior to 1986, circuit courts understood this phrase to be limited to loaded, operable guns, but in 1986 in *McLaughlin v. United States*, the Supreme Court "held that even an unloaded gun constitutes a dangerous weapon under the statute" (DeSanctis 2012, 160–61). So when the Ninth Circuit heard *United States v. Martinez-Jimenez*, they took into account the evolution of the law, and they did so in part by quoting *McLaughlin v. United States*: "The display of a gun instills fear in the average citizen; as a consequence it creates an immediate danger that violent response will ensue" (161).

In their own ruling, the Ninth Circuit agreed that "the dangerousness of a device used in a bank robbery is not simply a function of its potential to injure people directly, its dangerousness results from greater burdens that it imposes upon victims and law enforcement officers. Therefore an unloaded gun that only simulates the threat of a loaded gun is a dangerous weapon" (DeSanctis 2012, 162). This argument and the ruling are based upon a generalized narrative scene and character actions and responses.

Rule-based reasoning here is based upon a narrative illustration of how the rule has operated and a narrative of how the interpretation of that rule has expanded. It evokes characters (a robber, victims, police), actions and consequences (brandishing, threatening, injuring), and emotions (fear).

But what about a desk lamp? asks DeSanctis. Is it a dangerous weapon? Answering that question requires reinserting the object, the category, and the legal language back into a narrative situation and comparing that situation with one involving a more conventional weapon, a loaded gun. How do people respond? What is the danger? What legal scholars do in applying legal instruments is to enthymize their terms, reinserting them into hypothetical narratives and looking for nodal differentiators and situating these hypothetical narratives in the context of the history of the law's application. "Even a recitation of the law itself," says DeSanctis, "the fundamental jumping off point for rule based analysis, often entails narrative reasoning" (2012, 165).

Despite the differences between contemporary American and ancient Athenian law, argument in both systems relies heavily upon narrative. Examples like the one above could be cited for ancient legal reasoning and argument. In short, rhetorical narrative is not a preparation for or an alternative to argument but a mode of argument—in fact, a primary and ubiquitous mode of argument in ancient rhetoric. It is not that all narratives argue but that rhetorical narratives do, that the task of creating arguments relies on the ability to tell stories, and that skill at rhetorical narratives is central to ancient rhetorical artistry.

The enthymeme is just one of the tools of narrative argument and one example of the narrative basis of ancient rhetorical theory. Other ancient concepts and terms could be similarly reinterpreted and understood in new ways when approached from the perspective of legal storytelling and narrative theory: *kairos*, or opportunity; *pistis*, or proof; ethos, or character; pathos, or emotion; *paradeigma*, or example; *hupokrisis*, or delivery; and other parallel or subsidiary terms. A narrative orientation suggests new insights about these terms, but more importantly, it could suggest new terms, new concepts, and new approaches to ancient theory based on how orators argued. For example, while *nomos* is an important Greek term widely used to talk about the bases for legal reasoning (pace Cover 1983) and sources for persuasion, it has not entered the rhetorical lexicon in any significant way. But if speakers appeal to listeners' emotions and to the listeners' trust in the speakers as narrating characters, don't speakers also appeal to the normative world in which the audience lives and that the speech can evoke? Couldn't *nomos* stand alongside the other appeals as a central source for proofs that would make visible the important work done by cultural narratives as tools of justice, expediency, and praise?

RHETORIC AS PRACTICE

The second commitment is to rhetorical practice—in this case, to oratorical performance in narrative contests—as fundamental to the understanding of ancient rhetoric and of rhetorical theory for any period. Rhetorical theory in the form of a system laid out in treatises and textbooks, ancient or modern, is an insufficient tool for understanding the rhetoric of any period. Ancient rhetoric cannot be understood through Aristotle and Plato. The axiom is very old, but it is not always observed that rhetorical art is the offspring of eloquence and that rhetorical artistry resides in the communicative practices of a culture and the evolution of those practices (*De oratore* 1.32.146; Sutton 1988, 100–101; see also McGee 1982).

This means that theory is local and culturally situated. Whatever the enthymeme is, we cannot take for granted its universal applicability or indeed its relevance to any set of texts beyond the culture and genre within which it was developed. It is not that it does not have broader relevance but that its general applicability cannot be assumed; it must be demonstrated. Indeed, it was the very process of defining argument only in terms of logical form that allowed the enthymeme to be "universalized" in the first place, since logical forms themselves ignore cultural frameworks, knowledge, experience, and values. If theory has to be tied to practice, then the rhetorical theory that is confirmed through an analysis of practice should be presumed to have local use until it is shown to be more widely applicable.

If we do want to assert the more general relevance of a theoretical term, we should be required to explain why a concept developed for one genre or one situation in one cultural location should be relevant to another era or another kind of text. The specific features and operation of the enthymeme for which it evolved—the time-restricted adversarial, amateur, and oral nature of ancient legal arguments—will likely make it clumsy and counterproductive in other kinds of rhetorical interactions and other kinds of narratives, including perhaps contemporary legal arguments. The function performed by the enthymeme in the ancient legal case might be served by the introduction of exhibits in modern trials or by other linguistic features of written opinions and briefs.

Even if the view of the enthymeme sketched out here is incorrect, it seems to me important to consider the possibility that the enthymeme is a kind of rhetorical move that was useful and effective in one cultural location and a few related genres but not elsewhere. I consider this view to apply not only to the enthymeme but to all other rhetorical concepts: ethos, *kairos*, *eikos*, and the like. And regardless of the scholarly future of 1.0 as a rhetorical concept, I think it important that we move beyond a default reliance on syllogistic and deductive notions of reasoning and inference, beyond "missing-piece" arguments, and beyond both 3.0 and Aristotle to explore the enthymeme, rhetorical logos, and rhetorical artistry more generally. We will do better if we draw ancient rhetorical theory not simply from Aristotle or any other Greek, Latin, or modern rhetorical theory but from the orators and from the process of telling stories.

NOTES

Introduction

1. Not to be confused with that *other* imagined ancient rhetorical city, Sophistopolis. See Russell (1983).
2. Unless otherwise noted, all citations of the *Rhetoric* are followed by page numbers from Kennedy's 2007 translation, 2nd ed.
3. See *Rhetoric* 3.13.3–5.
4. *Antistrophe* has been read as referring to movements in choral dance, or to the term as used by Aristotle in the *Topics* (as *antistrephein* or "convert," see 4.4; Forster 1966, 452–53) and *Analytics*, or to Plato's comparison of rhetoric to cookery in *Gorgias*. See Green (1990), Price (1992), Brunschwig (1996), and McAdon (2001). Rhetoric is "like some offshoot [*paraphues*] of" and "partly [*morion ti*] dialectic, and resembles" it (1.2.7; 39). Green defines *antistrophos* as a "reciprocal and rule-governed transformation" (1990, 27).
5. Cope, with a different conceit, notes that it "will not admit of so high a finish" (1867, 11).
6. Raphael saw Aristotle's induction:example::deduction:enthymeme relationship to be "confused" and flawed (1974, 161).
7. On these differences between *Rhetoric* and *Dialectic*, see Brunschwig (1996). Grimaldi (1972) is a strong proponent of the *Rhetoric's* unity.
8. Bennet and Feldman's *Reconstructing Reality in the Courtroom* was one of the most influential works describing the law in terms of narrative and story, a project that rapidly grew into a significant field of legal studies in its own right.
9. Velleman speaks of an emotional "cadence" (2003, 6). Aristotle speaks of *peripateia* (reversal) and *anagnorisis* (recognition). I will use *periodos* in reference to legal plots because of its Greek associations with discursive movement "around" a thought (a *period*), to differentiate it from Aristotle's tragic plots, and to suggest that this movement is not simply emotional, as Velleman suggests.

10. The story has been attributed anecdotally to Hemingway, but the anecdote has never been verified. Versions of this "story" predate Hemingway. The episode is told in deGroot's *Papa*; see Wright (2014).
11. Gagarin (2003, 2007) asserts the centrality of storytelling to Athenian law and legal argument, though stops short of suggesting that rhetorical logos fundamentally is narrative argument.
12. Of course, other details prove that the event could not in reality have happened as they have been narrated (see 417 nn. 36–37, 418 n. 40).
13. I use the numeral designation simply as shorthand for the complex rhetorical frameworks that characterize each model and to suggest the linkages that have historically led from one to the next, like so many updated iterations of a piece of software. The decimal is included to allow and invite us to see intervening modifications to each framework.
14. In chapter 3, I'll discuss Bitzer's enthymeme as 3.1 and Barthes's enthymeme as 3.2.
15. Adapted from Kennedy (2007, 40). I have dropped Kennedy's use of *premise, conclusion*, and *syllogism*, which are not required by the original.
16. I discuss both of these derivations in chapter 1.

Chapter 1

1. He does not in fact say this, as will become clear in chapter 2, but this is the standard view. He does distinguish dialectical and contentious deduction from demonstration in *Topics* 1.1 (Smith 2003, 1–2).
2. Note that this and other rhetorical examples use an individual subject (Socrates or Caius) rather than a universal (all men) or particular (some men) subject. An alternative construction was noted by Woody Allen: all

men are mortal; Socrates is mortal; therefore, all men are Socrates.

3. I am here combining features of several versions of the enthymeme as elaborated by Bitzer and Barthes, for which, see below.

4. Supporting its status as the standard view, I could cite Burnyeat, for example, who finds general agreement that "an enthymeme is an abbreviated syllogism, that is, a categorical syllogism in which one of the premises or the conclusion is not stated but understood or held in mind (*en thumoi*)" (1994, 3). And of this writing, the Wikipedia entry defines *enthymeme* as "a rhetorical syllogism (a three-part deductive argument) used in oratorical practice" and divides the features of 3.0 in three different types: (1) with an unstated premise, (2) based on signs, and (3) where the audience supplies a premise. "Enthymeme," Wikipedia, last updated July 23, 2019, https://en.wikipedia.org/wiki/Enthymeme.

5. This is the most common approach, though a long tradition of scholarship distinguishes between enthymemes according to which statement is suppressed: the major premise (first form), the minor premise (second form), or the conclusion (third form). See, for example, Jevons (1888, 153–54), Madden (1952), and Lanigan (1974).

6. Thus Kennedy uses the Greek *gar* (for) as a formal clue for detecting enthymemes (2003, xiv; 2007, 30 n. 5).

7. See also McHendry (2017, 313).

8. This is the standard formulation, though there is also a tradition that speaks of three "modes" of the enthymeme, depending on whether the major premise, the minor premise, or the conclusion is suppressed. See, for example, Read (1906, 134–36).

9. One of the values of Kennedy's edition of Aristotle's *Rhetoric* is that he makes clear his own necessarily frequent editorial emendations through the use of brackets.

10. "If you ask why it is set forth in textbooks such as Irving Cope's *Introduction to Logic*," Burnyeat explains, "the answer is: because it was there in the books that Cope read, and for no other (good) reason" (1994, 4).

11. Cohen calls this "a blend, perhaps, of 'cognitive dissonance reduction' and 'adaptive preference formation'" (2006, 118).

12. See Erickson (1975). On the enthymeme, see Hood (1984) and Poster (2000).

13. See Mirhady's *Rhetoric to Alexander* (2011, 450–55). The pre-Aristotelian use of *enthumēma* is discussed by Grimaldi (1972), Conley (1984), Walker (1994), Bons (2002), and Piazza (2011).

14. Unless otherwise noted, all citations of *Rhetoric to Alexander* will be followed by page numbers from Mirhady's 2011 translation.

15. This is very close to what Aristotle says about *sullogismos* in the *Rhetoric* at 1.2.9.

16. Cicero's *De inventione* (1.34; Hubbell 1993, 99–123) discusses the parts of a deductive argument at length but does not use *enthymeme* in the sense of a shortened argument. *Ad C. Herennium* speaks of "reasoning by contraries" but not in terms of enthymeme (292–93, and see n. b).

17. Chapter 2 will include a review of comments in the *Prior Analytics* relevant to 2.0.

18. Kremmydas, for example, includes the *atelēs* in his discussion of the enthymeme (quoting the *Prior Analytics*): "An enthymeme is an incomplete syllogism from likelihoods and signs" (2007, 26). He later reverts to the standard view: "An enthymeme is understood as a truncated (or incomplete) form of syllogism, where one of the premises or the conclusion is omitted but can easily be understood by the audience" (27).

19. It is true that Whately does not mention Aristotle, but Whately—like Cope, Jevons, and others—relies directly or indirectly on Aristotle, who alone can be the source for 3.0. When Whately says that in the enthymeme one premise is "usually" suppressed, the source for this idea can only be Aristotle. It goes too far for Poster to say that because he does not cite Aristotle directly, Whately does not rely on him.

20. I will suggest in chapter 2 that this is the wrong way to think about the relationship between dialectical and rhetorical *sullogismos*.

21. Ironically, though Bitzer rejects Hamilton's definition of the enthymeme, he here agrees with Hamilton that it makes no logical difference whatsoever whether a premise is suppressed. Hamilton infers from this that the "missing premise" definition of the enthymeme must be rejected. Bitzer retains the definition in a "special sense."

22. I am not here differentiating between spoken and written arguments, as Bitzer makes no such distinction, though of course, how arguments are processed may differ substantially depending on the medium and mode through which they are received.

23. Within a decade, Bitzer's view of the enthymeme had resurrected and modernized the traditional view. It was picked up by Fisher (1964), Aly (1965), and Delia (1970), among others.

24. Barthes explains the puzzle-solution structure of narrative in terms of a "hermeneutic code" (2002, 31).

25. The frame story about a narrator at a party and a marquess who is curious about an old man in attendance need not concern us here.

26. Barthes had already written about rhetoric and the enthymeme in "The Old Rhetoric: An Aide-Mémoire" (1988, 57–64). See also Moriarty (1997).

Chapter 2

1. Scholarship on the root *thumos* is rather large and universally comments on the complexity of the term and its resistance to easy translation, though it is generally admitted to convey both emotional and cognitive qualities. See Adkins (1970, 14–26 passim), Warden (*thumos* and *noos*; 1971, 6–7), Darcus (1977), Darcus Sullivan (1980, 1981, 1996), Lynch and Miles (1980), Sharples (1983), Gay (1988), Casswell (1990), and Koziak (1999). The relationship between *thumos* and *enthumēma* has received less attention. Mirhady warns against seeing a direct connection between the two (2007, 54), but see Bertrand (2007) for an alternate view. A review of fifth- and fourth-century instances of the verb *enthumeisthai* betrays no special emphasis on affect or any tendency toward arousal of the emotions.

2. The debate about whether the enthymeme makes emotional or character appeals is ongoing. Miller and Bee (1972) and Grimaldi (1972) argue in favor; Gaines (2000) summarizes arguments against. Aristotle suggests that enthymeme is the "body" of proofs (*pisteis*) and that proofs are ethical, pathetic, and logical (*Rhetoric* 1.1.3, 1.1.11, 1.2.3; 13, 33, 38), but he later explicitly admonishes against using enthymemes for ethical or pathetic appeals (3.17.8; 243). Enthymemes in ancient oratory almost inevitably arouse emotions because they stipulate facts about human actions set in a normative world (see part 3). If they are passional, it is the narrative that makes them so.

3. Grimaldi roughly identifies logos (*en autō tō logō*) with *pragma*, calling it "the subject of discourse in its purely logical character which speaks to the intellect of the author" (1972, 62). I would instead translate *pragma* as "fact," "act," or "event." The *pragmata* are the narrative details (and inferences to and from them) that constitute the plot and address the law. The task of the litigant is simply to address the *pragma*, the matter at hand, showing what it is or is not, what happened or did not happen (*Rhetoric* 1.1.3–6; 31–32). On the range of meanings for *logos* in the *Rhetoric*, see Van Ophuijsen (2007).

4. All references to Thucydides are followed by page numbers from Strassler's *The Landmark Thucydides* (1996).

5. It is also worth noting that Antiphon make repeated use of *enthumios* across his Tetralogies. If the term and its emotional valence bear a relationship to the later *enthymeme*, here would be a good place to look.

6. In dialectic reasoning, for example, both the questioner and the respondent know the conclusion at which the questioner is aiming. In legal cases, the conclusion of each speaker will also be known in such form as "I am innocent (of X)" or "I am telling the truth" or "He is guilty (of X)" or "He is lying."

7. I overlook the problem of which premise the audience supplies—whether it was the one intended by the speaker, "needed" versus "used," and so on. See Burke (1985), Ennis (1982), Scriven (1976, 85–86), Gough and Tinsdale (1985), and Walton (2001).

8. In fact, it was Hamilton who, as Burnyeat states it, put "suppressed conclusion" enthymemes "on the map" (1994, 5).

9. We might compare the process of "supplying a premise" claimed by 3.0 with the description of probability in the *Rhetoric to Alexander*: "There is plausibility in what is being said when the audience has examples

in their thoughts." Statements seem probable when "everyone in the audience agrees that he himself has such desires," emotions, or beliefs (7.4; 515). That we recall or imagine familiar scenes and experiences that correspond to and personalize a speaker's statements is easily confirmed by self-reflection. That we "supply" premises to syllogisms that are missing them sparks no such recognition or correspondence.

10. We also have to resurrect a metaphysics of presence that has come under sustained attack from deconstruction and other strains of postmodernity. Because it is defined in terms of an unstated premise or opinion that "completes" the argument, 3.0 relies on a clear line separating the text and the required context (qua missing premise that supplements and completes the text) from any larger context that does not. But if postmodernity has taught us anything, it is that no such clear line can be maintained among text, context-that-is-part-of-the-text, and context. There is no "outside the text."

11. Walker (1994) does, but he also jettisons 3.0 for a more complex understanding of the enthymeme.

12. In the myth, Procrustes, a son of Poseidon, had a home on the sacred way from Athens to Eleusis. He would invite passersby to spend the night and then either stretch or cut them so that they fit the bed exactly (March 1998, 940–41).

13. See *Rhetoric of Motives* (Burke 1969).

14. McGee similarly observes that "discourse ceases to be what it is whenever parts of it are taken 'out of context'" (1990, 283).

15. In fact, it does of course have a context, but the context is not a discourse surrounding a crime and a trial but a textbook and its illustration of logical arguments. What the enthymeme "means" is not "Benny is guilty" but "Here is a real-life example of enthymematic reasoning." Benny is not a person but a logical place-filler like Caius or Socrates, or "X" or "A."

16. See, for example, the account of confessions, and specifically the confessions of four individuals of the so-called Central Park Five in Conlon (2014).

Chapter 3

1. In his *Commentary on the Posterior Analytics of Aristotle*, Aquinas notes that while syllogisms reason about universals, enthymemes are employed when universals are not available (1.1.1 71a8; see Seaton 1914, 118). Hamilton discusses Agricola's *De inventione dialectica*, Phrissemius's commentary on it, and Pace's commentary on the *Prior Analytics* (1852, 152–54), as does Seaton (1914, 118). Green presents the full reasoning of Pace (cr "Pacius"; 1995, 24–26). Conley (1984) and Walker (1994) consider pre-Aristotelian views in their criticism. Both introduce style as a feature of the enthymeme. Walker offers his own novel theory of the enthymeme (1994; 2000, chap. 6).

2. This observation is made by nearly all the commentators.

3. See *Posterior Analytics* 1.10.7 (76b23–27; Barnes 2002, 16; see Hamilton 1852, 152). Burnyeat observes that "a logic of incompletely expressed reasoning is as redundant as a logic of indignant reasoning" (1994, 5).

4. First observed by Pace and subsequently taken up by later commentators.

5. Aristotle will mention species of reasoning at *Topics* 1.1, but rhetorical is not one of them.

6. See Aristotle's *Categories* (Cooke 1996, chaps. 3 and 5) and Granger (1984).

7. We could compare this to Aristotle's *On Memory and Recollection*, where Aristotle says that "deliberation, too, is a kind of inference" (*sullogismos tis*; 453a13; Hett 1957, 310–11), or we could say, "Inference of a kind or in a particular context."

8. I take this to be the point of Burnyeat's discussion about the *tis* in "sullogismos tis," where he notes that "the *Rhetoric*'s definition of enthymeme is its definition of *sullogismos*" (1994, 17).

9. Tredennick betrays the power of 3.0 and its genus/species view of the enthymeme when he has Aristotle say in the *Posterior Analytics* that "rhetorical arguments . . . use either examples, which are a kind of induction, or enthymemes, which are a kind of syllogism" (71a11; Tredennick 1966, 25). But here Aristotle is not using the familiar *sullogismos tis* formulation. Rather, he says simply that

the enthymeme "hoper esti sullogismos" (is essentially deduction). The *hoper esti* is Aristotelian language for expressing identity: what a thing essentially is (see *Posterior Analytics* 83a24–25; Tredennick 1966, 120–21). Barnes's translation is not haunted with the spirit of 3.0, and so he can translate the passage more accurately: "Rhetorical arguments persuade . . . either through examples, which is induction, or through enthymemes, which is deduction" (2002, 1).

10. Aristotle is not ignoring rhetoric in the *Topics*. He compares it to dialectic at 1.3 (Smith 2003, 3).

11. Work on the topoi and their relationship to other Aristotelian concepts like *idia*, *stoikheia*, and *koina* is voluminous. I relied primarily on Rubinelli's *Ars Topica* (2009, part 1), Slomkowski's *Aristotle's Topics* (1997), Spranzi's *The Art of Dialectic between Dialogue and Rhetoric* (2011, chap. 1), and the introduction to Smith's *Topics* (2003). See also Brunschwig's "Rhetoric as a Counterpart to Dialectic" (1996) on the relationship between rhetorical and dialectical topics in the *Rhetoric* and *Topics*, respectively.

12. See Rubinelli (2009, 12–21). A topos includes a heading or name ("from the greater and the less"; 17), an applicability requirement ("if an accident which has a contrary is asserted"; 20), a law or rule ("if anything is predicated in a greater or less degree, it also belongs absolutely"; 18), an investigation instruction ("you must look whether what admits of the *accident* admits also if its contraries"; 20), an example ("for example, if your opponent has said that hatred follows anger"), and a purpose ("this method should be used in destructive criticism"; 20). Not all of Aristotle's topics include all of these elements, but most are, if not stated, understood or implied by the context.

13. Smith translates this as "standing off" (2003, 20–21, 108–9).

14. Forbes Hill states explicitly what is implicit in equating the enthymeme with *sullogismos* in the figures: "The various *dicta* about the enthymeme are unintelligible without knowledge of the *Prior Analytics*" (1981, 140). See, by contrast, the argument in Burnyeat (1994, 14–15). Aristotle is writing to students who are familiar with dialectic, but at no point is familiarity with syllogistic logic or the figures necessary or even helpful for understanding the *Rhetoric* or the enthymeme.

15. On rhetorical topics, see Braet (1999, 2005) and Brunschwig (1996).

16. Braet (2005) refers to a "logical" level of argumentation that is purely formal and a pragmatic level of argumentation that include "substantial terms" that resist complete formalization.

17. See also topic 16, "from consequences by analogy" (2.23.17; 179), and topic 18, "from contrasted choices" (2.23.19; 180).

18. Students of the *Organon* sometimes differentiate between the "inference" account of the Aristotelian *sullogismos* (which allows for the drawing of a new conclusion from given premises) and the "premise" account (which searches for premises leading to a known conclusion). By *inference* here, I do not mean to weigh in on this debate and would take the term to allow either of these two forms of logical movement. In practice, rhetorical audiences often perform some combination of these views, inferring new information from what has been said but also looking for "middle terms" (or narrative events) that can explain and lead to one or another conclusion. For a summary of these views, see Duerlinger (1969).

19. For Bitzer (1959) and others, the missing premise makes the enthymeme persuasive just as the fletching on an arrow makes it accurate. To say that an arrow *could* be made without fletching and still remain an arrow, or that an enthymeme *could* be made without a missing premise and still remain an enthymeme, robs Peter to pay Paul: what is denied as an essential feature is virtually required as a strategic one.

20. This is the sense of the comment at 1.2.12 (41), about hearers who are unable to "reason from a distant starting point" as happens in dialectic and scientific demonstrations (see 12.22.3; 168–69).

21. Aristotle did not compare the rhetorical *sullogismos* to dialectic here presumably because the dialectical *sullogismos* tends to be strategically elongated beyond what is necessary, and his point is rather that logically *necessary* propositions are often in rhetoric left unstated.

22. Freese (1982), like all translators of the *Rhetoric*, uses *syllogism* here and elsewhere.

23. In the *Prior Analytics*, for example, Tredennick offers a translation at 2.27 that invokes 3.0. He has Aristotle say that "if only one premise is stated, we got only a sign, but if the other premise is assumed as well, we get a syllogism" (1962, 525), adding a note that Aristotle's "syllogism" here is "strictly an enthymeme." But the passage is not about enthymemes; it is about the difference between signs (which conclude from one premise and are not deductions) and deductions (which require more than one premise). Smith translates the passage more accurately: "If one premise alone is stated, then it is only a sign, but if the other is taken in addition, then it is a deduction" (1989, 103).

Chapter 4

1. See topic 3 (from correlatives), 4 (from more and less), 4a (from analogy or precedent), 5 (from time), 6 (from turning against the opponent), 9 (from division), 10 (from induction), 13 (from consequence), 14 (from contrasting opposites), 15 (from hypothetical deception), 16 (from consequence by analogy), 17 (from results to cases), 18 (from contrasted choices), 19 (from identifying purpose with cause), 20 (from reasons for and against), 22 (from contradictions), 23 (from the cause of false impressions), 24 (from cause and effect), 25 (from a better plan), 26 (from comparison of contraries), and 27 (from what would have been a mistake).

2. This is topic 19, identifying purpose with cause: because curry's strong flavor hides the presence of opium, Holmes infers that curry was selected for just this purpose.

3. The Aeschines mentioned in Aristotle's *Rhetoric* at 3.16.10 is the Socratic Aeschines of Sphettos, not the orator (see Kennedy 2007, 241 n. 187).

4. There may be a reference to Lysias 34.11 at 2.23.19: "[It would be terrible] if when in exile we fought to come home, but having come home we shall go into exile in order not to fight" (180). The quotation is not exact, however, and it probably refers to the well-known mass exile of citizens when the Thirty took power so that this antithetical sentiment could have been in wide circulation by Aristotle's time.

5. Freese inserts *speech* (1982, 300–301) into example 4 where Kennedy adds *suit* in brackets (2007, 175). Trevett suggests *case* (1996, 374), noting that the passage does not imply that Aristotle saw the speech.

6. But see Usher (2004), who argues that there was a reading public for (some) forensic speeches. I find it less likely that an Athenian public would read a legal speech than that they would attend a legal trial. But some such speeches may have been popular. In chapter 8, I offer reasons for seeing Lysias 1 as being meant for wide consumption, as would any set speech (like Isocrates's *Encomium of Helen*) seek to attract a broad audience. Nevertheless, their use by Aristotle and his school may still have been limited to oral tradition and collections of sayings.

7. Trevett (1996) points out the contrast between this and Anaximenes's practice of inventing examples to illustrate his points.

8. Despite his criticism of democracy, Aristotle understood that the opportunity to appeal magistrate decisions to a popular court was one of the key elements of a democratic constitution and that the ability to go to court as litigant or juror was a defining feature of the democratic citizen (*Politics* 2.9.3, 3.1.4; Rackham 1998, 166–67, 174–75; and *Athenian Constitution* 9.1–2; Rackham 1996, 30–33).

Chapter 5

1. On abduction, see Burks (1946). On abduction and enthymemes, see Sabre (1990), Bybee (1991), and Lanigan (1994). On abduction in the law, see Schum (2001).

2. See Andocides's *On the Mysteries* (1.54, 60, 124, 128; Maidment 1941, 382, 386, 432, 436).

3. A clear example of an enthymeme introduced without the verb is in Antiphon's *On the Chorus Boy*, introduced at 6.41 as "pay close attention and think back" (*skepsasthe de kai moi mnēsthēte*; 86). This is a moment expressed at 6.43 as "clear evidence" (*megiston sēmeion*; 87). Antiphon does not tend to introduce his enthymemes with *enthumaomai*. I will argue in chapter 4 that this term came into vogue only with Lysias.

4. Eleven orators if we include Apollodorus, the likely author of several orations included in the work of Demosthenes. All translations are from the Oratory of Classical Greece series edited by Michael Gagarin from the University of Texas Press.

5. Thus I included Demosthenes 7: *On Halonnesus*, which was probably by Hegesippus from the mid-fourth century, and Antiphon's tetralogies, which were never meant to be delivered in court—but not Andocides 4: *Against Alcibiades*, which is likely to be a literary exercise from a later period (McDowell 1998, 159–60; Edwards 1995, 208–12).

6. Unless otherwise noted, all citations of "Antiphon" from *Antiphon and Andocides* are followed by page numbers from Gagarin's 1998 translation.

7. Unless otherwise noted, all citations of Isaeus are followed by page numbers from Edwards's 2007 translation.

8. On the persuasiveness of stories, see Fisher (1984, 1989); on legal stories in particular, see Bennet and Feldman (2014, chap. 6), Pennington and Hastie (1991), and Rideout (2008).

9. Holmes contrasts his perceptions from his deductions, but they invariably involve an inference of some sort—from what is seen to what else can be known (Doyle 2006, 220). On the "simplicity" of Holmes's perceptions when explained as deductions, see "A Scandal in Bohemia" (Doyle 2005, 9–10) and "The Red Headed League" (44).

10. From Doyle's "Sign of the Four" (2006, 222–24), Holmes "narrates" the history of Watson's family from a pocket watch that Watson inherited from his older brother. Holmes's rather immediate grasp of this little slice of Watson's family history has to be unpacked for Watson himself. Told as a stepwise progression, it feels more like deduction and less like perception and narrative inference.

11. The enthymeme—both 3.0 and 2.0—is always discussed in terms of deduction. So when Aristotle says that some enthymemes are drawn from signs, he implies that signs, and thus all aspects of semiotics and interpretation, form a subset of logic, a relation that I find unconvincing. Other forms of connection between one set of facts and another fact that "follows" are possible, including those that remain outside the realm of discourse.

12. Chekhov famously offered this as a requirement of narrative art: don't introduce a rifle in act 1 unless it's going to go off in act 3 (Bitsilli 1983, x).

13. See chapter 6 for an example (from Demosthenes's *Against Meidias*) used enthymematically.

Chapter 6

1. This is very close to the story of Lear and Cordelia and of Jacob and his brother Esau in Genesis 37–45.

2. On *eikos* as what is socially fitting and expected or what is similar to those things, see Hoffman (2008). The *Rhetoric to Alexander* says, "The thing being said is *eikos* when the audience has examples in their thoughts" (7.4; 514–15). For Hoffman (2008), this view expresses *eikos* more accurately than does the generalized frequency or statistical view of probability typical of many PC models: "most A is B" or "A is usually B." As a narrative, the *eikos* script is a prototypical, singular, imagined scene: this is what happens, not the generalized "major premise" commonly associated with the syllogistic figures.

3. Amsterdam and Bruner describe a "charter narrative" and the "scripts" that it authorizes (2000, 127, and chap. 5).

4. In addition to these two speeches, the affair of the Eleusinian mysteries and the herms is discussed in Plutarch's *Alcibiades* and Thucydides (6.27–29; 60). On this case and its background, see also MacDowell (1962), Marr (1971), Missiou (1992), Edwards (1995), Furley (1996), Todd (2004), and Carawan (2004). I do not concern myself here with the historical events or the nature of Andocides's involvement in either.

5. Parke (1986, 62) and Furley (1996, 48–52).

6. On Athenian clubs (*hetaireia*), see Connor (1971, 79–94) and Murray (1990).

7. On the herms, see Osbourne (1985) and Furley (1996, 13–28).

8. Demeter and Persephone were the two goddesses presiding over the cult of the Eleusinian Mysteries. On the Mysteries, see

Mylonas (1969), Parke (1986, 55–72), and Furley (1996, 31–40).

9. Thucydides suggests that popular opinion united these two events into one crime with the same perpetrators and a common purpose, but Andocides separates them as distinct. Osborne (1985, 67) and Furley (1996, 41–48) agree that they were in fact two separate crimes with different purposes. See also MacDowell (1962, 190–93).

10. Specifically, it prescribes that documents listing the *atimoi* (those who had lost their civic rights) be destroyed.

11. This is the view of MacDowell (1962, 200–203).

12. The speech is also available with good introduction and commentary in MacDowell (1962) and Edwards (1995). See also Missiou (1992).

13. Unless otherwise noted, all citations of "Andocides" from *Antiphon and Andocides* are followed by page numbers from MacDowell's 1998 translation.

14. This is a narrative marker and a moment of enthymizing, though without the term.

15. Here again, Andocides calls attention to a fact and suggests an interpretation without using a version of *enthumaomai* or any similar verb.

16. Andocides here switches to a version of *skopeō* (consider, contemplate) instead of *enthumaomai* to mark places for the jury's special attention. He uses this form elsewhere as well: "If any of you citizens think I informed on my friends to bring about their death and save my life," he says, "consider [*skopeisthe*] the actual facts" (1.54).

17. For an argument about how the orators use rhetoric to frame legal issues and address them (rather than using it to subvert the law and circumvent justice), see Harris (1994) and Sickinger (2007).

Chapter 7

1. This is "big rhetoric," or the notion that "everything ... can be described as rhetorical" (Schiappa 2001, 260).

2. All persuasive actions are rhetorical:

All symbol/language-use is persuasive.

Therefore: All symbol/language use is rhetorical. (Schiappa 2001, 261)

3. Narrative as a central paradigm for rhetoric was argued by Fisher (1984, 1989). On the bigness of narrative, see Barthes (1975), Mitchell (1981), Bruner (1986, 1991), and White (1978, 1980). Rhetorical definitions of narrative are offered by Chatman (1990, chap. 11) and Phelan (1996, 4).

4. Even reading a legal speech after the fact will only approximate the rhetorical function of the speech "at one remove," as it were, since it will no longer be an adversarial contest marked by the opposition of speeches and an immediate vote.

5. This outline is developed from models of rhetorical narratives by Fisher (1989), Lucaites and Condit (1985), Pennington and Hastie (1991), and Rideout (2008).

6. On storyworlds, see Herman (2009), 105–36). On the relationship of narrative gaps to cognitive studies, see Bernaerts et al. (2013).

7. On reasoning through mental models, see Johnson-Laird (2006).

8. On the process of raising a detail to the level of "fact" in history, see Carr (1964). On the process of raising a detail to the level of event in legal narrative, see Meyer (2014, 16–17).

9. In "Sign of the Four," Holmes observes, "Eliminate all other factors and the one which remains must be the truth" (Doyle 2006, 222).

10. The analogy fits in English in that we score points both in sports and in arguments. On the relationship between narratives and games, see Gallie (1968). On consequential games and contests, see Goffman (1967, 149–67). On ancient rhetorical contest and athletic games, see Hawhee (2004).

11. Burke (1969, 26–27) uses *drama* rather than *narrative*; Cover (1983) speaks of *nomos* as the normative world within which a people live and act, though this *nomos* is fundamentally narrative in its features, instructing its members in who they are to be, how they are to behave, what they are to strive for.

12. Aristotle gets at this at 2.23.30 (184) and 3.10.4 (219). Apsines says that enthymemes "give an impression of sharpness" (*Art of Rhetoric* 8.19; Dilts and Kennedy 1997, 181).

Chapter 8

1. Biographical material on Lysias comes largely from the essay by Dionysius of Halicarnassus, "Lysias," which is devoted primarily to the literary qualities of Lysias's speeches (Usher 1974, 16–99), and from the "Lysias" in the *Lives of the Ten Orators* included with the works of Plutarch (Fowler 1936, 360–69). On the life, career, and works of Lysias, see Dover (1968), Lateiner (1984), Carey (1989, 1–16), and Todd (2007, 5–17).

2. To be fair, it should be noted that Dionysius praised not only the narrative and style of Lysias but his skills at organization and argument as well. He was "adept at discovering the arguments inherent in a situation, not only those which any of us could discover, but those which would be beyond anyone else's imagination" (§15; 50–51). Bateman (1962, 1967) also reviews the arguments of Lysias but does not consider the place of the enthymeme.

3. On law as social feud and contest for honor, see Osborne (1985b) and Cohen (1995, esp. chaps. 5 and 6). I'll offer further reasons for seeing this as a teaching text below. The case does rely on existing social scripts and storyforms, but Eratosthenes in this speech claims no prior involvement with his opponent, Euphiletus (though of course he has reason to minimize any such connection). No knowledge of any prior hostilities or legal actions is necessary to understand the plot.

4. Influential early criticism of Lysias includes Demetrius §190 (Innes 1995, 462–63) and Dionysius (Usher 1974), who discusses stylistic virtues in "Lysias" at §2–14 (Usher 1974, 22–51) and characterization at §8 (32–35), the Lysian proem at §15–17 (50–59), narration at §18 (58–59), and proofs briefly at §19 (60–63). Blass (1893, 401–4) largely follows Dionysius, as did later commentators (see Edwards and Usher 1987, 128–29). On Lysian characterization, see also Devries (1892) and, more recently, Usher (1965) and Carey (1989, 10–11; 1994, 39–42). A review of Lysian criticism is in Todd (2007, 32–42).

5. Translations include Edwards and Usher (1987, with commentary), Carey (1997), and Todd (2000). Commentaries on Lysias include Carey (1989), Edwards (1999), Usher (1999, 55–126), and Todd (2007).

6. On *moichos*, see Cohen (1984), Wolicki (2007), and Cantarella (1991).

7. On legal aspects of adultery, see Cohen (1984; 1990; 1991, 98–132). Carawan (1998) specifically addresses Lysias 1 at 284–99. On the trial described in Lysias 1, see also Carey (1989, 17–24; 1997, 27–35). On punishments for adulterers, see Carey (1993) and Todd (1993).

8. On Demosthenes 23, Athenian homicide, and the "adultery law," see MacDowell (1963, 1978) and Gagarin (1981).

9. This reconstruction is based on Aeschines 1.91, Demosthenes 24.113 and perhaps 59.66, Lysias 1, and Aristotle's *Constitution of the Athenians* 52.1. See Cohen (1984) and Todd (1993, 361). Demosthenes 59.66 may refer only to a man who is seized (but not summarily executed), claims his innocence, and takes his opponent to court for false arrest. If he loses this case, Demosthenes says, his opponent may do what he likes to him "without a weapon," presumably because he was not subject to summary execution to begin with.

10. Todd (1993, 80–81, 117–18).

11. Carawan (1998, 287–91).

12. The speech also responds to the prosecutor's claim that the murder was motivated by prior enmity between the two (§43). Of course, Euphiletus offers us only a biased and partial account, and it is impossible to say for certain what the prosecutor's lines of argument were (if there was an opposing speaker) or how his construction of the events differed from Euphiletus's.

13. This begins a theme that runs throughout the speech: of where to place one's attention and how intently. This is exactly the question of enthymizing.

14. This example was introduced in chapter 7 of this work. The *andrōnitin* or *andrōn* was the men's living and dining or entertaining quarters, which was lined with couches for reclining and entertaining friends and guests and accessible through the courtyard. See *andrōn* in Liddell and Scott (1985).

15. The women's quarters were generally upstairs in a Greek house; the men's quarters downstairs and accessible through the courtyard. Converting the *andrōn* into women's quarters would make it more difficult and embarrassing for Euphiletus to entertain

friends for dinner or after-dinner drinking, enhancing in the mind of the audience Euphiletus's social isolation and folly. On Lysias 1 and the physical structure of Euphiletus's house, see Morgan (1982). On gendered separation of the *oikos*, see Wolpert (2001). On the Greek house and domestic space, see Nevett (1999).

16. The italicized words here and below will become significant when we consider how Euphiletus functions as an agent of the law.

17. Recall that Euphiletus must entertain Sostratus upstairs in the (former) women's quarters.

18. This is very close to the "rhetorical situation" posited by Bitzer (1968) and others. Like a rhetorical situation, the kind of situation that requires enthymizing presents a need or exigency that can be addressed or resolved by human interaction. This situation specifically requires attending to those details that will permit an advantageous response. This approach to the situation emphasizes the need for interpretation rather than communication.

19. Barthes describes the reality effect as one produced by narrative details that convey no symbolic import to the plot and thus have no reason to be mentioned other than that they "really happened" (1989, 141–48).

20. In a ring narrative (or chiastic structure or palistrophe), "the meaning is in the middle" (Douglas 2007, x). The central and most important moment and the key to interpreting the whole is placed at the center of the story around which the whole pivots.

21. As noted, this structure helps explain a few of the many repetitions in the speech noted by Todd (2007, 52, 110, 118, 136–37, 139 passim) and Usher (1999, 57 n. 14). Many details of the narrative will also be repeated later on in the refutative portion of the speech (1.37–42), when Euphiletus recalls them to demonstrate his innocence.

Chapter 9

1. On Athenian attitudes toward adultery in its social context, see Cohen (1990). On Lysias as a source for domestic arrangements, see Wolpert (2001). Most scholarship on Lysias 1 rests on the assumption that it accurately describes adultery and its consequences in ancient Athens, making it possible, for example, to speculate on the relative wealth of Euphiletus based on details in the speech (Todd 2007, 58–59). But from a purely artistic standpoint, Lysias would be advised for the sake of the plot to give Euphiletus one female slave (to assist the liaison) but no others (to minimize his wealth and simplify the plot) and to give him a farm some distance away that he would have to travel to, but no male slaves to work it.

2. Perotti (1989/90) argues for similar reasons that Lysias 1 was never delivered; see also Nyvlt (2013). Carey (1993) and Forsdyke (2008) explore the public shaming of adulterers in social rituals of popular justice, suggesting that the legal aspect of an adultery case and its ritual, theatrical, and even literary elements may not be entirely distinct.

3. Compare the adultery case Michael H. v. Gerald D. (491 U.S. 110) as combat myth discussed in Amsterdam and Bruner (2000, 77–109).

4. Gorgias told the story of Helen to advertise the power of speech and particularly of his favored techniques—the division of a topic into and elimination of alternatives and the concatenation of stylistic devices. Protagoras offered an account of human creation and the apportionment of justice and temperance, Antisthenes narrated the contest for Achilles as argued between Odysseus and Ajax, the Sisyphus poet tells of the invention of the gods, and across his tetralogies, Antiphon tells the story of murder pollution and its eradication (all in Gagarin and Woodruff 1995). Plato tells many narratives (Partenie 2009; Collobert et al. 2012) to forward his arguments. I do not here intend to enter into the *muthos*/logos question—merely to observe that in the period of the orators, sophistic and rhetorical argument (logos) was built upon narrative accounts (*muthoi* and logoi).

5. Cicero (*Brutus* §48; Hubbell 2001, 50–51) attributes this detail to Aristotle; see also Plutarch's *Lives of the Ten Orators* (Fowler 1936, 366–67). While he was a teacher, early in his career, Lysias was placed in the category of theorists alongside Tisias and Theodorus (see also Kennedy 1963, 54).

6. Porter's thesis has elicited a range of responses, mostly challenging or qualifying his claims. Nyvlt (2013), for example, recommends agnosticism on the question of the authenticity and reality of the speech.

7. This reading was proposed by Perotti, who calls Lysias 1 a "sort of parable" and a "political parody" (1989–90, 47–48).

8. Lysias 1 does not use the term *sykophantes*, but Lysias 12: *Against Eratosthenes* does so describe the Thirty who seized power: "The Thirty, who were criminals and sykophants, established themselves in office, claiming they needed to cleanse the city of wrongdoers and redirect the remaining citizens toward goodness and justice" (12.5; Todd 2000, 117).

9. In fact, Harmodius is the name of one of the "friends" that Euphiletus calls upon to help him confront Eratosthenes (*Lysias* 1.21; Todd 2000, 43).

10. The italicized words on pages 158–59 would all resonate in the realm of the courts as categories of legal procedure (*basanisēs* = evidentiary torture of slaves; *katēgorei* = formal accusation or charge of wrongdoing; *ep' autophōrō* = apprehension in the act of committing a crime) that Euphiletus undertook of his own accord or implications of litigious character (techne = skill at persuasion; *polupragmosunē* = one who frequents the courts) directed at others.

11. Nyvlt objects that the speech could not be a political parable because if it were, then Euphiletus (the democratic *politeia*) would by Athenian law be required to divorce his adulterous wife (the polis, the city itself), but obviously the *politeia* cannot "divorce" itself from the polis (2013, 160 n. 6). But this kind of objection expects strict allegorical correspondence from a form that was never designed on those terms. In a parable, not every detail of the story (told or implied) has allegorical significance.

12. For ancient sources, see Thucydides (2.40.2) and Aristophanes (*Ploutos* 898–925). See also Adkins (1976), Sinclair (1988, 202–8, 217), Osborne (1990), and Harvey (1990).

13. This is in line with the conclusions of Bakewell, who points out the "bad citizen, good metic" (1999, 6) trope in Lysias 12 and 31.

14. Since homicide cases allowed each litigant to deliver two speeches, the prosecution would speak both before and after Euphiletus's first speech so that the student could imagine himself either anticipating or responding to Lysias 1. See MacDowell (1978, 119).

15. See chapter 7 in this work.

16. Some scholars argue that the charge of *moichos*, typically translated as "adultery," applied not only to a man's wife but to any free woman under his protection, including a mother, daughter, sister, or concubine kept for purposes of procreation. The defense of having sex but not committing *moicheia* is mentioned by Aristotle to illustrate how defendants admit having done an action but not having committed a crime (*Rhetoric* 1.13.9; 98–99).

17. We are imagining that these students have already read Lysias 1. In an actual trial, the prosecution would speak first and would have only a thin understanding of the argument for the defense. In terms of developing skills, it is easier to respond to a known argument than to anticipate it in advance.

Conclusion

1. On narrative and argument as distinct modes of discourse, see Fisher (1984, 1989), Bruner (1986), and more recently, Kvernbekk (2003).

REFERENCES

Adkins, A. W. H. 1970. *From the Many to the One*. London: Constable.

———. 1976. "Polupragmosune and 'Minding One's Own Business': A Study in Greek Social and Political Values." *Classical Philology* 71 (4): 301–27.

Aeschines. 2000. *Aeschines*. Translated by Chris Carey. Austin: University of Texas Press.

Agricola, Rodolphus. 1521. *De inventione dialectica libri tres*. Argentina: Joannem Knoblouchum.

Aly, Bower. 1965. "Enthymemes: The Story of a Lighthearted Search." *Speech Teacher* 14 (4): 265–75.

Amsterdam, Anthony G., and Jerome Bruner. 2000. *Minding the Law*. Cambridge: Harvard University Press.

Andocides. 1941. *Andocides*. Translated by K. J. Maidment. In *Minor Attic Orators I*, 319–588. Cambridge: Harvard University Press.

———. 1998. "Andocides." In *Antiphon and Andocides*, translated by Michael Gagarin and Douglas M. MacDowell, 93–170. Austin: University of Texas Press.

Antiphon. 1998. "Antiphon." In *Antiphon and Andocides*, translated by Michael Gagarin and Douglas M. MacDowell, 1–92. Austin: University of Texas Press.

Antoine, Arnauld. 1850. *Logic, or The Art of Thinking; Being the Port-Royal Logic*. Translated by Thomas Spencer Baynes. Edinburgh: Sutherland and Knox.

Aquinas, Thomas. 1970. *Commentary on the Posterior Analytics of Aristotle*. Translated by F. R. Larcher. Albany, NY: Magi Books.

Aristophanes. 2002. *Ploutos*. Translated by Jeffrey Henderson. Cambridge: Harvard University Press.

Aristotle. 1957. *On the Soul. Parva Naturalia. On Breath*. Translated by W. S. Hett. Cambridge: Harvard University Press.

———. 1962. *Prior Analytics*. Translated by Hugh Tredennick. Cambridge: Harvard University Press.

———. 1965. *On Sophistical Refutations*. Translated by E. S. Forster. Cambridge: Harvard University Press.

———. 1966. *Posterior Analytics*. Translated by Hugh Tredennick. Cambridge: Harvard University Press.

———. 1980. *Metaphysics*. Translated by Hugh Tredennick. Cambridge: Harvard University Press.

———. 1982. *The "Art" of Rhetoric*. Translated by John Henry Freese. Cambridge: Harvard University Press.

———. 1989. *Prior Analytics*. Translated by Robin Smith. Indianapolis: Hackett.

———. 1995. *Poetics*. Translated by Stephen Halliwell. Cambridge: Harvard University Press.

———. 1996a. *Athenian Constitution*. Translated by H. Rackham. Cambridge: Harvard University Press.

———. 1996b. *Categories*. Translated by H. P. Cooke. Cambridge: Harvard University Press.

———. 1998. *Politics*. Translated by H. Rackham. Cambridge: Harvard University Press.

———. 2003. *Topics: Books I and VII*. Translated by Robin Smith. Oxford: Clarendon Press.

———. 2007. *On Rhetoric*. 2nd ed. Translated by George A. Kennedy. New York: Oxford University Press.

———. 2011. *Rhetoric to Alexander*. Translated by David C. Mirhady. Cambridge: Harvard University Press.

Avery, Harry C. 1991. "Was Eratosthenes the Oligarch Eratosthenes the Adulterer?" *Hermes* 119 (3): 380–84.

Bakewell, Geoff. 1999. "Lysias 12 and Lysias 31: Metics and Athenian Citizenship in the Aftermath of the Thirty." *Greek, Roman, and Byzantine Studies* 40:5–22.

Barnes, Jonathan. 1981. "Proof and the Syllogism." In *Aristotle on Science: The Posterior Analytics*, edited by Enrico Berti, 17–59. Padua: Editrice Antenore.

———, trans. 2002. *Aristotle Posterior Analytics*. By Aristotle. Oxford: Clarendon Press.

Barthes, Roland. 1975. "An Introduction to the Structural Analysis of Narrative." Translated by Lionel Duisit. *New Literary History* 6 (2): 237–72.

———. 1988. "The Old Rhetoric: An Aide-Mémoire." In *The Semiotic Challenge*, translated by Richard Howard, 11–94. New York: Hill and Wang.

———. 1989. *The Rustle of Language*. Translated by Richard Howard. Berkeley: University of California Press.

———. 2002. *S/Z*. Translated by Richard Miller. New York: Blackwell.

Bateman, John Jay. 1967. *A Study of the Arguments in the Speeches of Lysias*. Ann Arbor: University Microfilms International.

Bateman, John Jay. 1962. "Some Aspects of Lysias' Argumentation." *Phoenix* 16 (3): 157–77.

Beatty, John. 2017. "Narrative Possibility and Narrative Explanation." *Studies in History and Philosophy of Science* 62:31–41.

Bennet, W. Lance, and Martha S. Feldman. 2014. *Reconstructing Reality in the Courtroom: Justice and Judgment in American Culture*. 2nd ed. New Orleans: Quid Pro Books.

Bernaerts, Lars, Dirk de Geest, Luc Herman, and Bart Vervaeck, eds. 2013. *Stories and Minds: Cognitive Approaches to Literary Narrative*. Lincoln: University of Nebraska Press.

Bers, Victor, trans. 2003. *Demosthenes, Speeches 50–59*. By Demosthenes. Austin: University of Texas Press.

Bertrand, Denis. 2007. "Thymie et Enthymème." *Semiotica* 163 (1): 75–84.

Bitsilli, Petr Mikhailovich. 1983. *Chekhov's Art: A Stylistic Analysis*. New York: Ardis.

Bitzer, Lloyd. 1959. "Aristotle's Enthymeme Revisited." *Quarterly Journal of Speech* 45 (4): 399–408.

———. 1968. "The Rhetorical Situation." *Philosophy and Rhetoric* 1:1–14.

Blass, Friedrich. 1893. *Die Attische Beredsamkeit*. Vol. 2. Leipzig: Druck und Verlag von B. G. Teubner.

Blumer, Herbert. 1969. *Symbolic Interactionism: Perspective and Method*. Berkeley: University of California Press.

Bons, J. A. E. 2002. "Reasonable Argument Before Aristotle: The Roots of the Enthymeme." In *Dialectic and Rhetoric: The Warp and Woof of Argumentation Analysis*, edited by Frans H. Van Eemeren and Peter Houtlosser, 13–28. Dordrecht: Springer Science+Business Media.

Bourdieu, Pierre. 1977. *Outline of a Theory of Practice*. Translated by Richard Nice. New York: Cambridge University Press.

———. 1990. *The Logic of Practice*. Translated by Richard Nice. Stanford: Stanford University Press.

Braet, A. C. 1999. "The Enthymeme in Aristotle's *Rhetoric*: From Argumentation Theory to Logic." *Informal Logic* 19 (2/3): 101–17.

———. 2005. "Common Topics in Aristotle's *Rhetoric*: Precursor of the Argumentation Scheme." *Argumentation* 19:65–83.

Brandt, William J. et al. 1969. *The Craft of Writing*. Englewood Cliffs, NJ: Prentice-Hall.

Bruner, Jerome. 1986. *Actual Minds, Possible Worlds*. Cambridge: Harvard University Press.

———. 1991. "The Narrative Construction of Reality." *Critical Inquiry* 18 (1): 1–21.

Brunschwig, Jacques. 1996. "Rhetoric as the Counterpart to Dialectic." In *Essays on Aristotle's Rhetoric*, edited by Amélie Oksenberg Rorty, 34–55. Berkeley: University of California Press.

Burke, Kenneth. 1969. *A Rhetoric of Motives*. Berkeley: University of California Press.

Burke, Michael. 1985. "Unstated Premises." *Informal Logic* 7:107–18.

Burks, Arthur W. 1946. "Pierce's Theory of Abduction." *Philosophy of Science* 13 (4): 301–6.

Burnyeat, M. F. 1994. "Enthymeme: Aristotle on the Logic of Persuasion." In *Aristotle's Rhetoric: Philosophical Essays*, edited by David J. Furley and Alexander Nehamas, 3–53. Princeton: Princeton University Press.

———. 1996. "Enthymeme: Aristotle on the Rationality of Rhetoric." In *Essays on Aristotle's Rhetoric*, edited by Amélie Oksenberg Rorty. Berkeley: University of California Press.

Bybee, Michael D. 1991. "Abduction and Rhetorical Theory." *Philosophy and Rhetoric* 24 (2): 281–300.

Cantarella, Eva. 1991. "*Moicheia*: Reconsidering a Problem." In *Symposion 1990: Vorträge zur griechischen und hellenistischen Rechtsgeschichte*, edited by Michael Gagarin, 289–304. Köln: Böhlau.

Caplan, Harry, trans. 1989. *Ad. C. Herennium de ratione dicendi*. By [Cicero]. Cambridge: Harvard University Press.

Carawan, Edwin. 1998. *Rhetoric and the Law of Draco*. Oxford: Clarendon Press.

———. 2002. "The Athenian Amnesty and the 'Scrutiny of the Laws.'" *Journal of Hellenic Studies* 122:1–23.

Carey, Christopher, ed. and trans. 1989. *Lysias: Selected Speeches*. By Lysias. Cambridge: Cambridge University Press.

———, trans. 2000. *Aeschines*. By Aeschines. Austin: University of Texas Press.

———. 1995. "Rape and Adultery in Athenian Law." *Classical Quarterly* 45 (2): 407–17.

———. 1993. "The Return of the Radish, or Just When You Thought It Was Safe to Go Back into the Kitchen." *Liverpool Classical Monthly* 18:53–55.

———. 1994. "Rhetorical Means of Persuasion." In *Persuasion: Greek Rhetoric in Action*, edited by Ian Worthington, 26–45. New York: Routledge.

———. 1997. *Trials from Classical Athens*. New York: Routledge.

Carr, E. H. 1964. *What Is History?* New York: Penguin Books.

Carter, L. B. 1986. *The Quiet Athenian*. New York: Oxford University Press.

Casswell, Caroline. 1990. *A Study of Thumos in Early Greek Epic*. Leiden: Brill.

Chatman, Seymour. 1978. *Story and Discourse: Narrative Structure in Fiction and Film*. Ithaca: Cornell University Press.

———. 1990. *Coming to Terms*. Ithaca: Cornell University Press.

Chekhov, Anton. 2015. *The Cherry Orchard*. Translated by Richard Nelson, Richard Pevear, and Larissa Volokhonsky. New York: Theater Communications Group.

Chestek, Kenneth. 2008. "The Plot Thickens: The Appellate Brief as Story." *Journal of the Legal Writing Institute* 14:127–69.

———. 2010. "Judging by the Numbers: An Empirical Study of the Power of Story." *Journal of the Association of Legal Writing Directors* 7:1–35.

Cicero. 1942. *De oratore: Books I, II*. Translated by E. W. Sutton. Cambridge: Harvard University Press.

———. 1993. *De inventione, De optimo genere oratorum, Topica*. Translated by H. M. Hubbell. Cambridge: Harvard University Press.

———. 2001. *Brutus*. Translated by H. M. Hubbell. Cambridge: Harvard University Press.

[Cicero]. 1981. *Ad C. Herennium*. Translated by Harry Caplan. Cambridge: Harvard University Press.

Cohen, David. 1984. "The Athenian Law of Adultery." *Revue internationale des droits de l'antiquite* 31:147–65.

———. 1990. "The Social Context of Adultery at Athens." In *Nomos: Essays in Athenian Law, Society, and Politics*, edited by Paul Cartledge, Paul Millett, and Stephen Todd, 147–66. Cambridge: Cambridge University Press.

———. 1991. *Law, Sexuality, and Society: The Enforcement of Morals in Classical Athens*. Cambridge: Cambridge University Press.

———. 1995. *Law, Violence, and Community in Classical Athens*. New York: Cambridge University Press.

Cohen, G. A. 2006. "Deeper into Bullshit." In *Bullshit and Philosophy*, edited by Gary L. Hardcastle and George A. Reisch, 117–35. Chicago: Open Court.

Collobert, Catherine, Pierre Destrée, and Francisco J. Gonzalez, eds. 2012. *Plato and Myth: Studies on the Use and Status of Platonic Myths.* Leiden: Brill.

Conley, Thomas. 1984. "The Enthymeme in Perspective." *Quarterly Journal of Speech* 70 (2): 168–87.

———. 1994. "Notes on the Byzantine Reception of the Peripatetic Tradition in Rhetoric." In *Peripatetic Rhetoric After Aristotle,* edited by William W. Fortenbaugh and David C. Mirhady, 217–42. New Brunswick, NJ: Transaction.

Conlon, Edward. 2014. "The Myth of the Central Park Five." *Daily Beast,* October 19, 2014. https://www.thedailybeast.com/the-myth-of-the-central-park-five?ref=scroll.

Connor, W. R. 1971. *The New Politicians of Fifth-Century Athens.* Princeton: Princeton University Press.

Cooke, H. P., trans. 1996. *Categories of Interpretation.* Cambridge: Harvard University Press.

Cooper, Lane. 1932. *The Rhetoric of Aristotle.* New York: D. Appleton.

Cope, Edward Meredith. 1867. *An Introduction to Aristotle's Rhetoric.* London: Macmillan.

———. 1877. *The Rhetoric of Aristotle.* Revised and edited by J. E. Sandys. Cambridge: Cambridge University Press.

Copi, Irving, Carl Cohen, and Kenneth McMahon. 2014. *Introduction to Logic.* New York: Pearson.

Corbett, Edward P. J., and Robert J. Connors. 1999. *Classical Rhetoric for the Modern Student.* New York: Oxford University Press.

Cover, Robert M. 1983. "*Nomos* and Narrative." *Harvard Law Review* 97 (1): 4–69.

Crem, Theresa. 1956. "The Definition of Rhetoric According to Aristotle." *Laval Théologique et Philosophique* 12 (2): 233–50.

Crowley, Sharon, and Debra Hawhee. 2004. *Ancient Rhetorics for Contemporary Students.* New York: Pearson Longman.

Darcus, Shirley M. 1977. "-phrōn Epithets of Thumos." *Glotta* 55 (3/4): 178–82.

Darcus Sullivan, Shirley M. 1980. "How a Person Relates to θυμός in Homer." *Indogermanische Forschungen* 85 (January): 138–50.

———. 1981. "The Function of θυμός in Hesiod and the Greek Lyric Poets." *Glotta* 59 (3/4): 147–55.

———. 1996. "Disturbances of the Mind and Heart in Early Greek Poetry." *L'antiquité Classique* 65:31–51.

Delia, Jesse G. 1970. "The Logical Fallacy, Cognitive Theory, and the Enthymeme: A Search for the Foundations of Reasoned Discourse." *Quarterly Journal of Speech* 56 (2): 140–48.

Demetrius. 1995. *On Style.* Edited and translated by Doreen C. Innes. Cambridge: Harvard University Press.

Demosthenes. 2003. *Demosthenes, Speeches 50–59.* Translated by Victor Bers. Austin: University of Texas Press.

———. 2008. *Demosthenes, Speeches 20–22.* Translated by Edward M. Harris. Austin: University of Texas Press.

———. 2011. *Demosthenes, Speeches 1–17.* Translated by J. C. Trevett. Austin: University of Texas Press.

———. 2018. *Demosthenes, Speeches 23–26.* Translated by Edward M. Harris. Austin: University of Texas Press.

De Quincey, Thomas. 1897. *The Collected Writings of Thomas De Quincey.* Vol. 10. London: A&C Black.

DeSanctis, Christy. 2012. "Narrative Reasoning and Analogy." *Legal Communication and Rhetoric: JALWD* 9:149–71.

Devries, William Levering. 1892. *Ethopoiia: A Rhetorical Study of the Types of Character in the Orations of Lysias.* Baltimore: J. Murphy.

Dickstein, Louis S. 1978. "Error Processes in Syllogistic Reasoning." *Mind and Cognition* 6 (5): 537–43.

Dilts, Mervin R., and George A. Kennedy, eds. 1997. *Two Greek Rhetorical Treatises from the Roman Empire.* New York: Brill.

Dionysius of Halicarnassus. 1974. "Lysias." In *Critical Essays,* vol. 1, translated by Stephen Usher, 16–98. Cambridge: Harvard University Press.

Donaldson, J. W. 1864. "On the Origin and Proper Use of the Word Argument." *Transactions of the Cambridge Philosophical Society* 10 (4): 317.

Douglas, Mary. 2007. *Thinking in Circles: An Essay on Ring Composition*. New Haven: Yale University Press.

Dover, K. J. 1968. *Lysias and the Corpus Lysiacum*. Berkeley: University of California Press.

Doyle, Arthur Conan. 2005. *The New Annotated Sherlock Holmes*. Vol. 1. Edited by Leslie S. Klinger and John Le Carre. New York: W. W. Norton.

———. 2006. *The New Annotated Sherlock Holmes*. Vol. 3. Edited by Lisa Klinger. New York: W. W. Norton.

Duerlinger, James. 1969. "Sullogismos and Sullogizesqai in Aristotle's Organon." *American Journal of Philology* 90 (3): 320–28.

Edwards, Linda. 1996. "The Convergence of Analogical and Dialectic Imaginations in Legal Discourse." *Legal Studies Forum* 20:7–50.

Edwards, M. J., ed. 1999. *Five Speeches: Speeches 1, 12, 19, 22, 30*. Bristol: Bristol Classical Press.

Edwards, M. J., and S. Usher, eds. and trans. 1987. *Greek Orators I: Antiphon and Lysias*. Havertown, PA: Aris & Phillips.

Edwards, Michael, ed. and trans. 1995. *Greek Orators IV: Andocides*. By Andocides. Warminster: Aris & Phillips.

———, trans. 2007. *Isaeus*. By Isaeus. Austin: University of Texas Press.

Ennis, Robert. 1982. "Identifying Implicit Assumptions." *Synthese* 51:61–86.

Erickson, Keith. 1975. *Aristotle's Rhetoric: Five Centuries of Philological Research*. Meuchen, NJ: Scarecrow Press.

Evans, J. St. B. T. 1993. *Human Reasoning: The Psychology of Deduction*. Hove: Lawrence Erlbaum Associates.

Facciolati, Jacobi. 1728. "De Enthymemate." In *Acroases Dialecticae: Habitae in Gymnasio Patavino*, 3–21. London: John Manfré.

Fisher, Walter R. 1964. "Uses of the Enthymeme." *Speech Teacher* 13 (3): 197–203.

———. 1984. "Narration and Human Communication Paradigm: The Case of Public Moral Argument." *Communication Monographs* 51 (1): 1–22.

———. 1989. *Human Communication as Narration: Toward a Philosophy of Reason, Value, and Action*. Columbia: University of South Carolina Press.

Flannery, Kevin L. 1987. "A Rationale for Aristotle's Notion of Perfect Syllogisms." *Notre Dame Journal of Formal Logic* 28 (3): 455–71.

Forsdyke, Sara. 2008. "Street Theatre and Popular Justice in Ancient Greece: Shaming, Stoning and Starving Offenders Inside and Outside the Courts." *Past and Present* 201:3–50.

Forster, E. S., trans. 1966. *On Sophistical Refutations, On Coming-to-Be and Passing-Away*. By Aristotle. Cambridge: Harvard University Press.

Fowler, Harold North, trans. 1936. *Lives of the Ten Orators*. In *Moralia*, vol. 10, by Plutarch, 341–57. Cambridge: Harvard University Press.

———, trans. 1982. *Euthyphor, Apology, Crito, Phaedo, Phaedurus*. By Plato. Cambridge: Harvard University Press.

———, trans. 2007. *Cratylus, Parmenides, Greater Hippias, Lesser Hippias*. By Plato. Cambridge: Harvard University Press.

Freese, John Henry, trans. 1982. *Aristotle: The "Art" of Rhetoric*. By Aristotle. Cambridge: Harvard University Press.

Furley, William D. 1996. *Andokides and the Herms: A Study of Crisis in Fifth-Century Athenian Religion*. London: Institute of Classical Studies.

Gagarin, Michael. 1981. *Drakon and the Early Athenian Homicide Law*. New Haven: Yale University Press.

———, trans. 1998. "Antiphon." By Antiphon. In *Antiphon and Andocides*, 1–92. Austin: University of Texas Press.

———. 2003. "Telling Stories in Athenian Law." *Transactions of the American Philological Society*. 133:197–207.

———. 2007. "Rational Argument in Early Athenian Oratory." In *Logos: Rational Argument in Classical Rhetoric*, edited by Jonathan Powell, 9–18. London: Institute of Classical Studies.

Gagarin, Michael, and Douglas M. MacDowell. 1998. *Antiphon and Andocides*. The Oratory of Classical Greece 1. Austin: University of Texas Press.

Gagarin, Michael, and Paul Woodruff. 1995. *Early Greek Political Thought from Homer to the Sophists*. Cambridge: Cambridge University Press.

Gage, John T. 1983. "Teaching the Enthymeme: Invention and Arrangement." *Rhetoric Review* 2 (1): 38–50.

———. 1984. "An Adequate Epistemology for Composition: Classical and Modern Perspectives." In *Essays on Classical Rhetoric and Modern Discourse*, edited by Robert Connors, Lisa S. Ede, and Andrea A. Lunsford, 152–69. Carbondale: Southern Illinois University Press.

Gaines, Robert N. 2000. "Aristotle's *Rhetoric* and the Contemporary Arts of Practical Discourse." In *Rereading Aristotle's Rhetoric*, edited by Alan G. Gross and Arthur E. Walzer, 3–23. Carbondale: Southern Illinois University Press.

Gallie, W. B. 1968. *Philosophy and the Historical Understanding*. New York: Schocken Books.

Gay, Robert. 1988. "Courage and Thumos." *Philosophy* 63 (244): 255–65.

Genette, Gérard. 1980. *Narrative Discourse: An Essay in Method*. Translated by Jane E. Lewin. Ithaca: Cornell University Press.

Gerrig, Richard J. 2010. "Reader's Experiences of Narrative Gaps." *Storyworlds: A Journal of Narrative Studies* 2:19–37.

Goddu, G. C. 2016. "On the Very Concept of an Enthymeme." *OSSA Conference Archive* 84. http://scholar.uwindsor.ca/ossaarchive/OSSA11/papersandcommentaries/84.

Goffman, Erving. 1959. *Presentation of Self in Everyday Life*. New York: Anchor Doubleday.

———. 1967. *Interaction Ritual*. New York: Pantheon Books.

———. 1971. *Strategic Interaction*. Philadelphia: University of Pennsylvania Press.

Gough, James, and Christopher Tinsdale. 1985. "Hidden or Missing Premises." *Informal Logic* 7:99–106.

Green, Lawrence D. 1990. "Aristotelian Rhetoric, Dialectic, and the Traditions of Ἀτίστροφος." *Rhetorica* 8 (1): 5–27.

———. 1994. "The Reception of Aristotle's *Rhetoric* in the Renaissance." In *Peripatetic Rhetoric After Aristotle*, edited by William W. Fortenbaugh and David C. Mirhady, 320–48. New Brunswick, NJ: Transaction.

———. 1995. "Aristotle's Enthymeme and the Imperfect Syllogism." In *Rhetoric and Pedagogy: Its History, Philosophy, and Practice*, edited by Winifred Bryan Horner and Michael Leff, 19–42. New York: Routledge.

Grimaldi, William M. A. 1972. *Studies in the Philosophy of Aristotle's Rhetoric*. Wiesbaden: Franz Steiner Verlag GMBH.

Hamilton, Sir William. 1852. *Discussions on Philosophy and Literature, Education and University Reform*. London: Longman, Brown, Green and Longmans.

Harris, Edward M. 1994. "Law and Oratory." In *Persuasion: Greek Rhetoric in Action*, edited by Ian Worthington, 130–52. New York: Routledge.

———, trans. 2001. "Lycurgus." By Lycurgus. In *Dinarchus, Hyperides, and Lycurgus*, 153–218. Austin: University of Texas Press.

———, trans. 2008. *Demosthenes, Speeches 20–22*. By Demosthenes. Austin: University of Texas Press.

———, trans. 2018. *Demosthenes, Speeches 23–26*. By Demosthenes. Austin: University of Texas Press.

Harvey, David. 1990. "The Sykophant and Sykophancy: Vexatious Redefinition?" In *Nomos: Essays in Athenian Law, Politics, and Society*, edited by Paul Cartledge, Paul Millett, and Stephen Todd, 103–22. Cambridge: Cambridge University Press.

Hawhee, Debra. 2004. *Bodily Arts: Rhetoric and Athletics in Ancient Greece*. Austin: University of Texas Press.

Herman, David. 2002. *Story Logic: Problems and Possibilities of Narrative*. Lincoln: University of Nebraska Press.
———. 2009. *Basic Elements of Narrative*. Chichester: Wiley Blackwell.
Herman, Gabriel. 1993. "Tribal and Civic Codes of Behavior in Lysias 1." *Classical Quarterly* 43 (2): 406–19.
Hett, W. S., trans. 1957. *On the Soul. Parva Naturalia. On Breath*. By Aristotle. Cambridge: Harvard University Press.
Hill, Forbes. 1981. "The Amorality of Aristotle's Rhetoric." *Greek, Roman, and Byzantine Studies* 22 (2): 133–47.
Hoffman, David C. 2008. "Concerning *Eikos*: Social Expectation and Verisimilitude in Early Attic Rhetoric." *Rhetorica: A Journal of the History of Rhetoric* 26 (1): 1–29.
Homer. 1995. *The Odyssey: Books 13–24*. Translated by A. T. Murray. Revised by George E. Dimock. Cambridge: Harvard University Press.
Hood, Michael D. 1984. "The Enthymeme: A Brief Bibliography of Modern Sources." *Rhetoric Society Quarterly* 14 (3): 159–62.
Howland, Jacob. 2004. "Plato's Reply to Lysias: Republic 1 and 2 and Against Eratosthenes." *American Journal of Philology* 125 (2): 179–208.
Hubbell, H. M., trans. 1993. *De inventione, De optimo gerenre oratorum, Topica*. By Cicero. Cambridge: Harvard University Press.
———, trans. 2001. *Brutus*. By Cicero. Cambridge: Harvard University Press.
Innes, Doreen C., ed. and trans. 1995. *On Style*. By Demetrius. Cambridge: Harvard University Press.
Isaeus. 2007. *Isaeus*. Translated by Michael Edwards. Austin: University of Texas Press.
Iser, Wolfgang. 1972. "The Reading Process: A Phenomenological Approach." *New Literary History* 3 (2): 279–99.
Jackson, Matthew. 2006. "The Enthymematic Hegemony of Whiteness: The Enthymeme as Antiracist Rhetorical Strategy." *JAC: A Journal of Composition Theory* 26 (3/4): 601–41.
Jebb, Richard Claverhouse. 1876. *Attic Orators from Antiphon to Isaeus*. Vol. 2. London: Macmillan.
Jevons, Stanley W. 1888. *Elementary Lessons in Logic: Deductive and Inductive*. New York: Macmillan.
Johnson-Laird, P. N. 2006. *How We Reason*. New York: Oxford University Press.
Joyce, Christopher J. 2008. "The Athenian Amnesty and Scrutiny of 403." *Classical Quarterly* 58 (2): 507–18.
Kapparis, K. 1993. "Is Eratosthenes in Lys. 1 the Same Person as Eratosthenes in Lys. 12?" *Hermes* 121 (3): 364–65.
Keith, William M., and Christian O. Lundberg. 2008. *The Essential Guide to Rhetoric*. New York: Bedford St. Martin's.
Kennedy, George A. 1963. *The Art of Persuasion in Greece*. Princeton: Princeton University Press.
———, trans. 2003. *Progymnasmata: Greek Textbooks of Prose Composition and Rhetoric*. Atlanta: Society of Biblical Literature.
———, trans. 2007. *On Rhetoric*. 2nd ed. By Aristotle. New York: Oxford University Press.
Knudsen, Rachel Ahern. 2014. *Homeric Speech and the Origins of Rhetoric*. Baltimore: Johns Hopkins University Press.
Koziak, Barbara. 1999. "Homeric Thumos: The Early History of Gender, Emotion, and Politics." *Journal of Politics* 61 (4): 1068–91.
Kremmydas, Christos. 2007. "Logical Argumentation in Demosthenes *Against Leptines*." In *Logos: Rational Argument in Classical Rhetoric*, edited by Jonathan Powell, 19–34. London: Institute of Classical Studies.
Kvernbekk, Tone. 2003. "On the Argumentative Quality of Explanatory Narratives." In *Anyone Who Has a View: Theoretical Contributions to the Study of Argumentation*, edited by Frans van Eemeren, J. Anthony Blair, Charles A. Willard, and A. Francisca Snoeck Henkemans, 269–82. Dordrecht: Springer Science+Business Media.

Lakoff, George, and Mark Johnson. 1980. *Metaphors We Live By*. Chicago: University of Chicago Press.

Lamb, W. R. M., trans. 1952. *Meno*. By Plato. Cambridge: Harvard University Press.

Langer, Susan. 1948. *Philosophy in a New Key: A Study in the Symbolism of Reason, Rite, and Art*. New York: New American Library.

Lanigan, Richard L. 1974. "Enthymeme: The Rhetorical Species of Aristotle's Syllogism." *Southern Speech Communication Journal* 39 (3): 207–22.

———. 1994. "From Enthymeme to Abduction: The Classical Law of Logic and the Postmodern Rule of Rhetoric." In *Recovering Pragmatism's Voice: The Classical Tradition, Rorty, and the Philosophy of Communication*, edited by Lenore Langsdorf and Andrew R. Smith, 49–70. New York: State University of New York Press.

Lateiner, Donald. 1984. *Lysias and Athenian Politics*. Ann Arbor: University Microfilms.

Levi, Don S. 1995. "The Case of the Missing Premise." *Informal Logic* 17 (1): 67–88.

Liddell, H. G., and R. Scott. 1985. *An Intermediate Greek-English Lexicon*. Oxford: Clarendon Press.

Lloyd, G. E. R. 1966. *Polarity and Analogy: Two Types of Argument in Ancient Greek Thought*. Cambridge: Cambridge University Press.

Lloyd, Keith. 2014. "Reinterpreting the Enthymeme to Include the Nonverbal." *JAC: A Journal of Composition Theory* 33 (3/4): 732–49.

Lucaites, John Louis, and Celeste Michelle Condit. 1985. "Re-constructing Narrative Theory: A Functional Perspective." *Journal of Communication* 35 (4): 90–108.

Lycurgus. 2001. *Dinarchus, Hyperides, Lycurgus*. Translated by Edward M. Harris. Austin: University of Texas Press.

Lynch, J. P., and G. B. Miles. 1980. "In Search of Thumos: Toward an Understanding of a Greek Psychological Term." *Prudentia* 12:3–9.

Lysias. 2000. *Lysias*. Translated by S. C. Todd. Austin: University of Texas Press.

MacDowell, Douglas. 1962. *Andokides: On the Mysteries*. Oxford: Clarendon Press.

———. 1963. *Athenian Homicide Law in the Age of the Orators*. Manchester: Manchester University Press.

———. 1978. *The Law in Classical Athens*. Ithaca: Cornell University Press.

———, trans. 1998. "Andocides." By Andocides. In *Antiphon and Andocides*, 93–170. Austin: University of Texas Press.

Madden, Edward H. 1952. "The Enthymeme: Crossroads of Logic, Rhetoric, and Metaphysics." *Philosophical Review* 61 (3): 368–76.

Maidment, K. J., trans. 1941. *Andocides*. By Andocides. In *Minor Attic Orators I*, 319–588. Cambridge: Harvard University Press.

Mansel, H. L. 1856. *Artis Logicae Rudimenta from the Text of Aldrich*. 3rd ed. Oxford: Oxford University Press.

March, Jenny. 1998. *Dictionary of Classical Mythology*. Oxford: Oxbow Books.

Marr, J. L. 1971. "Andokides' Part in the Mysteries and Hermai Affairst 415 BC." *Classical Quarterly* 21:326–38.

McAdon, Brad. 2001. "Rhetoric Is the Counterpart of Dialectic." *Philosophy and Rhetoric* 34 (2): 113–50.

McGee, Michael Calvin. 1982. "A Materialist's Conception of Rhetoric." In *Explorations in Rhetoric: Studies in Honor of Douglas Ehninger*, edited by Ray E. McKerrow, 23–48. Glenview, IL: Scott Foresman.

———. 1990. "Text, Context, and the Fragmentation of Contemporary Culture." *Western Journal of Speech Communication* 54 (3): 274–89.

McHendry, George F., Jr. 2017. "Instagrams That Wound: Punctum, Visual Enthymemes, and the Visual Argumentation of the Transportation Security Administration." *Argumentation and Advocacy* 53 (4): 310–26.

Mead, George Herbert. 1943. *Mind, Self, and Society*. Chicago: University of Chicago Press.

Meyer, Philip M. 2014. *Storytelling for Lawyers.* New York: Oxford University Press.

Miller, Arthur B., and John D. Bee. 1972. "Enthymemes: Body and Soul." *Philosophy and Rhetoric* 5 (4): 201–14.

Mink, Louis. 1970. "History and Fiction as Modes of Comprehension." *New Literary History* 1 (3): 541–58.

Mirhady, David C. 2007. "Aristotle's Enthymeme, Thymos, and Plato." In *Influences on Peripatetic Rhetoric,* edited by David C. Mirhady, 53–64. Boston: Brill.

———, trans. 2011. *Rhetoric to Alexander.* By Aristotle. Cambridge: Harvard University Press.

Mirhady, David C., and Yun Lee Too. 2000. *Isocrates I.* By Isocrates. Austin: University of Texas Press.

Missiou, Anna. 1992. *The Subversive Oratory of Andokides: Politics, Ideology and Decision-Making in Democratic Athens.* New York: Cambridge University Press.

Mitchell, W. J. T., ed. 1981. *On Narrative.* Chicago: University of Chicago Press.

Momigliano, Arnaldo. 1993. *The Development of Greek Biography.* Cambridge: Harvard University Press.

Morgan, Gareth. 1982. "Euphiletos' House: Lysias 1." *Transactions of the American Philological Association* 112:115–23.

Moriarty, Michael. 1997. "Rhetoric, Doxa, and Experience in Barthes." *French Studies* 51 (2): 169–82.

Moss, Jessica. 2014. "Right Reasoning in Plato and Aristotle: On the Meaning of Logos." *Phronesis* 59:181–203.

Murray, A. T., trans. 1995. *Homer: Odyssey Books 13–24.* By Homer. Revised by George E. Dimock. Cambridge: Harvard University Press.

Murray, Oswyn. 1990. "The Affair of the Mysteries: Democracy and the Drinking Group." In *Sympotica: A Symposium on the Symposion,* edited by Oswyn Murray, 149–61. Oxford: Clarendon Press.

Mylonas, George E. 1969. *Eleusis and the Eleusinian Mysteries.* Princeton: Princeton University Press.

Nemesi, Attila L. 2013. "Implicature Phenomena in Classical Rhetoric." *Journal of Pragmatics* 50:129–51.

Nevett, Lisa C. 1999. *House and Society in the Ancient Greek World.* Cambridge: Cambridge University Press.

Nyvlt, Pavel. 2013. "Killing of Eratosthenes Between Reality and Mime (or, Was Lysias 1 Really Pronounced?)." *Graeco-Latina Brunensia* 18 (1): 159–70.

Ong, Walter J. 1958. *Ramus: Method and the Decay of Dialogue.* Cambridge: Harvard University Press.

Osborne, Robin. 1985a. "The Erection and Mutilation of the Hermai." *Proceedings of the Cambridge Philological Society* 31:47–73.

———. 1985b. "The Law in Action in Classical Athens." *Journal of Hellenic Studies* 105:40–58.

———. 1990. "Vexatious Litigation in Classical Athens: Sykophancy and the Sykophant." In *Nomos: Essays in Athenian Law, Politics, and Society,* edited by Paul Cartledge, Paul Millett, and Stephen Todd, 83–102. Cambridge: Cambridge University Press.

Pace, Giulio. 1584. *Aristotelis Stagiritae peripateticorum principis organum.* Geneva: Guilelmus Laimarius.

———. (1597) 1966. *In Porphyrii Isagogen et Aristotelis Organum Commentarius Analyticus.* Hildesheim: G. Olms.

Papillon, Terry L., trans. 2004. *Isocrates II.* By Isocrates. Austin: University of Texas Press.

Parke, H. W. 1986. *The Festivals of the Athenians.* London: Thames and Hudson.

Partenie, Catalin, ed. 2009. *Plato's Myths.* Cambridge: Cambridge University Press.

Pennington, Nancy, and Ried Hastie. 1991. "A Cognitive Theory of Juror Decision Making: The Story Model." *Cardozo Law Review* 13:519–57.

Perelman, Chaim, and L. Olbrechts-Tyteca. 1971. *The New Rhetoric: A Treatise on Argumentation.* Translated by John Wilkinson and Purcell Weaver. Notre Dame: University of Notre Dame Press.

Perotti, Pier Angelo. 1989/90. "La I Orazione Di Lisia fu mai Pronunciata?" *Sandalion* 12–13:43–48.

Phelan, James. 1996. *Narrative as Rhetoric: Technique, Audiences, Ethics, Ideology.* Columbus: Ohio State University Press.

Piazza, Francesca. 2011. "*Pisteis* in Comparison: Examples and Enthymemes in the *Rhetoric to Alexander* and in Aristotle's *Rhetoric*." *Rhetorica* 29 (3): 305–18.

Pierce, Charles Sanders. 1935. *Collected Papers of Charles Sanders Pierce*. Vols. 5 and 6. Edited by Charles Hartshorne and Paul Weiss. Cambridge: Belknap Press.

Plato. 1952. *Meno*. Translated by W. R. M. Lamb. Cambridge: Harvard University Press.

———. 1982. *Phaedrus*. Translated by Edward North Fowler. Cambridge: Harvard University Press.

———. 2007. *Cratylus*. Translated by Edward North Fowler. Cambridge: Harvard University Press.

Plutarch. 1936. *Lives of the Ten Orators*. In *Moralia*, vol. 10, translated by Harold North Fowler, 341–57. Cambridge: Harvard University Press.

Porter, John R. 2007. "Adultery by the Book: Lysias 1 (*On the Murder of Eratosthenes*) and Comic *Diēgēsis*." In *Oxford Readings in the Attic Orators*, edited by Edwin Carawan, 60–88. Cambridge: Oxford University Press.

Poster, Carol. 1994. "A Historicist Recontextualization of the Enthymeme." *Rhetoric Society Quarterly* 22 (2): 1–24.

———. 2000. "The Enthymeme: A Preliminary Bibliography of Secondary Sources." *Journal for the Study of the Rhetoric of the New Testament*. October 2000. http://www.academia.edu/6161063/The_Enthymeme_A_Preliminary_Bibliography_of_Secondary_Sources.

———. 2003. "Theology, Canonicity, and Abbreviated Enthymemes: Traditional and Critical Influences on the British Reception of Aristotle's *Rhetoric*." *Rhetoric Society Quarterly* 33 (1): 67–103.

Prenosil, Joshua D. 2012. "The Embodied Enthymeme: A Hybrid Theory of Protest." *JAC: A Journal of Composition Theory* 32 (1/2): 279–303.

Price, Robert. 1992. "Some Antistrophes to the Rhetoric." *Philosophy and Rhetoric* 25 (Supplement): 29–47.

Prince, Gerald. 1988. "The Disnarrated." *Style* 22 (1): 1–8.

Quintilian. 2001. *The Orator's Education*. Translated by Donald A. Russell. Cambridge: Harvard University Press.

Rabinowitz, Peter. 1987. *Before Reading: Narrative Conventions and the Politics of Interpretation*. Ithaca: Cornell University Press.

Rackham, H., trans. 1996. *Athenian Constitution, Eudemian Ethics, Virtues and Vices*. By Aristotle. Cambridge: Harvard University Press.

———, trans. 1998. *Politics*. By Aristotle. Cambridge: Harvard University Press.

Raphael, Sally. 1974. "Rhetoric, Dialectic and Syllogistic Argument: Aristotle's Position in *Rhetoric* I–II." *Phronesis* 12:153–67.

Ratcliffe, Krista. 2007. "In Search of the Unstated: The Enthymeme and/of Whiteness." *JAC: A Journal of Composition Theory* 27 (1/2): 275–90.

Raymond, James C. 1984. "Enthymemes, Examples, and Rhetorical Method." In *Essays on Classical Rhetoric and Modern Discourse*, edited by Robert Connors, Lisa S. Ede, and Andrea A. Lunsford, 140–51. Carbondale: Southern University Press.

Read, Carveth. 1906. *Logic: Inductive and Deductive*. London: Alexander Moring.

Rideout, Christopher. 2008. "Storytelling, Narrative Rationality, and Legal Persuasion." *Journal of the Legal Writing Institute* 14:53–86.

Roberts, W. Rhys, trans. 1924. *Rhetoric*. By Aristotle. 1924. Oxford: Clarendon Press.

Rosch, Eleanor. 1978. "Principles of Categorization." In *Cognition and Categorization*, edited by Eleanor Rosch and Barbara Bloom Lloyd, 1–25. Hillsdale, NJ: Erlbaum.

Rossolatos, George. 2014. "On the Pathology of the Enthymeme: Accounting for

Hidden Visual Premises in Advertising Discourse." *Signs and Society* 2 (1): 1–27.

Rubinelli, Sara. 2009. *Ars Topica*. Lugano, Switzerland: Springer.

Russell, Donald A. 1983. *Greek Declamation*. New York: Cambridge University Press.

———, trans. 2001. *The Orator's Education*. By Quintilian. Cambridge: Harvard University Press.

Sabre, Ru Michael. 1990. "Abductive Argument and Enthymeme." *Transactions of the Charles Pierce Society* 26 (3): 363–72.

Scenters-Zapico, J. 1994. "The Social Construct of Enthymematic Understanding." *Rhetoric Society Quarterly* 24 (3/4): 71–87.

Schiappa, Edward. 2001. "Second Thoughts on the Critique of Big Rhetoric." *Philosophy and Rhetoric* 34 (3): 260–74.

Schum, David A. 2001. "Species of Abductive Reasoning in Fact Investigation in Law." *Cardozo Law Review* 22 (5/6): 1645–81.

Scriven, Michael. 1976. *Reasoning*. New York: McGraw-Hill.

Seaton, R. C. 1914. "The Aristotelian Enthymeme." *Classical Review* 28 (4): 113–19.

Sharples, R. W. 1983. "'But Why Has My Spirit Spoken with Me Thus?': Homeric Decision-Making." *Greece and Rome* 30 (1): 1–7.

Sickinger, James P. 2007. "Rhetoric and the Law." In *A Companion to Greek Rhetoric*, edited by Ian Worthington. Malden, MA: Blackwell.

Sinclair, R. K. 1988. *Democracy and Participation in Athens*. Cambridge: Cambridge University Press.

Slomkowski, Paul. 1997. *Aristotle's Topics*. Leiden: Brill.

Smith, Robin, trans. 1989. *Prior Analytics*. By Aristotle. Indianapolis: Hackett.

———. 1994. "Dialectic and the Syllogism." *Ancient Philosophy* 14 (3): 133–51.

———, trans. 2003. *Topics: Books I and VII*. By Aristotle. Oxford: Clarendon Press.

Solmsen, Friedrich. 1941. "The Discovery of the Syllogism." *Philosophical Review* 50 (4): 410–21.

Sorensen, Roy A. 1988. "Are Enthymemes Arguments?" *Notre Dame Journal of Formal Logic* 29 (1): 155–59.

Spranzi, Marta. 2011. *The Art of Dialectic Between Dialogue and Rhetoric*. Philadelphia: John Benjamins.

Strassler, Robert B., ed. 1996. *The Landmark Thucydides*. By Thucydides. Translated by Richard Crawley. New York: Free Press.

Sutton, E. W., trans. 1988. *De oratore: Books I, II*. By Cicero. Cambridge: Harvard University Press.

Thucydides. 1996. *The Landmark Thucydides*. Edited by Robert B. Strassler, translated by Richard Crawley. New York: Free Press.

Todd, S. C. 1993. *The Shape of Athenian Law*. Oxford: Clarendon Press.

———, trans. 2000. *Lysias*. By Lysias. Austin: University of Texas Press.

———. 2007. *A Commentary on Lysias, Speeches 1–11*. Oxford: Oxford University Press.

Tredennick, Hugh, trans. 1962. *Prior Analytics*. By Aristotle. Cambridge: Harvard University Press.

———, trans. 1966. *Posterior Analytics*. By Aristotle. Cambridge: Harvard University Press.

———, trans. 1980. *The Metaphysics*. By Aristotle. Cambridge: Harvard University Press.

Trenker, Sophie. 1958. *The Greek Novella in the Classical Period*. New York: Cambridge University Press.

Trevett, J. C. 1996. "Aristotle's Knowledge of Athenian Oratory." *Classical Quarterly* 46 (2): 371–79.

———, trans. 2011. *Demosthenes, Speeches 1–17*. By Demosthenes. Austin: University of Texas Press.

Usher, Stephen. 1965. "Individual Characterization in Lysias." *Eranos* 63:99–119.

———, trans. 1974. "Lysias." In *Critical Essays*, vol. 1, by Dionysius of Halicarnassus, 16–98. Cambridge: Harvard University Press.

———. 1999. *Greek Oratory: Tradition and Originality*. New York: Oxford University Press.

———. 2004. "Lysias for Pleasure?" In *Law, Rhetoric, and Comedy in Classical Athens*, edited by D. L. Cairns and R. A. Knox, 113–21. Swansea: Classical Press of Wales.

Van Ophuijsen. 2007. "Reason in Speech? *Logos* and Means of Persuasion in Aristotle's *Rhetoric*." In *Influences on Peripatetic Rhetoric*, edited by David C. Mirhady, 65–86. Leiden: Brill.

Velleman, J. David. 2003. "Narrative Explanation." *Philosophical Review* 112 (1): 1–25.

Walker, Jeffrey. 1994. "The Body of Persuasion: A Theory of the Enthymeme." *College English* 56 (1): 46–65.

———. 2000. *Rhetoric and Poetics in Antiquity*. New York: Oxford University Press.

Walton, Douglas. 2001. "Enthymemes, Common Knowledge, and Plausible Inference." *Philosophy and Rhetoric* 34 (2): 93–112.

Warden, J. R. 1971. "The Mind of Zeus." *Journal of the History of Ideas* 32 (1): 3–14.

Welsh, Joshua. 2014. "Common Sense and the Rhetoric of Technology." *Poroi* 10 (1): 1–31.

Whately, Richard. 1848. *Elements of Logic*. Cambridge: James Munroe.

White, Hayden. 1978. *Tropics of Discourse: Essays in Cultural Criticism*. Baltimore: Johns Hopkins University Press.

———. 1980. "The Value of Narrativity in the Representation of Reality." *Critical Inquiry* 7 (1): 5–27.

White, James Boyd. 1985. *Heracles' Bow: Essays on the Rhetorics and Poetics of the Law*. Madison: University of Wisconsin Press.

Wolicki, Aleksander. 2007. "*Moicheia*: Adultery or Something More?" *Palamedes* 2:131–42.

Wolpert, Andrew. 2001. "Lysias 1 and the Politics of the Oikos." *Classical Journal* 96 (4): 415–24.

Wright, Frederick A. 2014. "The Short Story Just Got Shorter: Hemingway, Narrative, and the Six-Word Urban Legend." *Journal of Popular Culture* 47 (2): 327–40.

Young, Stephanie L. 2015. "Running Like a Man, Sitting Like a Girl: Visual Enthymeme and the Case of Caster Semenya." *Women's Studies in Communication* 38 (3): 331–50.

Yunis, Harvey, trans. 2005. *Demosthenes, Speeches 18 and 19*. By Demosthenes. Austin: University of Texas Press.

INDEX

abduction (logic), 89, 95, 182, 194
accuse (*kategorei*), 97, 119, 120, 122, 131, 155, 168, 199
Adkins, A. W. H., 46, 191, 199
adultery, 150–52, 157, 163–65, 167, 172–76, 197–99
Aeschines, 79, 91, 116, 131, 132, 197
Aeschines Socraticus, 82, 194
Agricola, Rodolphus, 35, 59, 192
Alcibiades, 117, 118
Alcidamas, 82, 106
Aly, Bower, 191
amnesty (ancient Greece), 118, 119, 121, 126
Amsterdam, Anthony G., 90, 195, 198
anagnorisis, 96, 157, 189
Anaximenes, 29, 60, 101, 108, 194
Andocides, 79, 90, 92, 101, 117–27, 130–32, 137, 140–42, 148, 150, 153, 154, 194–96
Antiphon, 3, 5, 79, 82, 91, 92, 94, 97, 140, 141, 166, 170, 180, 191, 194, 195, 196, 198
Antisthenes, 166, 170, 198
Antoine, Arnauld, 34
Aquinas, Thomas, 192
Aristophanes, 199
Aristotle, 1, 3, 5, 6, 14–16, 18, 19, 23, 25–39, 44–48, 52, 59–84, 87, 88, 95, 106–8, 128, 133, 150, 157, 177–84, 187–99
    Athenian Constitution, 84, 194
    Categories, 192
    Metaphysics, 29
    On Memory and Recollection, 192
    Poetics, 6, 18, 76, 82, 157
    Politics, 83, 194
    Posterior Analytics, 63, 71, 72, 192, 193
    Prior Analytics, 23, 26, 27, 30–36, 59, 67, 69–73, 183, 190, 192–94
    Rhetoric, 1–4, 14, 15, 23, 25–27, 30–37, 46, 61, 65, 67–69, 71–73, 75–84, 87, 107, 183, 189–94, 199
    Rhetoric to Alexander, 29, 30, 101, 107, 108, 171, 190, 191, 195
arrangement, 7, 52, 65, 66, 74, 77, 138, 158, 170
Athens, 6, 28, 83, 92, 97, 100, 101, 119, 120, 124, 125, 148–50, 166, 168, 171, 174, 176, 192, 198
audience, 5–11, 14–17, 19, 24–27, 36–40, 42–45, 47–54, 60, 61, 62, 70, 72–75, 77, 78, 83, 88–90, 93–100, 101, 103–5, 107, 108, 110–14, 116, 120, 121, 123, 126, 127, 130–35, 137–39, 143, 144, 147, 151, 153–58, 160, 162, 166, 175, 180, 184, 187, 190–95, 198
Avery, Harry, 167

Bakewell, Geoff, 199
Barnes, Jonathan, 63, 67, 71, 192, 193
Barthes, Roland, 14, 36, 40–44, 51, 60, 70, 134, 137, 159, 189–91, 196, 198
basanos/basanisēs. *See* torture
Bateman, John Jay, 197
Beatty, John, 137
Bennet, W., and Martha Feldman, 5, 88, 100, 147, 180, 181, 189, 195
Beraerts, Lars, Dirk de Geest, Luc Herman, and Bart Vervaeck, 196
Bers, Victor, 133, 151, 175, 176
Bertrand, Denis, 191
Bitsilli, Petr Mikhailovich, 195
Bitzer, Lloyd, 14, 25, 36–40, 42, 44, 48, 51, 60, 70, 87, 134, 189–91, 193, 198
Blass, Friedrich, 197
Blumer, Herbert, 38
Bons, J. A. E., 29, 190
Bourdieu, Pierre, 6, 147
Braet, A. C., 193
Brandt, William J., et al., 36
Bruner, Jerome, 90, 184, 195, 196, 198, 199
Brunschwig, Jacques, 62, 68, 189, 193
Burke, Kenneth, 53, 142, 192, 196
Burke, Michael, 191
Burks, Arthur W., 194
Burnyeat, M. F., 25, 29, 32, 45, 47, 52, 59, 62, 67, 190–93
busybody (*polupragmosunē*), 150, 154, 159, 162, 168, 169
Bybee, Michael D., 194

cadence. See *periodos*
Cantarella, Eva, 197
Caplan, Harry, 30

Carawan, Edwin, 118, 195, 197
Carey, Christopher, 91, 116, 197, 198
Carr, E. H., 196
Carter, L. B., 169
Casswell, Caroline, 191
Chatman, Seymour, 137, 196
Chekhov, Anton, 88, 105, 195
Chestek, Kenneth, 184
chiasmus. *See* ring composition
Cicero, 5, 30, 184, 190, 198
    Ad C. Herennium, 30, 190
    De inventione, 30, 190, 192
club (*hetaireia*), 117, 118, 122, 125, 131, 132, 195
Cohen, David, 197, 198
Cohen, G. A., 190
Collobert, Catherine, Pierre Destrée, and Francisco J. Gonzalez, 198
conclusion
    logical, 3, 4, 9, 15–17, 20, 23–26, 29, 30, 34, 35, 47–52, 55, 60, 64–66, 68–71, 76, 77, 84, 94, 96, 98, 99, 111, 112, 147, 189–91, 193, 199
    peroration, 8, 120, 122, 127, 165, 175
Conley, Thomas, 29, 32, 59, 67, 87, 190, 192
Conlon, Edward, 192
Conner, W. R., 195
constitution (*politeia*), 84, 167, 168, 169, 194, 199
contest, 2, 19, 30, 62, 63, 65, 75, 89, 97, 109, 115, 128, 129, 141–44, 158, 159, 182, 187, 196, 197, 198
Cooke, H. P., 192
Cooper, Lane, 51, 69, 72
Copi, Irving, Carl Cohen, and Kenneth McMahon, 36
Corbett, Edward P. J., and Robert J. Conners, 24, 36, 52
Cover, Robert, 142, 180, 186, 196
Crem, Theresa, 2, 45
Crowley, Sharon, and Debra Hawhee, 36, 46

Darcus, Sullivan Shirley M., 191
deduction (*sullogismos*), 2, 3, 8, 14, 15, 18, 23, 27, 29–31, 42, 44, 61–66, 68–79, 83, 84, 88, 89, 95, 96, 107, 111, 120, 127, 134, 179, 182, 183, 189, 190, 192–95
    primary, 36, 72, 73
    topical (dialectical), 14, 15, 64, 65, 66, 67, 68, 72, 189
Delia, Jesse G., 191
Demades, 1, 79

Demetrius, 31, 197
democracy/democratic, 2, 4, 6, 20, 62, 83, 84, 118, 119, 121, 123, 126, 148, 149, 166–69, 176, 177, 194, 199
Demosthenes, 1, 3, 5, 83, 92, 93, 97, 101–4, 133, 150, 151, 175, 176, 195, 197
De Quincey, Thomas, 14, 33, 59, 87
DeSanctis, Christy, 185, 186
Devries, William Levering, 197
dialectic, 2–5, 9, 18, 23, 27, 31, 35, 36, 38, 39, 42, 61–76, 79, 81, 84, 95, 107, 183, 189–93
Dickstein, Louis S., 48
Dilts, Mervin R., and George A. Kennedy, 30, 196
Dionysius of Halicarnassus, 148, 149, 166, 197
disnarration, 133, 139–41, 182
Donaldson, J. W., 33
Douglas, Mary, 160, 198
Dover, K. J., 197
Doyle, Arthur Conan, 11, 78, 195, 196
Duerlinger, James, 193

Edwards, Linda, 184
Edwards, Michael J., 195–97
eikos. See probability
endoxa. See reputable opinion
Ennis, Robert, 191
enthumios, 46, 191
enthymeme, 2, 3, 14, 15, 17, 19, 74, 76, 77, 84, 87, 88, 108, 171, 181, 182, 187, 190, 192, 194–97
    1.0 (narrative enthymeme, enthymizing), 11, 13–17, 19, 20, 62, 88–115, 117, 119–22, 125, 126, 128–31, 133–35, 137, 140–44, 147, 148, 150, 153–63, 165, 168–71, 177, 178, 181, 182, 184, 186–88, 194, 196–98
    2.0 (topical deduction), 14, 15, 17, 18, 35, 59–75, 78, 83, 84, 107, 129, 133, 183, 189, 191–93
    3.0 (truncated syllogism), 11, 14, 15, 17, 18, 23–55, 59, 60, 69, 70, 78, 134, 147, 179–82, 189–94
enthymizing, types of
    mediacy (immediate/ mediate), 91, 94–100, 111
    mood (indicative/ imperative), 91–94, 108, 122, 123, 127, 156
    novelty (mnemonic/ didactic/ heuristic), 91, 103–5, 108, 110, 111, 126, 143, 156, 159, 171

stance (supportive/ contradictory), 31, 91, 98, 100–103, 107, 108, 110, 111, 115, 122, 133, 159, 170, 171
ep' autophōrō (red-handed), 151, 155, 168, 199
Eratosthenes, 19, 105, 147–57, 160–62, 165–77, 197, 199
Erickson, Keith, 190
ethopoiia, 149, 150, 165
ethos (character appeal), 3, 7, 27, 127, 128, 179, 186, 188
Euripides, 82
Evans, J. St. B. T., 48
example. *See* induction
exetasis (examination), 60, 108

Facciolati, Jacobi, 33, 59
Fisher, Walter, 39, 184, 191, 195, 196, 199
Flannery, Keith, 59
Forsdyke, Sarah, 198
Forster, E. S., 66, 71, 189
Fowler, Harold North, 29, 197, 198
Freese, John Henry, 69, 70, 73, 74, 194
Furley, William D., 195, 196

Gagarin, Michael, 184, 189, 195, 197, 198
Gage, John, 36, 39
Gaines, Robert N., 46, 59, 60, 191
Gallie, W. B., 196
game, 6, 19, 65, 134, 141–44, 196
gaps (narrative), 8, 17, 19, 39, 47, 49, 133–37, 154, 180, 196
Gay, Robert, 191
Genette, Gérard, 134, 139
Gerrig, Richard, 134
Goddu, G. C., 60, 87
Goffman, Erving, 37, 153, 154, 196
Gorgias, 5, 82, 166, 170, 189, 198
Gough, James, and Christopher Tinsdale, 191
Green, Lawrence D., 29, 31–34, 47, 59, 60, 189, 192
Grimaldi, William M. A., 46, 189, 190, 191

Hamilton, William, 33–35, 52, 59, 67, 190–92
Harris, Edward, 101, 102, 150, 196
Harvey, David, 199
Hawhee, Debra, 196
hegemony, 42, 43
Hemingway, Ernest, 6, 189
herm, 117, 118, 120–25, 130, 195
Herman, David, 134, 196
Herman, Gabriel, 159, 160

hetaireia. *See* club
Hett, W. S., 192
Hill, Forbes, 193
Hoffman, David, 195
Holms, Sherlock, 11–13, 78, 95, 135, 138, 140, 194–96
Homer, 46, 82, 116, 147
Hood, Michael, 190
Howland, Jacob, 149
Hubbell, H. M., 30, 190, 198
humiliate (*hubrizein*), 154, 168

ideology, 41, 42
impiety. *See* sacrilege
induction, 2, 3, 8, 25, 27, 69, 89, 107, 122, 179, 182, 186, 189, 192–95
inference, 8–11, 14–17, 29, 31, 47, 62, 64, 65, 68, 69, 74, 75, 77–79, 89, 95, 98, 110–14, 120, 122, 127, 134–38, 144, 171, 183, 188, 191–93, 195
Innes, Doreen C., 31, 197
introduction (*proemium*), 82, 122, 127, 165, 175, 197
Iphicrates, 79, 80, 81, 82
Isaeus, 3, 79, 93, 102, 109–16, 120, 127, 131, 180, 195
Iser, Wolfgang, 134
Isocrates, 5, 29, 60, 82, 104, 106, 108, 170, 194
Isotimides, decree of, 118, 119, 121

Jackson, Matthew, 43
Jebb, Richard Claverhouse, 30, 69
Jevons, Stanley W., 34, 45, 190
Johnson-Laird, P. N., 48, 181, 196
Joyce, Christopher, 118

Kapparis, K., 167
kategorei. *See* accuse
Keith, William M., and Christian O. Lundberg, 36, 52
Kennedy, George, 30, 69, 70, 72, 73, 76, 81, 166, 189, 190, 194, 196, 198
kernel, 113, 133, 137, 138, 139, 182
Knudsen, Rachel Ahern, 24, 147
Koziak, Barbara, 191
Kremmydas, Christos, 27, 60, 190
Kvernbekk, Tone, 199

Lakoff, George, and Mark Johnson, 181
Lamb, W. R. M., 88
Langer, Susan, 181

Lanigan, Richard, 190, 194
Lateiner, Donald, 197
Levi, Don S., 25, 53, 54, 75
liaison, 16, 95, 96, 99, 182, 198
Liddell, H. G., and R. Scott, 89, 197
Lloyd, G. E. R., 98, 103
Lloyd, Keith, 28
logismos/logizomai, 63, 64, 77, 106
logos, 4, 7–9, 18, 27, 42, 71, 72, 77, 88, 133, 135, 144, 179–81, 183, 184, 188, 189, 191, 198
Lucaites, John Louis, and Celeste Michelle Condit, 7, 128, 129, 132, 184, 196
Lycurgus, 1, 102, 105
Lynch, J. P., and G. B. Miles, 191
Lysias, 3, 5, 19, 20, 79, 82–84, 92–94, 97, 101, 103–6, 117, 119–21, 135, 148–80, 194, 197–99

MacDowell, Douglas, 118, 195–97, 199
Madden, Edward H., 36, 190
Maidment, K. J., 194
Mansel, H. L., 59
March, Jenny, 192
Marr, J. L., 118, 195
McAdon, Brad, 189
McGee, Michael, 42, 43, 51, 187, 192
McHendry, George F., 46, 190
Mead, George Herbert, 38
metic, 83, 149, 167, 169, 199
Meyer, Philip M., 196
Miller, Arthur B., and John D Bee, 46, 191
Mink, Louis, 6
Mirhady, David, 46, 108, 190, 191
Missiou, Anna, 195, 196
Mitchell, W. J. T., 196
moichos. *See* adultery
Momigliano, Arnaldo, 81
Morgan, Gareth, 198
Moriarty, Michael, 191
Moss, Jessica, 69
Murray, A. T., 46
Murray, Oswyn, 195
Mylonas, George, E., 196
myth, 99, 116, 192, 198

narrative, adversarial, 4, 7, 11, 17, 19, 62, 89, 115, 127–44, 158, 181, 182, 187, 196
narrative enthymeme. *See* enthymeme: 1.0 (narrative enthymeme, enthymizing)
narrative features
    brevity, 132, 133, 135, 138, 175
    coherence, 8, 63, 95, 108, 113, 131, 139

    correspondence, 95, 131, 132
    uniqueness, 132, 133, 137, 138
narrative reasoning, 4, 8, 9, 10, 11, 14, 75, 77, 96, 180–82, 185, 186
Nemesi, Attila L., 87
Nevett, Lisa, 198
nomos, 7, 10, 52, 99, 100, 112, 116, 121, 128, 132, 181, 186, 187, 196
Nyvlt, Pavel, 198, 199

Ong, Walter, 26, 33, 36
Osborne, Robin, 197, 199

Pace, Giulio, 33, 34, 35, 59, 192
Papillon, Terry L., 104
parable, 166–69, 177, 199
paradeigma. *See* induction
Parke, H. W., 195, 196
Partenie, Catalin, 198
pathos (emotional appeal), 3, 6, 7, 16, 27, 46, 53, 76, 78, 89, 94–96, 99, 107, 116, 120, 125–27, 130, 135, 154, 157, 165, 186, 189, 191, 192
PC (premise-conclusion) sequence, 4, 15, 16, 18, 25, 51, 53–55, 66, 75–78, 96, 100, 111, 147, 195
Pennington, Nancy, and Ried Hastie, 133, 195, 196
Perelman, Chaim, and L. Olbrechts-Tyteca, 16, 89, 93, 96, 99
periodos, 6, 7, 17, 76, 110, 114, 127, 130, 135, 137, 189
Perotti, Pier Angelo, 167, 168, 198, 199
Phaedrus, 29, 82, 83, 149
Phelan, James, 196
Piazza, Francesca, 190
Pierce, Charles Sanders, 95, 182
Plato, 5, 29, 82, 88, 149, 166, 170, 187, 189, 198
plot, 6–8, 11, 13, 14, 16–18, 82, 92, 96, 99, 105, 106, 108, 112–16, 120, 123, 125–27, 129, 132, 133, 135–38, 141, 154, 159, 164, 165, 176, 177, 189, 191, 197, 198
Plutarch, 195, 197, 198
politeia. *See* constitution
polupragmosunē. *See* busybody
Porter, John R., 163, 164, 165, 167, 199
Poster, Carol, 29, 34, 190
Prenosil, Joshua D., 43, 60
presence, 89, 93, 99, 108
Price, Robert, 189
Prince, Gerald, 139, 140
probability (*eikos*), 23, 24, 26, 35, 46, 54, 61, 62, 115, 116, 180, 188, 192, 195

INDEX 217

Procrustes, 53, 192
prototype, 2, 181

Quintilian, 30, 87, 132

Rabinowitz, Peter, 138, 139
Rackham, H., 194
Ramus, 33, 35
Raphael, Sally, 189
Ratcliffe, Krista, 42, 43
Raymond, James C., 40
Read, Carveth, 190
reputable opinion (*endoxa*), 2, 17, 23–26, 36, 41, 42, 50, 60, 66, 71, 81
Rideout, Christopher, 184, 195, 196
ring composition (chiasmus), 159–62, 165, 198
Roberts, W. Rhys, 69
Rosch, Eleanor, 181
Rossolatos, George, 46
Rubinelli, Sara, 193
Russell, Donald A., 31, 87, 189

Sabre, Ru Michael, 194
sacrilege (*asebeia*), 117–19, 121, 126, 131, 140, 141
Scenters-Zapico, J., 43
Schiappa, Edward, 129, 196
Schum, David A., 194
Scriven, Michael, 191
Seaton, R. C., 33, 59, 192
Sharples, R. W., 191
Sickinger, James, 196
Sinclair, R. K., 199
Slomkowski, Paul, 193
Smith, Robin, 23, 31, 36, 59–67, 70, 77, 81, 189, 193, 194
Solmsen, Friedrich, 67
Sorensen, Roy A., 87
Spranzi, Marta, 193
story, 4–13, 16, 17, 63, 64, 99, 100, 106–17, 121–44, 147, 152, 154, 160, 167, 168, 169, 176
storyworld, 6–8, 10, 16, 76, 96, 112, 114, 120, 124, 129, 135

Strassler, Robert B., 191
sullogismos, 2, 14, 15, 18, 23, 29–31, 44, 61–78, 183, 190, 192, 193
Sutton E. W., 187
syllogism (categorical) / syllogistic, 14, 16–18, 23, 25–35, 37, 38, 42, 46–49, 52, 59–63, 66–74, 77, 95, 107, 128, 134, 179, 182, 183, 185, 188–90, 192–95

theory (rhetoric), 5, 7, 28, 39, 60, 88, 89, 106, 147, 166, 177–79, 181, 182, 184, 186–88
Thucydides, 5, 46, 92, 117, 170, 191, 195, 196, 199
thumos, 19, 24, 40, 45, 46, 47, 88, 191
Todd, S. C., 97, 101, 103–5, 120, 135, 161, 163, 168, 195, 197–99
torture (*basanos*), 97, 98, 154, 155, 160, 161, 171–75, 199
Tredennick, Hugh, 26, 29, 71, 192–94
Trenker, Sophie, 164
Trevett, J. C., 79, 81–83, 92, 93, 97, 183, 194
tyranny, 118, 148, 149, 166–69, 176, 177

Usher, Steven, 149, 166, 194, 197, 198

Van Ophuijsen, 191
Velleman, J. David, 189

Walker, Jeffrey, 29, 46, 59, 60, 87, 108, 142, 190, 192
Walton, Douglas, 191
Warden, J. R., 191
Welsh, Joshua, 40, 45, 60
Whately, Richard, 34, 60, 190
White, Hayden, 116, 196
White, James Boyd, 5, 181
Wolicki, Aleksander, 197
Wolpert, Andrew, 198
Wright, Fredrick A., 189

Young, Stephanie, 25
Yunis, Harvey, 103

CPSIA information can be obtained
at www.ICGtesting.com
Printed in the USA
BVHW031807020420
576611BV00002BA/3

9 780271 086132